Regional American Food Culture

Regional American Food Culture

LUCY M. LONG

FOOD CULTURES IN AMERICA

Ken Albala, Series Editor

GREENWOOD PRESS
An Imprint of ABC-CLIO, LLC

A B C ☰ C L I O

Santa Barbara, California • Denver, Colorado • Oxford, England

Library of Congress Cataloging-in-Publication Data

Long, Lucy M., 1956–
  Regional American food culture / Lucy M. Long.
      p. cm. — (Food cultures in the United States)
  Includes bibliographical references and index.
    ISBN 978-0-313-34043-7 (hard copy : alk. paper) — ISBN 978-0-313-08806-3 (ebook) 1. Cookery, American. 2. Diet—United States. 3. Food habits—United States. I. Title.
  TX715.L81874 2009
  394.1′20973—dc22   2009028335

13 12 11 10 09   1 2 3 4 5

This book is also available on the World Wide Web as an eBook.
Visit www.abc-clio.com for details.

ABC-CLIO, LLC
130 Cremona Drive, P.O. Box 1911
Santa Barbara, California 93116-1911

This book is printed on acid-free paper ∞

Manufactured in the United States of America

The publisher has done its best to make sure the instructions and/or recipes in this book are correct. However, users should apply judgment and experience when preparing recipes, especially parents and teachers working with young people. The publisher accepts no responsibility for the outcome of any recipe included in this volume.

Contents

Food Cultures in the United States

If you think of iconic and quintessentially American foods, those with which we are most familiar, there are scarcely any truly native to North America. Our hot dogs are an adaptation of sausages from Frankfurt and Vienna; our hamburgers are another Germanic import reconfigured. Ketchup is an invention of Southeast Asia, although it is based on the tomato, which comes from South America. Pizza is a variant on a Neapolitan dish. Colas are derived from an African nut. Our beloved peanuts are a South American plant brought to Africa and from there to the U.S. South. Our french fries are an Andean tuber, cooked with a European technique. Even our quintessentially American apple pie is made from a fruit native to what is today Kazakhstan.

When I poll my students about their favorite foods at the start of every food class I teach, inevitably included are tacos, bagels, sushi, pasta, fried chicken—most of which can be found easily at fast-food outlets a few blocks from campus. In a word, American food culture is, and always has been, profoundly globally oriented. This, of course, has been the direct result of immigration, from the time of earliest settlement by Spanish, English, French, and Dutch to slaves brought by force from Africa, to later arrival by Germans, Italians, Eastern Europeans (including Jews), and Asians, and up until now with the newest immigrants from Latin America and elsewhere.

Although Americans have willingly adopted the foods of newcomers, we never became a melting pot for these various cultures. So-called ethnic cuisines naturally changed on foreign soil, adapting to new ingredients and popular taste—but at heart they remain clear and proud descendants of their respective countries. Their origins are also readily recognized by Americans; we are all perfectly familiar with the repertoire of Mexican, Chinese, and Italian restaurants, and increasingly now Thai, Japanese, and Salvadoran, to name a few. Eating out at such restaurants is a hallmark of mainstream American culture, and despite the spontaneous or contrived fusion of culinary styles, each retains its unique identity.

This series is designed as an introduction to the major food cultures of the United States—Jewish American, Hispanic, Asian American, African American, and regional. Each volume delves deeply into the history and development of a distinct ethnic or regional cuisine. The volumes further explore these cuisines through their major ingredients, who is cooking and how at home, the structure of mealtime and daily rituals surrounding food, and the typical meals and how they are served, which can be dramatically different from popular versions. In addition, chapters cover eating out, holidays and special occasions, as well as the influence of religion, and the effect of the diet on health and nutrition. Recipes are interspersed throughout. Each volume offers valuable features, including a timeline, glossary, and index, making each a convenient reference work for research.

This series is important for our understanding of ourselves on several levels. Food is central to how we define ourselves, so in a sense this series will not only recount how recipes and foodways serve as distinct reminders of ethnic identity, binding families and communities together through shared experiences, but it also describes who we have all become, as each food culture has become an indispensable part of our collective identity as Americans.

Ken Albala
University of the Pacific

Introduction

Anyone who travels across the United States quickly becomes aware of differences in landscape, climate, and people. Even with all the generic shopping malls and housing developments, national food chains and commercial outlets, regions are evident, and each region still displays something of its own culture. Food is one of the most common ways of expressing that culture and often helps us to recognize different regions. Places often become known for their food, and these foods are in turn markers of that place—sweet tea and barbecue in the South, baked beans and clam chowder in the Northeast, red and green salsas in the Southeast, fusion cuisine in California, and salmon bakes in the Pacific Northwest.

Regional foods in the United States, however, are complex and often difficult to identify. Frequently, we do not recognize that they are unique until we contrast them with other regions: for example, New England hot dog rolls open from the top, in contrast to nationally distributed hot dog buns that open from the side. Some foods seem to automatically represent a region, such as grits in the South or king crab and cedar-planked salmon in the Pacific Northwest; but sometimes the food icons that symbolize a specific place are found in other regions as well, for example, chili in Texas and Cincinnati, barbecue in Memphis and Kansas City, or a choice of red or green salsa in New Mexico. Also, some regional foods that are unique to an area may not be attractive to mainstream America, such as Philadelphia scrapple and pepper pot soup, St. Louis snoot sandwich, or North Carolina Brunswick stew made the traditional way with squirrel. These foods are often not advertised or marketed to "outsiders." Similarly, cities, states, and regions often invent foods that can represent that place, for example, buck-eye candies and ice cream in Ohio and garlic in Gilroy, California—or they highlight a tradition that may attract positive attention, even though most residents of the region do not participate in the tradition, for example apple butter festivals in Ohio and Indiana, sorghum stirrings in southern Appalachia, and chuck wagon suppers and Rocky Mountain oysters in the western plains. To further complicate matters, commercially produced, mass-distributed foods that are available nationally can also become regional culinary traditions, for example, green bean casserole and Jell-O salads in the eastern Midwest and Spam in Hawaii.

What exactly then is a regional food? Regions are a mixture of natural features (climate, topology, soil type), natural resources (flora, fauna), and human history—settlement by various peoples, the ways in which people have adapted the land, and the ways in which people have adapted to the land. This sounds straightforward enough, but defining regions is actually very complex. Physical boundaries are not always clear, and human history has a way of ignoring or transcending them. For example, the lines defining the 50 states are political rather than physical or cultural, but they in turn have shaped the ways in which the natural resources have been used,

Whoopie pies are traditional to Pennsylvania, where they originated with Amish settlers. They can be homemade with fresh ingredients and are usually eaten as a festival or holiday snack. Courtesy of author.

agricultural industries been developed, and culinary culture treated. Frequently, cultural features, such as foodways traditions, overlap those boundaries.

Geographer Yi-Fu Tuan suggests that cultural regions are areas in which the residents feel "local patriotism … that rests on the intimate experience of place, and on a sense of the fragility of goodness; that which we love has no guarantee to endure."[1] This "topophilia" (love of place) is then reflected in residents holding onto traditions that represent that place. Participating in those traditions, in turn, can create a sense of place and loyalty to it.

Americans often use food to both recognize and celebrate a region. Some foods become public symbols or icons of a place and are often featured at festivals and tourist sites, for example, crawfish in Louisiana, lobster in Maine, or roasted chilies in New Mexico. Images of those foods are used on souvenirs, meals and parties feature them, and they become associated with festivity and regional identity.

This book defines regional foods as those foods and foodways that reflect the history of humans settling and interacting with the land within a given geographic area. The result will be both distinctive foods—those that are unique to a region—and representative foods—those that are found elsewhere but somehow embody a region's history and foodways.

The word "food" itself is actually rather general and vague and can mean foodstuff, ingredients, or the dishes and meals being consumed. The word "cuisine" usually refers to a publicly recognized (i.e., through cookbooks, cooking schools, or other official channels) set of dishes, ingredients, and preparation methods that represent a group of people, whereas the term "food culture" refers to the totality of learned behaviors and understandings around food. Furthermore, scholars often use the word "culture" to mean the learned resources for interpreting and acting in the world, so a food culture is a specific set of meanings for food and eating, proscribing what is edible and palatable as well as when, where, how, and why food should be eaten. Meanwhile, the word "foodways" refers to all the activities surrounding food, as well as the ways in which people think and talk about food. Foodways broadens the focus from specific dishes to all the behind-the-scenes activities involved in producing that dish—procurement, preservation, preparation, distribution, consumption, and even cleanup.

Many regional traditions, for example, display variations in foodways rather than the actual food consumed. For example, shopping at the corner grocery run by Korean immigrants in New York City is a very different experience from going to a national chain supermarket or even to a regional supermarket such as Piggly Wiggly in the South—even though the shopper might end up with the same item. Similarly, the same food can have different names in different regions. Carbonated soft drinks, for example, are called "tonic" in New England, "soda" in the Mid-Atlantic, "pop" in the Midwest, and "coke or something" in the South. A "milkshake" in New England is a glass of milk with a flavored syrup mixed into it. Elsewhere, it is an ice cream, milk, and flavoring concoction (called a "frappé" in New England). Similarly, regions may give their own meanings to a food found elsewhere, so that a dish is used differently and evokes different feelings in each region. Spam, for example, is a commercially processed food available everywhere in the nation, but it became a standard ingredient in Hawaii after World War II and is referred to as "Hawaiian steak." Chicken-fried steak is common throughout the South but is considered iconic of Texas and the western plains region. Similarly, the word "barbecue" is used everywhere, but it has different meanings as well as different recipes and techniques according to the region.

Another issue in discussing American regional foods is defining what American food is in the first place. On one hand, it can be anything that Americans eat, but that would include almost all possible foodways from around the globe. It is more useful to describe American foods and foodways as those that reflect the landscape, history, and present conditions (economics, politics, culture) of the nation. For American food, it is useful to think of it as a series of layers. Beginning with Native American, a pioneer culinary culture of British and German tradition overlaid that for the foundation. This foundation adapted to each specific region, opening the way for the development of regional cuisines. Then immigrants brought their various ethnic traditions, some of which were blended into regional ones, whereas others retained their Old World identities. A national layer of American food began in the mid-1800s with the development of transportation systems (particularly canals, railroads, and refrigerated train cars) and the food industry (canning, processing, and advertising). This popular culture layer has united Americans in their eating experiences, so that we can all share some common foods—fast-food hamburgers, hot dogs, pizza, popcorn, chips, and so on. This dimension has also taken over in many places, so that everyday foods no longer seem to represent regions. People often adapt those popular foods, however, to regional tastes and resources, so that people in Pittsburgh may put gravy on french fries, Utah residents might use fry sauce, and New Englanders might use malt vinegar, but "everyone else" uses ketchup. Part of what is seen in regional foods, then, is different mixings of those layers.

American food regions may be grouped and classified in numerous ways. The Slow Food Raft Project has divided the country into nations based on their historical foods, for example, the Taro Nation is Hawaii, the Gumbo Nation is the coastal South, and the Clambake Nation is the Northeast Coast. Meanwhile, the U.S. Census Bureau divides the country into four regions: Northeast, South, Midwest, and West. Some of these census regions seem too broad for discussing food traditions, however. The South, for example, extends from Maryland and Delaware to Oklahoma.

This book uses four basic regions that are then divided into subregions: the East (New England, Mid-Atlantic), the South (the Southeast, Florida, the upland South, Louisiana, and the Gulf Coast), the Midwest (the eastern Midwest, the upper Midwest, the Great Plains), and the West (the Mountain region, the Southwest, California, the Pacific Northwest, Alaska, Hawaii). Because states can be in more than one region, firm maps cannot be drawn for these regions, and states are sometimes listed more than once.

The following chapters discuss the general patterns in each region. Many local traditions are included, but not all can be mentioned. That is a task left up to the reader—and a challenge as well. This book provides a blueprint for exploring the connections between food and place wherever readers may be.

NOTE

1. Yi-Fu Tuan, *Topophilia: A Study of Environmental Perceptions, Attitudes, and Values* (New York: Columbia University Press, 1974).

Chronology

1519	Spanish conquistador Hernán Cortés brings cattle to Mexico and Florida.
1538/9	Spanish explorers Pánfilo de Narváez and Hernando de Soto bring oranges to Florida.
1600s	Europeans settle along the eastern seaboard and establish European food patterns and adapt such Native traditions as cornbread varieties, pumpkins, cranberries, and wild game. African foods are introduced.
1607	Jamestown in Virginia is the first permanent English settlement in North America.
1607	The first Africans are brought to America (Virginia) as indentured servants.
1611	Cows are brought to Jamestown.
1612	The first commercial brewery is established in New York.
	The first vineyards are planted in New York.
1620	The *Mayflower* brings Pilgrims to Massachusetts where they establish the Plymouth (Plimoth) Colony.
1621	Plymouth Plantation celebrates its first Thanksgiving.

1624	Cows arrive in Plymouth Plantation.
1654–1865	Slavery is legal in the United States.
1680	The cranberry industry is established in New Jersey.
1690	The rice industry is established in South Carolina.
1700s	Continued colonization by British, German, and French.
1700s	Cow peas are brought from Africa via the Caribbean.
1742	The first cookbook in America is printed in Virginia, a reprint of the English publication *Compleat Housewife* by Eliza Smith.
1760s	Pralines are made in Louisiana. New Orleans is the hub for pecan commerce.
1765–1785	In Louisiana, Acadian settlers (French Catholics from Nova Scotia) become known as Cajuns.
1769	Grapes are planted at the Spanish Franciscan missions in California.
1770s	Thomas Jefferson plants gardens at his Monticello estate in Virginia, introducing vegetables and fruits from France and experimenting with gardening techniques.
1776	The American Revolution begins. Coffee replaces tea as the favored beverage.
Late 1700s	Wine grapes are established in Cincinnati, Ohio.
1796	The first American cookbook is published, Amelia Simmons' *American Cookery* (Hartford, CT: Hudson & Goodwin).
1830s	Industrialization brings new transportation systems (canals, railroads), scientific agriculture, advertising, and refrigerated cars.
Early 1800s	American immigration extends into the Mexican Southwest.
1810s	Dutch colonists in New York introduce the doughnut.
1821	The United States acquires Florida, and the citrus industry begins.
1823	Grapefruit are brought from Barbados to Florida.
1826	The Union Oyster House restaurant is established in Boston.

1827	The icebox is invented and replaces root cellars.
1828	Cranberries are brought from Massachusetts to Wisconsin.
1829	The Ruby Red grapefruit variety is developed in Texas.
1830s	Iron ranges replace hearth fires for cooking.
1830	Indian River citrus hybrids are established in Florida.
1830	The Indian Removal Act moves Native Americans west of the Mississippi River.
1838	The Trail of Tears marks the removal of the Cherokee from North Carolina and Georgia.
1837	Wisconsin cheese production begins.
1840s	The commercial cranberry industry begins in Massachusetts.
1840s	The Oregon Trail spreads pioneer foodways to the Pacific Northwest.
1840	Antoine's restaurant opens in the French Quarter of New Orleans.
1841	California's first commercial orange grove is planted.
1847	Chinese food is introduced to California.
1849	The California Gold Rush begins.
1850s	Beer industries (Anheuser-Busch) are established in St. Louis, Missouri.
1847–1900	Immigration begins from Asia (primarily China and Japan) to the West Coast.
Mid-1800s	The Southwest is annexed, and Mexican citizens become ethnic Americans.
Mid-1800s	Immigration begins from Europe (primarily Ireland and Germany) to the East (particularly the Northeast) and Midwest.
Mid-1800s	The Wisconsin dairy industry is established.
1855	The first Creole cookbook is published in New Orleans, *La Cuisine Creole: A Collection of Culinary Recipes*, by Lafcadio Hearn.

1856	Vanilla cream soda is invented in Wisconsin.
1860s	The wine industry begins in Cincinnati.
1860s–1870s	Beer production (Schlitz, Pabst, Blatz, Miller) begins in Milwaukee, Wisconsin.
1870s	Immigration begins from Asia and Russia to the Pacific Northwest.
1870s	West Texas sees significant German immigration. Chili mixes are developed.
1870s	The wine industry develops in the Firelands area of Ohio and in California.
1870	Valencia oranges are introduced to Florida, and the juice industry begins.
1870	Navel oranges are established in California and Arizona.
1870	John Harvey Kellogg markets granola in Battle Creek, Michigan.
1870–1901	In the Southwest, Fred Harvey Houses are the first chain restaurants.
1871	Cranberry growers organize.
1872	Luther Burbank begins seed experimentation in California.
Mid-1870s	Freed slaves migrate to northern and midwestern urban centers.
1880s	Mobile food wagons (forerunners of diners) appear in Rhode Island.
1880s	Jewish immigrants establish delicatessens in New York City.
1880s	Chicago becomes the meatpacking capital of nation.
1885	Dr. Pepper is invented in Texas.
1886	Coca-Cola is invented in Atlanta.
1890s	The cattle industry is established in the West. Buffalo are decimated.
1893	At the World's Columbian Exposition in Chicago, Cracker Jack, ice cream cones, shredded wheat, and Juicy Fruit gum are introduced.

1893	Vermont Maple Sugar Makers' Association sets standards.
1893	Hot dogs are associated with St. Louis Brown Stockings' baseball games (the team owner, Chris Von der Ahe, is German).
1894	Pepsi is invented in New Bern, North Carolina.
1894	The Hershey Chocolate Company is established in Pennsylvania.
1894	Cornflakes are invented in Battle Creek, Michigan.
1896	*The Boston Cooking-School Cook Book* by Fannie Merritt Farmer (Boston, MA: Little, Brown, & Company) is published.
1897	Grapenuts are invented by C.W. Post.
Late 1800s	In the urban centers of the Northeast, social reforms for immigrants include attempts to Americanize them through their foodways.
Late 1800s	Immigrants from Eastern Europe and southern Europe arrive in the East (particularly the Northeast) and Midwest.
Late 1800s	Immigrants from Scandinavia and northern Europe arrive in the upper Midwest.
1900s	Nationalism is on the rise, and there is a push for people to lose their ethnic traditions and become "American."
1904	In St. Louis, at the Louisiana Purchase Exposition, a concessionaire from Bavaria introduces hot dogs on a bun.
1904	The largest wholesale maple sugar company (Cary MS Company) is established in Vermont.
1905	Permanent diners begin to appear in Rhode Island and New York.
1906	The Kellogg Foundation is started in Michigan.
1912	A&W Root Beer, perhaps the first fast-food establishment, opens in Lodi, California.
1916	The White Castle System of Eating Houses begins in Wichita, Kansas.
1916	Piggly Wiggly, the first self-service grocery store, opens in Memphis, Tennessee.

1920–1933	The Prohibition era begins, and alcohol is banned.
1920s	In New York City, bagels and cheesecake are introduced in delis.
1921	The first drive-in restaurant, the Pig Stand, opens in Dallas, Texas.
1927	Kool-Aid is invented in Nebraska.
1930s	The California wine industry emerges as the largest in the nation.
1940s	Pizza parlors open in New York City Italian neighborhoods.
1942	Norman Rockwell's painting, "Freedom from Want," depicts his family's New England Thanksgiving meal and becomes the iconic image for Thanksgiving dinners throughout the country.
1950s	During the era of suburbia and conformity, processed foods and kitchen gadgets are invented.
1950s	Tex-Mex cuisine is adopted by mainstream America.
1955	The first McDonald's opens in Des Plaines, Illinois.
1960s	The Celestial Seasonings tea company is founded in Boulder, Colorado.
1960s	The counterculture revolution in food encompasses macrobiotic diets, vegetarian diets, and whole grain and natural foods. Yogurt, tofu, and other new foods are associated with the "crunchy granola" lifestyle.
1964	Japanese steak houses are introduced in New York City.
1964	Soul food emerges in California as a political and social statement of black identity.
1970s	Thai food is introduced on the West Coast.
1970s	Vietnamese food is introduced on the East Coast.
1971	Chez Panisse is founded in Berkeley, California, introducing local, fresh, and organic food.
1971	Starbucks is founded in Seattle.
1980s	Microbreweries begin to appear.

1980s	American chefs reclaim ethnic roots.
1984	Paul Prudhomme's *Louisiana Kitchen* cookbook is published.
1980s	California cuisine is dominated by chefs Jeremiah Tower, Wolfgang Puck, and Alice Waters.
1988	"Floribbean" cuisine (a fusion of Florida and Caribbean cuisine) is celebrated in *Feast of Sunlight* by Norman Van Aken.
1988	*Chez Panisse Cooking*, by Alice Waters, is published.
1988	*Wolfgang Puck Cookbook* is published.
2000s	"Eat local" and organic movements begin, farmers' markets proliferate, and community-supported agriculture begins. Americans eat more international foods but also become more aware of regional traditions. Star chefs, cooking shows, and mainstream interest in food also emerge.

1

Historical Overview

The fourth-largest country in the world, the United States, stretches 3,717,813 square miles between the Atlantic and Pacific oceans and the countries of Canada and Mexico. It includes Alaska and Hawaii, states that do not join the mainland. The United States has historically contained rich natural resources of timber, mineral, minerals, and wildlife. It has a mostly temperate climate, a vast central plain, smaller coastal plains, and plentiful fresh water supplies (181,519 square miles of water). This translated into bountiful food from the wild for Native peoples and early European settlers, as well as rich farmland capable of sustaining a nation today.

From a geographic perspective, the United States is divided into three main regions: the eastern seaboard, the Midwest (interior plains), and the western seaboard. (The southern states cut across the eastern seaboard to the beginnings of the West.) Each has distinctive topographies, climates, soils, and different habitat for animals and vegetation. These regions combine with the cultural history of the United States to give the four major culinary regions: East, South, Midwest, and West. Each region reflects a unique combination of natural resources, the Native American cultures originally inhabiting it, settlement by various ethnic groups, and different political and economic developments. Because much of this history is shared across regions, this chapter gives broad overviews of those commonalities before addressing each region and its subregions. All of these descriptions are general summaries, focusing on the highlights.

NATIVE AMERICAN CULTURES AND FOODWAYS

Native American peoples are thought to have entered the North American continent from Asia through the Bering Strait in Alaska between 15,000 and 13,000 years ago. They then spread throughout the continent, adapting to local resources and developing distinctive cultures with their own worldviews, languages, social structures, and food traditions. Although there was wide variety among the Native American cultures, they all tended to share a sense that humans needed to live in respectful harmony with nature. They carefully used local resources, mixing hunting and gathering with farming. Corn (maize) cultivation began around 400 CE and allowed more reliance on farming, which then led to more permanent settlements. Corn became a staple crop, and it was usually grown and cooked with squash and beans. These "three sisters" were integral to Native American foodways and are one of their most significant legacies.

European exploration and colonization beginning in the late 1400s introduced new foods, animals, and technologies but also brought tremendous upheaval. Native cultures were disrupted—and, in some cases, exterminated—and many cultural traditions and skills were lost. The Indian Removal Act of 1830 forced Native Americans into reservations west of the Mississippi, further disrupting traditional cultures.

The rich diversity of Native American cultures can be categorized into four primary regions: Eastern Woodland Cultures, Plains Cultures, Far West Cultures (including the Pacific Northwest, Alaska, and Hawaii), and Southwest Cultures.[1] The lasting influence of each culture varies. In many cases, the European settlers adapted the skills and traditions of the culture, but their original identity was lost; in others, the traditions from a number of cultures were blended together.

Eastern Woodland Cultures

The tribes of the Woodland cultures lived in the eastern part of the continent, where, as the name suggests, forests and woodlands dominated. The region included all of the East Coast and extended west as far as the Mississippi River. The Woodland cultures apparently developed in the Southeast and then moved north, where the food traditions shifted because of the colder climate and rockier habitat. Some of the most iconic American foods today can be traced directly to Eastern Woodland traditions—succotash, baked beans, clambakes, and popcorn.

A variety of indigenous peoples lived throughout the Southeast before European exploration. The Mississippian culture, for example, flourished from about 800 to 1500 CE when European settlement occurred. Referred to by archaeologists as Mound Builders, they were primarily hunter–gatherers. Their descendents include the Chickasaws, Choctaws, Creeks, Cherokees, and Seminoles, cultures that were thriving when European settlement began. Today, only the Cherokees (North Carolina) and Seminoles (Florida) have large populations in their original homelands. The Cherokees in particular had a significant effect on southern Appalachian culture, often marrying European settlers and teaching them Native traditions.

The southeastern Woodland cultures used corn not only as a vegetable but also as a staple for bread and porridge, often drying and parching it for preservation. Corn kernels soaked in ashes lose their outer hull and expand. The resulting product, called hominy, was then eaten in stews or dried and ground into grits for porridge. The Seminoles of Florida also made a drink from roasted corn or grits called *sofk*. Along with the three sisters, the Woodland groups in the Southeast may have grown crops from Central America: sweet potatoes, sweet peppers, and possibly even tomatoes.

Southeastern Native peoples also frequently gathered food from the wild: fruit (plums and cherries), berries (blackberries and blueberries), nuts (hickory, acorns), and vegetation (wild onions, greens such as poke and dandelion, sassafras and other tree barks). Plants were used extensively for medicinal purposes. The Seminoles gathered plants distinctive to the Florida swamplands, such as swamp cabbage, now known as hearts of palm. They also gathered the roots of the coontie or *Zamia* plant, dried them, and ground them for bread.

The Woodland peoples also fished and hunted, using bows and arrows, spears, clubs, and various traps and snares. Large game included black bear and white-tailed deer; smaller game included rabbit, squirrel, opossum, beaver, and raccoons. Wild birds were plentiful, including large, slow-moving turkeys, waterfowl (ducks and geese), and smaller game birds (partridge, quail, doves). Alligator was unique to the swamplands. Meat was dried and made into jerky, a tradition that was passed along to white settlers, along with customs of storing food in gourds and skins.

Moving north to the Mid-Atlantic, the peoples of the Eastern Woodland cultures thrived on the rich coastal fishing and shellfish as well as what they found in the vast forests. The Delaware (Lenni Lenape), Montauk, and Powhatan peoples farmed and fished extensively.

At the time of European exploration and settlement of the New World, Native peoples in the Northeast had extensive political and social institutions. The Iroquois Confederacy (uniting the Five Nations of the Mohawks, Onondagas, Cayugas, Oneidas, and Senecas) was established by 1500 and functioned partly to provide food assistance to each other if needed. Algonquian-speaking peoples were also thriving in the region.

These groups made extensive use of wild plants, which they both gathered and cultivated—including amaranth, marsh elder, and goosefoot—whose seeds they ground into flour. Berries (cranberries, blueberries, blackberries), nuts (chestnuts, walnuts, acorns), roots (Jerusalem artichokes), stalks, and leaves were a large part of their diet. Tree sap, particularly from maple trees, was collected in early spring and boiled down into syrup and sugar, which was used as a seasoning and a preservative. Beans flavored with maple syrup (and bear fat) were often slow-cooked in a stone-lined pit, a technique taught to the settlers.

Like the cultures in the Southeast, the Woodland peoples hunted extensively: deer, rabbit, squirrel, beaver, moose, elk, and bear as well as various birds, such as turkey, partridge, duck, and goose. They also depended heavily on the many inland rivers, streams, and ponds for fish, and those living along the coast consumed shellfish, particularly clams (both hard-shelled and soft-shelled quahogs) and oysters. Lobsters and crabs were also eaten. These foods were often boiled, smoked, or roasted. Native Americans also dug pits in the sand, lined them with stone, and—after building a fire and letting it die down—would slow cook shellfish in the pit, a technique used in modern-day clambakes and lobster bakes.

The three sisters were the staple, and the tradition of growing them together was taught to the Pilgrims and later European settlers. Native Americans also taught the settlers to grind the corn into flour, first using lye to remove the hulls. The Iroquois also taught the settlers to prepare succotash (corn, beans, and, if possible, bits of meat), roasted corn, boiled corn, and hominy. Native peoples in Maine still make a bean and corn dish, called "hull corn soup," made of hominy, yellow-eye beans, and meat. Legend also claims that a Native named Quadequina brought popcorn to the Thanksgiving dinner in 1621, introducing it to the Pilgrims. Pumpkins were the most common type of squash and quickly became a staple of the European settlers.

The Woodland cultures extended as far west as the Mississippi. Before European settlement, the natural resources of the eastern Midwest provided abundant hunting, fishing, and gathering for Native American cultures. These Woodland tribes tended to have semipermanent dwellings with small gardens to raise crops, particularly corn, beans, and squash that supplemented hunting and fishing. Many of them gathered foods from the wild with variations depending on their locale. Wild game included deer, moose, bear, porcupine, beaver, rabbit, muskrat, and raccoon, along with wild birds: partridge, duck, pigeons, snowbirds, and coot. Turtles, turtle eggs, and seagull eggs were also eaten.

Fish was a mainstay of the Native American diet and was caught all year round, usually with nets and hooks, although spears and hooks were used with ice fishing. Lake Superior supplied trout and whitefish, and the inland lakes offered northerns, walleye, sunfish, suckers, and bullheads. Fish were preserved by smoking or, during the winter, by freezing in snow or the cold air. These Woodland peoples depended primarily on foods from the wild: berries (strawberries, June berries, raspberries, pin cherries, blueberries), mushrooms, greens (fiddlehead ferns, milkweed stems, watercress, dandelion pigweed, leeks, camas bulbs, Jerusalem artichokes), nuts (hazelnuts, walnuts), and herbs. They also tapped maple trees for sap, which was turned into syrup and sugar. Wintergreen or labrador leaves were used for tea.

A distinctive Native American food in the upper Midwest that was incorporated into European-American foodways was wild rice. Actually the kernel of an aquatic grass, it is the only grain indigenous to North America. The rice grows in the lakes and rivers of the upper Midwest (Minnesota, Michigan, Wisconsin) and was a staple of the Sioux, Chippewas, and Ojibwas. These cultures gave it symbolic meanings and ceremonial uses, and it played a significant role in their foodways. Among the Ojibwas, wild rice was harvested by shaking the tall grasses over a canoe. The kernels were then parched lightly and the hulls loosened by men gently dancing on them. These were then boiled in water and eaten with butter or bacon fat or are used in breads and soups. The kernels could also be popped in hot fat and eaten either lightly salted or mixed with maple sugar.

Like other midwestern Native Americans, some of the tribes living in the southern parts of the Midwest raised corn, much of which was dried into hominy for use during the winter months as well as for bartering. Wheat flour may have been introduced with government allotments in the mid-1800s, and became the breads that are staples in Native American foodways. Two distinctive types were found among the Ojibwas: bannock, a heavy, baked biscuit-like dough made of flour, baking powder, water, salt, and lard or bacon fat; and fry bread, a bread probably originating in the Southwest that used government rations of wheat flour, salt, baking powder or yeast, and milk or water.

Native Americans were moved out of the eastern states in the 1830s to lands west of the Mississippi. Pioneers often adopted their traditions; however, there was little opportunity to learn from them in the eastern Midwest. Upper Midwest tribes were able to maintain some of their traditions, but many skills were purposely lost, blended with other traditions, or adapted to the new physical and cultural environments of the western Plains and of the reservations.

Plains Cultures

The Native American Plains cultures were found from the Mississippi River to the Rocky Mountains. Tribes included the Arapahos, Blackfeet

Cheyennes, Crows, Comanche Dakotas, Kiowas, Pawnees. Shoshones, and Sioux. These groups have been stereotyped as the American Indian; fierce and aggressive, raiding pioneer caravans and scalping settlers. The reality was that the region was not suited to agriculture and lacked the rich forests and water sources that characterized the eastern part of the United States. The cultures developed nomadic and seminomadic lifestyles, living in tepees and, for part of the year, they cultivated crops (three sisters but also tomatoes and melons) in settlements along the rivers and streams, particularly the Mississippi and Missouri Rivers, but traveled looking for food the rest of the year. They ate whatever they could find from the wild—game included bison (buffalo), elk, antelope, whitetail deer, rabbit (hare), fish, and birds; vegetation included onions, wild rice, berries, cherries, wild greens, camas root, and scarlet buffalo berries. Large game would often be driven off a cliff or into a ravine where they could then be killed.

European colonists introduced horses in the 1600s, allowing Native peoples to develop a more hunting-based nomadic culture in which tribes lived in tepees (skin tents) while following the buffalo. The animal then became the staple food. All of the buffalo was used, not only the meat. The liver and kidneys were eaten raw, and strips of meat were dried in the sun. Known as "jerky," these strips could be kept for several years and were also ground up and mixed with fat and berries to make pemmican. Bone marrow was used in stews and soups, which were often "stone-boiled," that is, cooked in a lined pit with hot stones. Buffalo skins were used to make shelters, clothing, and food containers. Even the dung was used as fuel.

The Plains cultures, however, stood in the way of western expansion by the United States. The Homestead Act of 1862 allowed white settlers to farm Indian lands, and the completion of the Transcontinental Railroad in 1869 gave access to these lands to even more settlers. During this time, the vast herds of bison were decimated (dropping from 60 million in 1800 to 750 in 1890), destroying the means of survival for the Plains cultures. In the 1860s, reservations were allocated to them and to the Woodland Indians dislodged by Andrew Jackson's 1830 Indian Removal Act. On the reservations, they were dependent on the government and the largesse of charities and churches. They no longer had access to their traditional foods and lost much of the culture surrounding those foods. Children were often sent to government schools where they learned the white people's ways and their own cultures were systematically dismantled.

Southwest Cultures

Stretching from Texas through Southern California, north to southern Colorado and south to Mexico, the Southwest cultures developed out of a distinctive climate and topography of arid semidesert river valleys with seasonal rainfall, and forests at higher elevations. Summer rains and river valleys allowed for some farming. Three distinct cultures with highly sophisticated governments, religions, and social institutions emerged around 300 BCE, all of which practiced strict control of water: the Anasazis (known as cliff dwellers) in Arizona, New Mexico, Utah, Colorado; the Mogollons, in western New Mexico and eastern Arizona, who hunted and farmed along the rivers; and the Hohokams who developed sophisticated irrigation systems in central Arizona. These peoples mixed with those coming north from Mexico and developed into groups that have survived today, including the Hopis, who boast the oldest continuously inhabited village in the United States, Old Oraibi, in Northern Arizona; the Pueblos, the descendants of the Anasazis and known for their adobe houses built along cliff terraces; the Mojaves; the Pimas; the Yumis; the Zunis; and the nomadic hunting tribes, Apaches and Navajos.

These groups cultivated the three sisters along with chilies, pumpkins, and melons. Corn was central to their foodways and considered sacred. They developed different varieties of corn and often attached symbolic meanings to each variety. The Zunis raised five colors, each associated with a different direction and specific uses: white, associated with east, was used in gruels and breads; yellow, associated with north and eaten roasted; red, associated with south; blue, associated with west and used for a special flat bread known as piki; and black, associated with center, was rare and used in special ceremonial foods. The Hopis had 20 varieties of corn and also gave significance to the colors. Corn was usually dried and ground into cornmeal, which was then used to make flat breads or stuffed dough. Corn was also soaked in ashes to soften the husk. Rinsed and boiled, the kernels swelled into posole (also known as hominy). Beans, including the indigenous tepary and pinto beans, were second to corn in importance.

Foods gathered from the wild included cactus leaves (napoles) and cactus fruits (usually called cactus pears), nuts from the piñon pine tree, and small game, such as turkey, rabbit, armadillos, and desert reptiles (lizards, snakes). Many of these have become integral to the regional cuisine of today.

Spanish explorers in the 1600s introduced sheep and horses to the Southwest. The Navajos then became sheepherders, whereas the Apaches adopted the horse for use in hunting and raiding, living much like the tribes of the Plains cultures. Spanish, which later became Mexican, settlement in the Southwest created social hierarchies with Native Americans at the bottom. They were often treated virtually as slaves, and Native cultures, including foodways, were seen as uncivilized and kept separate from the Spanish and Mexican culinary habits. Although the inhospitable land protected the Southwest cultures from the American colonization occurring in other regions, reservations were established in the 1860s that isolated Native peoples and forced them to acculturate to Anglo-American ways. Rations were given to them, for example, that reflected "American" food-ways rather than Native American foodways. Fry bread and much later, "Indian tacos," were developed out of the wheat flour and lard provided to them. Interestingly, a large number of the Southwest cultures established relatively stable economies based on selling crafts (silver and topaz jewelry, beadwork, woven blankets) and performing dances and religious ceremonies for tourists. Today, 20 percent of all Native Americans live in New Mexico and Arizona, and the largest nation, the Navajo, is in the Southwest.

Far West (Pacific Northwest) Cultures

The Far West cultures ranged from northern California through Oregon and Washington to southern Alaska, westward to Idaho, Montana, and Wyoming, and east to the Pacific Ocean. The temperate, moist climate along the coast west of the Cascades supported lush rain forests rich in wild foods, and the seacoast offered abundant food, so that agriculture was not necessary. East of the Cascades, the land was much colder and windier, and of little use agriculturally.

Native Americans in the region included Kwakiutls, Chinooks, and Tlingits. These groups had distinctive large wooden carvings (totem poles), long houses and canoes made of red cedar, and a rich decorative art tradition. They also had a tradition of giving feasts as a display of generosity and wealth (called potlatches). Almost all of their food came from the wild. The forests supplied berries (blackberries, blueberries, chokecherries, huckleberries, raspberries), nuts (acorns, hazelnuts), roots (camass), and greens (desert parsley, mint, salal). Acorns were particularly important and were often used to make bread. The woods also provided game—bear, deer, elk, mountain goats, waterfowl, and game birds. The ocean, inlets, and streams supplied fish—salmon, cod, clams, crabs, halibut, herring, shrimp sole, smelt, sturgeon, and trout—as well as water mammals—otter, seal, and whale. Fish were often caught with nets made of cedar fibers, and clans camped next to rivers when the salmon were running upstream to spawn.

As with other Native American cultures, the Pacific Northwest groups used local resources with respect. Nothing was wasted, and nature was ceremonially thanked. For example, the bones of the first salmon caught in the spring were thrown back in the river to bring the salmon back the next year. Whales and other sea mammals that washed up on the beach were usually eaten, or used in some way—their bones and fat were used to make tools and oil for lamps.

American settlement of the Pacific Northwest began with the annexation of California in 1848 and the opening of the Transcontinental Railroad in 1869. The prospect of gold and lumber brought pioneers to the region, who encroached on Native lands. Reservations were established, and by the 1880s, almost every Native American had been forced to move there. Although they also experienced attempted assimilation and faced corruption among the reservation management, Native peoples in this region were able to continue many of their food traditions into the present. Salmon bake, for example, was salmon filleted and boned, tied to alder branches and then smoke cooked over an alder wood fire. Salmon "candy" (also called "squaw candy") was salmon jerky—thin strips of salmon dried in the sun (or in a low-heat oven for 12 hours). Smoked salmon, considered a delicacy to many throughout the United States, was a common food, and a soup made of smoked salmon and spinach was distinctive to the area. Fiddlehead fern tops were used as a green vegetable, steamed or boiled, and oftentimes served in a manner similar to asparagus. Oolichan grease, an oil from fermented oolichan fish, was often mixed with meats and berries or used as a sauce, similar to melted butter. Another Northwest Indian tradition was "fishy duck," a wild duck that lived off fish, which gave its flesh a fishy flavor. It would be slow roasted over an outdoor fire. A common dessert was wild berries (e.g., raspberries, blackberries, loganberries, cherries, blueberries) mixed traditionally with oolichan grease, but today they are usually mixed with honey. Nuts and mushrooms were also gathered from the wild.

Alaskan Natives

Native peoples in Alaska adapted to its environment of permafrost and tundra and its climate of ice and snow. The Inuit peoples developed culinary traditions that gave them the large amounts of protein and fat they needed to survive. Because they were unable to cultivate crops, their diet depended largely on game animals (caribou, moose, polar bear, arctic hare), sea mammals (whales, walrus, seals), fish from the Arctic Sea (salmon), birds, wild berries (lingonberries), and greens and roots (rosewort, beach asparagus, goosetongue). Meat and fish, including blubber, blood, and intestines, were usually eaten raw or lightly boiled. The Inuits usually consumed the entire animal, receiving vitamins from the stomach contents. Stews often contained a whole carcass along with whatever else was available. Meat and fish were preserved by drying or freezing and then were buried in the tundra. Meat and fish were also mixed with fat and berries for pemmican. Favorite treats that are still eaten today are muktuk (raw whale skin with a thick coating of blubber); *aguduk*, also called "Eskimo ice cream," which is made of whipped seal oil mixed with snow, berries, and roots; and jerky made from salmon or caribou.

Hawaiian Natives

Although considered Polynesian rather than Native American, the ancient Hawaiians made respectful use of the surrounding sea and tropical forests as well as the year-round growing climate and plentiful rainfall. They ate fish, shellfish (squid, limpets, crabs), seaweed, wild birds and domesticated chickens, dogs (which are no longer eaten), and pigs. They cultivated yams, arrowroot, breadfruit, bananas, coconuts, raspberries, strawberries, "mountain apples," taro, and sugar cane, and they ate wild plants, such as tree fern and fan palm. One of their main staples was poi, a highly nutritious paste made from taro root, which today is treated as a symbol of native Hawaiians.

ETHNIC GROUPS AND THEIR SETTLEMENT HISTORIES

Each region in the United States has a distinctive history of colonization and immigration. Each incoming group adapted differently according to the natural resources and the other cultures in a particular region. Some cultures quickly assimilated, leading to a so-called melting pot of American culture; others retained their individual identities, maintaining cultural forms (such as language, food, religious beliefs) and social groupings and creating more of a "salad bowl."[2] Food was often used as a way to mark boundaries, express identity, create community, pass along beliefs and worldviews among ethnic groups, nurture, and oftentimes to make money. The ways in which ethnic foods were used often differed by region. In some cases, immigrant foodways entered mainstream American foodways and are no longer thought of as ethnic.[3]

The United States saw several waves of settlement. After the initial arrival of Spanish explorers in the late 1400s, the first wave of settlement in the East lasted from the early 1600s through the early 1800s. Settlement was by western Europeans—primarily British, Dutch, and German in 1700s. These cultures laid the foundation for what later became the American culture, and their foods have for the most part become mainstream American food. The forced immigration of slaves from Africa during this period until the Civil War in the mid-1860s significantly influenced the southern United States—shaping its economy, agricultural, social structures, and foodways. Spanish colonization of Mexico during this time included parts of what later became the American Southwest.

A second wave of immigration took place in the 1800s, when industrialization and accompanying economic opportunities attracted numerous

European immigrants. Many initially settled in urban centers in the Northeast and the Mid-Atlantic, but new transportation systems (canals and trains) also took them to the Midwest and beyond, again mostly to larger cities. These groups included the Irish (from Catholic Ireland, rather than the Protestant north), southern and eastern Europeans, and European Jews. When Texas and southern California were claimed from Mexico in the 1840s, suddenly Mexican citizens in those areas became ethnic Americans. The California Gold Rush (1848–c.1864) and similar opportunities in the Pacific Northwest attracted immigrants from southern China and other Asian countries as well as Russia. Immigration laws in the 1910s and 1920s, however, limited the number of immigrants to the United States, shutting out some ethnicities altogether. Migrant workers from Mexico were still brought into the United States as an inexpensive labor force.

A final wave of immigration began in the 1960s with refugees from international conflicts (Korea, Vietnam, Southeast Asia, Somalia, Ethiopia, Central America) as well as educated professionals from around the world. Many people settled along the coasts, but some also went to urban centers throughout the country, particularly Atlanta, Houston, Minneapolis, Cleveland, St. Louis, and Chicago. This influx of cultures has expanded the foods available in the United States, but acceptance of new ingredients and styles of cooking varies widely among the regions.

AMERICAN REGIONS

The four primary American regions—the East, South, Midwest, and West—grew out of these Native American and immigrant cultures. Although each region developed differently, the regions were also united by national trends in economics and politics, particularly with the rise of industrialization, transportation, and communication networks as well as the increasing commercialization of the food system. Developments in refrigeration, canning, self-serve supermarkets, and marketing created a national culinary culture that has been further developed through mass media. This media in turn highlighted regional traditions, making people aware of the local as well as encouraging the invention of symbolic regional foods. This section of the chapter gives a brief history of each region and its subregions and describes the primary cultural groups and historical events shaping that region.

The East

The Eastern United States, which stretches from Maine to Maryland and extends from the Atlantic coastline to the Appalachian Mountains, contains some of the original British colonies and is often considered (along with Virginia) the foundation of American heritage. It is divided into New England and the Mid-Atlantic.

New England

New England comprises Maine, Vermont, New Hampshire, Massachusetts, Connecticut, and Rhode Island. The inland areas of New England were historically heavily wooded, and although this required backbreaking work in clearing the land, the forests provided plentiful game, particularly deer, elk, and moose, and birds, such as ducks, geese, and turkeys. Trapping was a major occupation of early settlers, and pelts were oftentimes used for trade. The woods also provided lumber and firewood for cooking, so that early settlers could roast meat and bake bread without worrying about whether they had sufficient fuel. Wood was also burned down to charcoal, which could be used for slow baking, and into potash, which was used for lye soaps. Wild berries grew throughout New England—strawberries, blueberries, cranberries, and blackberries—as did wild mushrooms, particularly in the northern parts of Vermont and New Hampshire.

The foodways of early New Englanders were based largely on the Native American three sisters, as well as British traditions, and emphasized bread (wheat preferably, but corn was used initially), meat (beef), cheese, butter, and dark ale. Although the early Puritans actually brought with them the complex dishes and taste for spices common in Europe, life in the New World required a more austere diet. They also maintained the English social class divisions of gentry and commoners (which included tradespeople and the poor). The gentry preferred imported food from England and used the locally produced salt cod for export. This Anglo diet dominated up through the Revolutionary War.

Because wheat did not grow well in New England, the colonists adopted maize, which they called "Indian corn," using the European idea of corn as grain. Cornmeal was used to make unleavened flat cakes—usually a simple blend of meal and water. These were similar to oatmeal bannocks of the British Isles, but called different names (e.g., johnnycake in Rhode Island). They also adapted porridges to corn instead of wheat, using cornmeal to make mush or hasty pudding. It could be boiled in a bag in water (similar to English puddings). For a special treat, the cornmeal would be cooked with milk and molasses as an "Indian pudding."

Colonists also grew rye and combined it with corn for "rye and Indian," which was used for everyday meals. They also made bread of grains such as oats, barley, and wild seeds. Boston brown bread is a legacy of those times—technically a steamed pudding, it is rye and Indian bread leavened with sour milk and baking soda and sweetened with molasses. Wheat, however, was valued above other grains and was often used for special occasions in pastries and cakes. When wheat from the Midwest became available in the mid-1800s through the building of the canal system, New Englanders shifted back to wheat bread, and corn breads are rarely used today. Cakes from refined wheat flour became a favorite, and even today are central to celebrations.

The other two plants of the three sisters have continued to be mainstays in New England foodways. Peas were common in the European diet, but they did not grow well in New England because of the weather, so the colonists borrowed numerous bean varieties from Native Americans, eating them fresh in season and dried in winter. They stewed dried beans with salted meat into pottage, combined them with corn into succotash, and learned to bake them with maple syrup. Boston baked beans grew out of the Native American tradition but molasess replaced maple syrup in the recipe. The beans also fit well with the Puritan rules of not working on Sundays. They could be baked all day Saturday, eaten at sundown and then the following day. Boston became known as "Beantown" because of the many entrepreneurs who would bake and sell pots of beans for this purpose during the colonial era. In Maine, loggers continued the Native American tradition of baking the beans in pits, or "bean holes." The yellow-eye variety was the most popular there, though the small white navy or pea bean became popular nationally. Squash translated into pumpkins, and these were used extensively by early colonists. They stewed them as a vegetable and often used them in place of apples—boiled down as sauce for meat, as a filling for tarts, pies, and puddings, and even baked whole.

Meat was a large part of the daily menu. New Englanders preferred beef, but they also ate a good deal of mutton, pork, lamb, and veal. The meat was often salted for preservation, although richer households preferred fresh meat year round. Two iconic dishes grew out of this era: the New England boiled dinner (corned beef, potatoes, carrots, onions, cabbage, beets, and turnip, served with horseradish) and Yankee pot roast (beef joint roasted with potatoes, carrots, and onions.)

The English colonists preferred domesticated meat to the many wild meats available. Venison had been available only to the gentry in England, and the common people had neither a taste for it nor a tradition of hunting. Some historians also think there was an association of hunting with the Native Americans, who were viewed as savages, and New Englanders felt a strong need to keep themselves apart.

The early colonists preferred fresh fish, both saltwater species from the Atlantic (cod, shad, salmon, pollack, bluefish, mackerel, herring) and freshwater fish from the inland streams and lakes (trout, bass, walleye, perch, pike, salmon). Salt-preserved fish, particularly salt cod, was usually eaten only by the poor or used for export. Fishermen's stews were made of whatever fish and vegetables, usually potatoes, were available. These came to be called chowders, probably from the French work for the large cauldron (*chaudière*) used for making them. Often thickened with potato or flour and seasoned with bacon or salt pork, these milk- or cream-based chowders were a mainstay of the common people, particularly along the coast. Corn or potato chowders could be made without fish.

The early colonists did not always appreciate the plentiful shellfish found along the coasts, possibly because of its association with Native Americans. Legends also suggest that early colonists sickened from mussels and inland clams. Be that as it may, it was primarily commoners who ate clams, often in the form of chowder. Lobsters, similarly, were not immediately welcomed into the Anglo-American diet and were not considered a luxury food until the 1900s. Maine's famous boiled lobster dinners and lobster rolls were originally simple fishermen's fare. The now-iconic New England clambake, featuring lobster, clams, sausage, corn on the cob, and potatoes, probably derived from Native traditions. Oysters, however, were plentiful and much appreciated. They were prepared in a variety of ways and often accompanied special occasions.

The colonists continued the British taste for dairy products. Every family had a cow, and it was a standard part of women's work to milk the cow and make butter and cheese. Dairying developed into a commercial enterprise early in New England (and the Mid-Atlantic) because of the urban and later industrial centers growing up along the coasts.

Apples did very well in New England's climate, and numerous orchards were established in the 1700s and 1800s, partly because homestead claims included planting an orchard. (Johnny Appleseed came from New England.) Apples were used as a fresh fruit and in cooking, particularly for pies. They were also dried or made into sauce and cider. The cider was then boiled down into "apple molasses" and used as a sweetener. Hard cider (cider allowed to ferment) was a significant staple. Pears and cherries were also cultivated in orchards and used in ways similar to apples. Wild fruits, strawberries, blueberries, cranberries, and blackberries were also used. Cranberries were unique to the region and became associated with the heritage of New England. Cape Cod growers began marketing cranberry juice and, more recently, sweetened dried cranberries. These various fruits were often used in pies, cakes, and muffins.

Foods were sweetened in a variety of ways. Refined sugar could be imported, but it was expensive. Maple syrup, used inland, was originally processed into sugar, but it was replaced by molasses, which was introduced through trade with the West Indies. Molasses was also the basis for rum.

The early colonists maintained the European custom of drinking beer and spirits rather than water, and rum, gin, home-brewed beer, and cider were part of everyone's diet, regardless of their age. The 1919 Great Molasses Flood, in which a holding tank broke, drowning 21 people in molasses, ended New England's production of molasses, and today molasses is found—other than in baked beans and Indian pudding—only in the back country. Maine boasts a molasses doughnut, for example.

As a leader and purveyor of American culture, New England shaped American attitudes toward food. In the 1800s, various reform movements emphasized controlling basic instincts (including hunger) and civilizing social behaviors. Meat, for example, was prepared so it was not obvious what animal the meat came from. The 1896 *Boston Cooking-School Cook Book*, which mimicked French dishes and was aimed at the middle class, was very influential throughout the nation. The early industrialization and urbanization of New England lead to the development of food-processing industries, including ice production and canning. Boston shipped ice all over the world, establishing itself as the center of the industry. Nineteenth-century immigration brought in vast numbers of Irish, Italians, Germans, Eastern Europeans, and Portuguese. Although reformers attempted to teach these new Americans to rely on the Anglo-American foodways of meat, bread, potatoes, and dairy, many of them retained their ethnic traditions. Industries continued to attract waves of migrants who have added to the rich mix of cuisines available today.

The Mid-Atlantic

The Mid-Atlantic region, which consists of New York, New Jersey, Pennsylvania, Maryland, and Delaware, is similar to New England in that it stretches from the Atlantic Ocean to the Appalachian Mountains in the west. Its climate, however, offers a longer growing season with cold, snowy winters, and the soil ranges from rocky to very fertile and flat to sandy along the coast. The plentiful rainfall and inland streams ensure plenty of water. The seaboard has numerous ports—New York, Philadelphia, and Baltimore—which developed early into urban and industrial cities. The coast also offers rich clam, crab, and oyster beds, as well as fishing in the various bays and inlets, which allowed it to develop into one of the nation's richest fishing areas. Extensive farming developed in the fertile plains, and orchards thrived on the mountain slopes.

Although the Mid-Atlantic had a strong English colonial culinary culture, similar to New England, it also had more diversity. German and Dutch settlers in particular gave it a different flavor. As a refuge for religious minorities, Maryland attracted Roman Catholics, and Pennsylvania

welcomed the Quakers (Friends) and Anabaptists. Many of these early settlers tended to be "common folk"—farmers, traders, fisherman—creating a
more egalitarian society than in New England. The region was also significant in the political history of the United States, because Philadelphia was
home to the Continental Congress, the Declaration of Independence
(1776), and the Constitutional Convention (1787).

New York was settled in 1625 by the Dutch, who established a tradition
of commerce and left a legacy of food, including waffles, pancakes, cookies,
and coleslaw. The city they built on the Hudson River, New Amsterdam,
grew into one of the largest in the country. The English conquered it in
1664 and renamed it New York but kept its commercial character, which
was solidified in 1825 when the Erie Canal connected it to inland markets.
Early in the 1800s, the city attracted numerous immigrants who transformed
it into a city of ethnic neighborhoods. This gave a distinctive international
flavor to its culinary culture. Clam chowder was transformed into a tomato-
based stew, sausages were transformed into all-American hot dogs, Italian
pies were Americanized into pizza, and eastern European breads were shared
with other ethnicities.

New York City and other urban centers of the Northeast were also home
to Jewish immigrants, who had a significant impact on the local food culture. Beginning in the mid-1880s, these immigrants frequently worked as
vegetable and fruit peddlers, later opening small food businesses, including
delicatessens that carried kosher foods. These also offered carryout sandwiches and preprepared side dishes. They quickly gained a reputation for
high-quality meats, exotic food items, and European dark breads, all of
which attracted non-Jewish clientele. One of the most significant Jewish
contributions to American foodways is the bagel. Originally a bread that
could be eaten by peddlers while working, typically with little access
water—the rules of Kashrut require handwashing before eating a meal, but
bagels technically did not count as bread because they were boiled, then
baked, so they did not have to wash their hands before eating it—bagels
tended to be a Sunday morning treat for Jewish families. In 1927, Harry
Lender started mass-producing "authentic New York–style" bagels, but
bagels were not introduced to the general American public until the 1960s
and later, when Lender started distributing frozen bagels. Varieties of flavorings and ingredients were developed along with toppings. Bialys, a roll similar to bagels, are still made in New York but are unique to Brooklyn.

The Catskills Mountains in upstate New York began in the early 1900s
attracting large numbers of Eastern European Jewish residents of New York
City. Escaping the heat of the city, families would spend summers at camps
and boarding houses that recognized the Jewish rules of Kashrut (observ-
ances surrounding food and eating). Known informally as the borscht belt,

the area featured numerous resorts and restaurants that mixed entertainment, particularly comedy acts, and good food based on eastern European Jewish culinary heritage.

Along with English Quakers from New England, Pennsylvania was heavily settled by German immigrants before the Revolutionary War. Many of these people moved inland and retained their language and culture. Known now as the "Pennsylvania Dutch," they maintained a distinctive cuisine. In contrast to the New England Puritans, the Pennsylvania Dutch tended to think of food as a gift from God, rewarding them for their labor. Food was therefore to be enjoyed, and sweets were a large part of the cuisine. Wheat flour and molasses were used in many creative ways—shoofly pie, sticky buns, funnel cake, fastnachts, doughnuts, apple pandowdy, and other dishes that have continued until today.

Philadelphia, meanwhile, was a major port for immigration until the early 1800s and for trade up to the present. The city was settled initially by English Quakers as the City of Brotherly Love. The English working-class cuisine was overlaid by German foods. As one of the largest and most important colonial cities in the United States, Philadelphia was a center for the emerging new nation as well as for commerce and trade. This supported the rise of fine restaurants and public eating houses. One of the city's most famous citizens, Benjamin Franklin, may have shaped the local foodways through his admonitions to eat and drink in moderation, and to live frugally—rules he did not always follow himself. One of the city's most famous dishes reflects its history as well as the contradictory impulses seen in Franklin. Pepper pot—a stew of tripe, beef, vegetables, and black peppercorns—by legend was created in 1777 by a cook in the Continental Army and helped win the Revolutionary War. It was made of scraps and leftovers. It was later served in fine restaurants. Later immigrants, particularly Italians, added to this mix.

At the western end of Pennsylvania, the city of Pittsburgh developed where three rivers converged (actually, the Alleghany and Monongahela rivers meet to form the Ohio River). The British, French, and Native Americans fought for control of the area. The French built Fort Duquesne in 1754, but the British took over in 1758 and renamed it Fort Pitt. By the time of the Revolutionary War, Pittsburgh was a gateway to the westward expansion, and by 1815, it had become a major industrial city, producing iron, brass, glass, and tin. Its steel industry identified it in the 20th century. These industries attracted Eastern European immigrants, a heritage reflected in the city's foodways—hearty "working man's" dishes, such as Ukrainian specialties, pierogis, and french fries with gravy.

Also part of the Mid-Atlantic, New Jersey was nicknamed "the Garden State" in 1876 because it supplied food to the cities of New York and

Philadelphia. A distinctive subregion within the state is the Pine Barrens, a 1.1 million acre area along the coast whose pinewoods and sandy soil were unsuitable for agriculture. The area has a long history of settlement by people trying to hide out or live apart from mainstream society: Tories, Quakers, Hessian deserters from the British army, and French Huguenots in 1700s, and Native Americans in the 1800s. These settlers valued self-sufficiency and resourcefulness, and their food traditions reflect that. In addition to standard rural American pioneer foodways, they relied heavily on hunting, fishing, gathering wild plants, and growing small kitchen gardens. Duck hunting was particularly prominent, but other small game mammals (rabbit, raccoons, squirrel) and birds (quail, grouse) were a standard part of the diet, as was venison (oftentimes poached). Freshwater and saltwater fish were also a major part of the cuisine, often as chowders. Catfish were called "freshwater chicken," and eels were both eaten and exported. Berries grew wild there, and cranberry cultivation became a major business in the 1860s. In 1978, the Pine Barrens was made into a national reserve.[4]

Delaware's food was similar to that of New York and Pennsylvania with its mixture of British, Dutch, and German traditions and a heavy reliance on seafood. Crab was historically favored, as was chicken.

Wealthy English Catholics settled Maryland in 1634 in the Chesapeake Bay area. These settlers brought lavish lifestyles and established plantations with West African slaves. Their rich cooking was an adaptation of local resources (wild turkey, venison, oyster stuffing, wild strawberries) with African (sweet potatoes, peanuts, okra) and British traditions. English steamed puddings were a common dessert. Terrapins (turtles) were plentiful, and terrapin stew was famous. Crab was also used to develop distinctive soups and chowders—particularly Maryland crab soup (with beef base and bacon flavoring) and she-crab soup, a delicate cream soup containing crab eggs, crabmeat, and sherry. Similar to Delaware, chickens were also raised, and used for an iconic dish: Maryland fried chicken with cream gravy. Oystering was a leading industry until the 1920s when typhoid outbreaks were thought to come from oysters, and blue crabs replaced them in popularity.

Central and western Maryland were settled much later (1740s) than the coast and primarily by Pennsylvania Germans who brought their cuisine—meats stewed and roasted with spices (ginger, cloves, allspice, mace), primarily pork, beef, and lamb. They also grew herbs in kitchen gardens (thyme, savory, marjoram) and greens (lettuce). They favored English "pot salads" (cooked greens with a dressing) but preferred a sweet and sour German dressing. These areas also attracted families migrating from the southern mountains in the 1920s through the 1940s who brought their own traditions of pork, dairy, and corn-based foods.

The South

The South contains subregions with distinctive histories and natural resources—the Southeast (which includes coastal Virginia, the Carolinas, and Florida as well as the flatlands east of the Appalachian Mountains), the upland South, the Deep South (Mississippi River Delta), and the Gulf Coast (including Louisiana). Within these subregions were distinctive cultures that retained traditions separate from the mainstream—South Carolina Gullahs, Appalachian and Ozark mountain people (including the Melungeons), and Louisiana Cajuns and Creoles. Distinctive cuisines developed among these peoples, but they also shared some commonalities in their histories.

Southern food culture developed out of a British Protestant heritage with an overlay of African culture from the slaves that toiled the fields to support a largely agricultural economy. Other cultures also contributed, particularly German and, in specific regions, Spanish and French. The confederacy during the American Civil War (1861–1865) united the states politically, and the region still tends to be lumped into one homogenous blend "south of the Mason-Dixon line." The South as a whole also developed an ethic of generosity with food and an emphasis on socializing around food—what became known as "southern hospitality."

Southeast

The Southeast runs from the Atlantic Coast to the Appalachian foothills and includes Virginia, North Carolina, South Carolina, Georgia, Florida, and Tennessee. The first Europeans in the South were the Spanish, who arrived in Florida in 1513 when Ponce de León landed on the northeast coast. He returned with colonists to the southwest coast in 1521, but native peoples fought him off. In 1539, the Spanish explorer Hernando de Soto traveled as far north as western North Carolina, and some scholars believe the Melungeons (a mixed-race group of people living in parts of Appalachia) are descendants of de Soto's crew. He also brought what became one of the most important foods to the South when he introduced pigs during his explorations from Florida to the Mississippi River. The descendents of these pigs flourished in the wild and provided a food source for the early pioneers. These wild boars or razorbacks were omnivorous and could be quite vicious. British settlers later brought their own domesticated varieties, and frequently left them in the woods to fatten off the plentiful acorns. Virginia and parts of Appalachia became famous for their sugar- and salt-cured hams.

Florida proved to be an ideal location for trade with the Caribbean, and the Spanish, French, and English vied for ports there. The Spanish controlled the southeastern United States until 1763 when Britain traded Cuba for Florida. In 1784, Spain with the help of France recaptured Florida and held it until 1821, when it was ceded to the United States. Plantations modeled on those from the Southeast were established, and Florida quickly became a major agricultural producer. After the Civil War, Florida developed extensive cattle and citrus industries, the latter becoming even more important as it became known as "the Sunshine State." Although heavily Anglicized, the state maintained its culinary connections to the Spanish and Caribbean cultures, developing a distinctive cuisine based on seafood, rice, and citrus. Although the historical Spanish influence is found only in Florida, with traces in New Orleans, recent immigration has brought in numerous laborers, particularly to the Carolinas and Georgia, where families and villages have transplanted to rural areas to work on farms.

British Protestants were the predominant European ethnic group to settle the South, and although other ethnicities and religions also came there, they were usually assimilated into the British culture. The first permanent settlement was by the English at Jamestown, Virginia, in 1607. It was located at the entrance to the Chesapeake Bay, a swampy area with lots of mosquitoes, undrinkable river water, and poor hunting. The settlers hoped to trade for food with the Native Americans, but were not successful until 1614, when John Rolfe married Pocahontas, the daughter of a chief of the Powhatan Confederacy, and relations improved. In 1646, the first reservation in the New World was established specifically for the Powhatans in King William County.

Founded by the Virginia Company of London, Jamestown was a business venture and the sponsors had to repay investors, so they encouraged cash crops in the New World while sending food supplies from England. Rolfe introduced tobacco, which grew well there. Large plantations developed, leading to the extensive use of indentured servants, including women and men from Europe, particularly the lower classes in England, and Africa. The 1619 census listed 32 Africans, and in 1619, 20 black men were purchased from a Dutch slave ship. Indentured servants could earn their freedom after a set amount of time, and many went on to become landowners (and even slave owners) themselves. Jamestown also recruited skilled craftspeople from Europe, particularly Germany and Poland, including a team of glassmakers from Italy.

More land was colonized, and plantations were established up and down the coast and in the interior flatlands. Cotton was added as a cash crop and became, in the late 1700s, the major force behind the southern economy (and behind the perceived need for slaves). Land grants given by the English king George II, however, made sure the English maintained their higher status and control. British food traditions also dominated, emphasizing the basic core of bread and meat and heavy use of dairy products.

Porridges, made from whatever grain was available, tended to be a staple food, and drink tended to be beer. Other cultures' food traditions were anglicized, and their ethnic heritage was often not recognized. For example, the German origins of frying, sauerkraut, apple butter, and reliance on pork were forgotten. Wheat was also grown in Virginia starting in 1618, and the upper classes quickly moved from corn to wheat bread. They also shied away from the wild game that fed the Native Americans. African food traditions were also incorporated into southern cooking, particularly the use of legumes, such as cowpeas and peanuts, and vegetables, such as yams (often confused with sweet potatoes), okra, and greens. African slave women usually did the cooking for the "big house," as the plantation's main residence was called, and learned to cook the English way.

The Virginia Piedmont areas especially retained the English sense of genteel society and social classes. There in 1768, Thomas Jefferson began building his 5,000-acre plantation, Monticello, where he imported plants, garden designs, and philosophies from France. There he cultivated more than 250 varieties of vegetables, introducing items from Europe and Africa into the American food system, particularly cauliflower, broccoli, eggplants, and tomatoes. He also subsisted on a diet based more on vegetables than animal food and promoted salads of fresh greens, a radical novelty to most Americans, who were suspicious of raw vegetables. His attempts to refine American tastes helped to establish French cooking as the model for cultured cooking in the United States.

Scots-Irish and Scottish settlers were also numerous, either migrating from Pennsylvania or coming through the port of Charleston, South Carolina. The peak of migration from Scotland and Northern Ireland lasted from 1720 to 1770. These individuals fit easily into the protestant South and adapted local resources to replace their traditions of oatcakes, porridges, and mutton. They also brought traditions of distilling spirits, skills that were particularly put to use in the mountain regions.

Meanwhile, the Low Country of the Carolinas and Georgia developed into a distinctive culture. The city of Charleston was founded in 1670, along the coast of South Carolina and was an oasis of diversity, accepting French Huguenots (Protestants) and Sephardic Jews (from Spain) as well as Catholics. As a port, it saw a great deal of trade with Bermuda and the Caribbean and had a large African American population. By the mid-1750s, it was the largest and wealthiest city in the South and had developed a reputation of gentility and sophistication. It was also a stewpot of culinary traditions, blending West African, British, and French foodways. The Huguenots brought customs of using honey in place of sugar and relying on home cultivation of vegetables and fruits. West Africans brought okra, peas, and rice cultivation.

Rice was first introduced to Virginia in the mid-1600s as an export cash crop, but it grew best in the humid, low-lying lands farther south. Slaves were imported from West Africa, where there was long tradition of rice cultivation. They grew indica types of rice, a high-quality long-grain rice referred to as "Carolina gold." Rice was commonly substituted for potatoes in Low Country meals. It was also adapted to English and French recipes for puddings of milk and egg and was often called Carolina rice pudding in historical cookbooks. Dishes of rice combined with beans (black-eyed peas or cowpeas) were also commonly eaten. The dish known as Charleston red rice also reflected the Caribbean influence of hot peppers in its recipe of rice cooked with bacon, ham, onions, tomatoes, and hot pepper sauce. The coastal areas provided a wealth of seafood, and shrimp, oysters, and fish were a significant part of the diet. These were oftentimes stewed or creamed and served over rice or hominy grits. Rice production in South Carolina ended by the 1920s and shifted to the west to Arkansas, Texas, and California.

The Sea Islands of South Carolina and Georgia were home to the distinctive Gullah culture of the Low Country. which was developed by West African slaves. The humid, subtropical climate of the coastal Low Country was similar to their homes on the west coast of Africa, so they were able to maintain their African food traditions, cultivating rice, sweet potatoes, tomatoes, collards, turnips, beans, peas, okra, and eggplant and relying on creatures from the sea. They emphasized boiled, one-pot stews (such as Frogmore stew, which contains potatoes, sausage, shrimp, and corn—but no frogs) as well as cooking foods in ashes. Hopping John, the rice and black-eyed pea dish eaten throughout the South for New Year's Day, may have come from there; the first known published recipe is in the 1847 cookbook, *The Carolina Housewife*.

The food traditions of African slaves influenced American food traditions extensively, particularly in the Southeast, Gulf Coast, and Mississippi Delta. More than 645,000 black Africans were shipped to the United States between 1654 and 1865, and the slave population had grown to almost 4 million by 1860. The South had land suitable for large farms and agricultural industries (tobacco, later, cotton), and these in turn supported slavery. As the primary food producers and cooks for the plantations, slaves used West African cooking techniques (deep frying, one-pot stews, boiling greens) and introduced some foods (okra, cowpeas, greens, eggplant, sesame seeds, sorghum, sweet potatoes, field peas, peanuts, and melons) to their white owners. These cooks then adapted British, French, and German recipes, so that even today southern white and southern black cooking share many ingredients, dishes, and techniques.

African Americans also developed a culinary culture of their own that was based on poverty and "making do" with scraps not considered palatable by wealthier people. The slave diet tended to be sparse and often depended on the whims of the master. Slaves were usually allocated small portions of cornmeal, rice, vegetables, salt, molasses, coffee, and maybe some pork or fish, so many supplemented this by hunting, fishing, and cultivating a small vegetable garden. Sweet potatoes were a staple, replacing the yams central to West African diets. They also gathered wild greens, including one called poke sallet (also called polk salad), which became the stuff of songs and skits. Chickens were often raised for "egg money." Two distinctive foods that grew out of these conditions were chitlins (intestines) and pig's feet, both of which were associated with black culture. Similarly, catfish, a bottom feeder with numerous bones and a spiny skin, was considered undesirable by many but was relished by African Americans (and actually many whites in the Delta area). In the second half of the 1800s, fried chicken and watermelon became stereotypes of southern black foods, displayed being stolen or eaten with the hands, portraying African Americans as happy-go-lucky and childlike but also dishonest and lacking civilized manners. Another food that developed in southern black culture was barbecue, meat slow cooked in a pit or an above-ground roaster, and then slathered with sauce. Although there is much variety, African American sauces were generally tomato based, whereas European Americans tended to use vinegar-based ones.

After the Civil War, many blacks stayed in the South, oftentimes as tenant farmers to their former owners. In the Reconstruction era (1865–1877), the southern states were restored to the Union, but in many cases were disenfranchised and exploited by carpetbaggers from the North. The result was increased tensions between races and economic classes, and the establishment of Jim Crow laws that legalized segregation. Many blacks left for Northern cities, looking for employment, social freedom, and new lives far from the fields that reminded them of their slave heritage. In the late 1800s and early 1900s, northern and midwestern cities seemed to welcome them. However, between 1916 and 1930, more than 7 million southern blacks migrated out of the South, and cities grew fearful of the increasing population. Tensions also developed between blacks already established in the North and the newcomers, many of whom were uneducated and unskilled. Discrimination became common in housing and education, as well as in food. For example, blacks could not eat in white restaurants (although they could work in the kitchens), could not shop in white grocery stores, and were often depicted as eating in an uncouth manner (e.g., eating watermelon and fried chicken with their hands).

In the 1960s, the term "soul food" was introduced to celebrate the African American culinary culture. Many of the dishes on a soul food menu could also be found on southern white tables, particularly those of working classes and Appalachian mountain residents—cornbread, macaroni and cheese, rice, biscuits, butter beans, black-eyed peas, sweet potatoes, fried chicken, greens, cakes, and pies. Some foods became iconic celebrations of the hardships of the past, symbolizing the resourcefulness but also the poverty of their lives as these were foods that were undesirable (in some cases, even discarded as garbage) or inexpensive—chitlins, pig's feet, cornbread, catfish, collards, or turnip greens. In 1958, The National Council of Negro Women published a cookbook, *The Historical Cookbook of the American Negro*, that helped establish a canon of soul foods. In the 1990s, they also began a series of cookbooks by well-known African Americans. Other authors, such as Edna Lewis, Sallie-Ann Robinson, and Joyce White have published books that weave recipes with family memories, helping to write a social history of African Americans through their food.

Gulf Coast

The Gulf Coast includes parts of Florida, Alabama, Mississippi, Louisiana, and Texas. In this area, native seafood (crab, oysters, shrimp, fish, and crayfish) was central to the food traditions of Native Americans and later the Spanish, French, and British colonizers. As the gateway to the Mississippi River, New Orleans was a melting pot of cultures. Founded by the French in 1718, it was under Spanish control from 1763 until 1801 when it went back to the French. The Louisiana Purchase in 1803 made New Orleans part of the United States, but it maintained its cultural and economic ties with Europe and the Caribbean. It also had the largest slave market in the nation. Its culture, like its people, was a mixture of races and ethnicities and tended to be more progressive than elsewhere in the United States, giving free blacks and mulattos much personal freedom and economic power. The food of New Orleans is a similar mixture. Heavily rice based but also with a strong bread-making tradition, it incorporated a great deal of seafood and often cooked okra (brought by African slaves) with French and Spanish colonial methods and tastes.

The term "Creole" originally meant anything native to the city but soon began referring to this mixture of traditions. Creole food tended to be urban food—elegant and delicate. One of the most distinctive dishes, gumbo, combined African stews (rice and okra) and French bouillabaisse (seafood and tomato) with a Native American tradition of filé (ground sassafras leaves) as a thickener. Gumbo was also made with whatever meats were available—venison, squirrel, sausage—and etouffe developed out of French sauces into a seafood stew thickened with file. Filling everyday dishes included rice mixed with beans and sausage (known as "dirty rice") and bread rolls filled with sliced meats or sausage. The Spanish dish paella

probably evolved into jambalaya, and Latin American cultures also contributed their spicy hot peppers and pepper sauces. French desserts also became
a fixture, and the native pecans were often used for pie and candied
pralines.

Another distinctive culinary culture in Louisiana was Cajun. Cajuns were
French-speaking people forced out of the Acadia region of Nova Scotia in
eastern Canada in the 1750s. As French Catholics, they sought refuge in
Louisiana but were relegated to the more rural areas southwest of New
Orleans. Their foods tended to be more "down home," often depending on
ingredients from the wild. Crawfish, in particular, became central to their
diet, and became a symbol of the scrappy resourcefulness of the Cajun people. Alligator was also eaten. Cajuns also borrowed from the various local
food traditions, particularly hot peppers, rice, and okra, and rice was often
the base for a meal.

New Orleans has long been known for its fine restaurants, colorful Mardi
Gras parades, and vibrant jazz scene. Its reputation is attached to Cajun and
Creole cooking, styles that became celebrated in the 1980s through chef
Paul Prudhomme.

Upland South

The upland South refers to the southern parts of the Appalachian Mountains and the Ozark Mountains. As a cultural region, the Appalachians
include all of West Virginia, parts of Virginia, Kentucky, Tennessee, North
Carolina, South Carolina, Georgia, and the Ozarks include northern Arkansas
and southern Missouri.

Native Americans had long thrived in the mountains, using the plentiful
natural resources. The Cherokee Nation was a highly organized, democratic,
matrilineal culture that cultivated crops and had extensive knowledge of
the medicinal uses of local plants. They developed their own writing system
in the 1820s, and many members assimilated with the incoming European
cultures, becoming Christian and intermarrying. Although 4,000 died in
the forced removal of the Cherokee in 1838 to Oklahoma (referred to as
the Trail of Tears), a large population stayed behind, primarily in the Great
Smoky Mountains of western North Carolina. A reservation was established
there, and a museum and living history village were constructed in Cherokee, North Carolina, in 1948 to preserve traditional ways of life and educate
the many tourists who flocked to the area. European settlers adopted many
of the Cherokee agricultural traditions, raising corn, beans, and squash and
learning to make hominy and to dry vegetables for preservation, including
"leather britches," strings of dried green beans. Settlers learned to gather
wild plants, including the distinctive onion known as ramps. Cherokee

herbal lore was passed along, including the use of ginseng, bark teas, and poultices made of fat and wild plants.

The Appalachian region was settled by a mixture of Scots-Irish, German, and English people who established a food culture centered on bread, corn, pork, and milk. They came partly from Pennsylvania following an Indian path, the Occaneechi Trail, that went into the interior of the mountains all the way to Georgia. Similar groups also came west from Charleston, seeking land and, sometimes, a haven from the law or colonial mainstream culture (indentured servants, convicts, Hessian mercenaries from the British army, Tory sympathizers). These settlers were staunchly Protestant and often fiercely independent. The mountainous terrain kept out all but the hardiest people, although parts of it were no more isolated than most of the rural south. Daniel Boone explored the mountains, blazing trails—most notably, the Wilderness Road in 1775 that led into Kentucky.

The terrain also limited settlers to foods that could be grown, gathered, and hunted. Pigs thrived on the acorns of the oak forests and were central to the diet, although oftentimes pigs were used more as a flavoring than as a main course. Lard was a basic ingredient in baking, frying, making gravies, and cooking vegetables. During the 1800s, cattle were raised for flatland markets, and cattle drovers created many of the paths that later became the major roads throughout the Appalachians. Although beef was too expensive to eat, milk was considered a staple food. Sweet milk and butter-milk were drunk, butter was considered a delicacy, and cheese was even made in some communities. Men hunted bear and deer or smaller game (squirrel, raccoon, possum, groundhogs), and the latter frequently showed up in stews and gravies. Mountain streams offered trout and other fish. As elsewhere in the country, women often raised chickens. They were usually valued for their eggs and eaten only on special occasions (such as a wedding, funeral, or visit from the preacher).

Out of necessity, every home had a garden. The three sisters were staple foods, and beans were often slow cooked into a thick soup and served as the main protein. Corn, in particular, was significant. It was eaten as a vegeta-ble, pickled into a relish, dried and ground into cornmeal, or turned into hominy. The meal was then used to make raised baked breads (corn bread or corn pone) or flat ones cooked over a flame (hoecakes or corn cakes). Oftentimes, soup beans and corn bread was a basic meal. Hominy was fried in lard or ground into grits, which were then cooked into porridge. Wheat, when available, was used to make biscuits, and biscuits served with gravy of-ten made an entire meal. These gravies were often bits of meat in a thick-ened milk and flour mixture, but were also made of "pot liquor," that is, the liquid left over from cooking greens, or coffee (for red-eye gravy). Families also raised potatoes, cabbage, squash, onions, and greens (collards, kale, turnips) along with fruit trees, especially apples. Cabbage was often turned into sauerkraut and apples into apple butter, two traditions from the German settlers. Families also gathered wild berries and fruits (blackberries, blueberries, mulberries, persimmons) and nuts (chestnuts, hickory, black walnuts). In fact, chestnuts were often used to make bread until blight in the first part of the 1900s wiped out most of the trees. Foods were often sweetened with honey or molasses.

Because travel was difficult, food had to be preserved through the winter, so traditions of canning and drying developed. Most homesteads included root cellars to store vegetables and a springhouse for milk and meat. Although stores brought in processed foods, most mountain people relied on them only for staples they could not raise—sugar, salt, pepper, coffee, flour, baking powder, baking soda, spices, and, later in the 1900s, tinned fish and meat. Stores often worked on a barter system, accepting eggs, animal skins, ginseng, and other medicinal roots. The mountains also developed a reputation for whiskey. Corn was distilled into moonshine, which could then be taken to flatland markets more easily than loads of fresh corn. It was also used as medicine. Other grains were also distilled—wheat, rye, and barley. Bourbon was developed in Kentucky, first simply as a generic name for corn whiskey, but the process was later refined with specific requirements for the mash and number of barrels used.

In the late 1800s, coal mining and other industries brought immigrants to Appalachia from Italy, Poland, and various eastern European countries. Settling primarily in the mining regions of West Virginia and Kentucky, these groups often maintained strong communities and ties to their native food traditions, which even today have not been assimilated into Appalachian foodways. Scattered throughout the mountains were also small communities of African Americans, freed slaves or even runaways. These communities tended to keep to themselves, oftentimes being on the other side of a mountain or holler from a white community. They tended to eat the same foods as the "mountain whites," but had even less money, so used more of the food scraps in their cooking.

For a variety of reasons, the Appalachian Mountain region has long been economically depressed. Local-color writers and "home missionaries" (church-sponsored reformers and educators) discovered the region in the mid and late 1800s, both romanticizing its isolation and attempting to preserve its quaintness. Others, particularly those who could benefit from exploiting the mineral deposits and lumber, emphasized what they saw as the backwardness of the people. Food was often used to stereotype mountain residents and still is today, with moonshine, corncob pipes, possum meat, medicinal herbs, and pigs characterizing "hillbilly" food. Aside from the stereotypes, poverty was rampant throughout the upland South (and still is in some parts), giving rise in the 1960s to John F. Kennedy's War on Hunger program. The Appalachian Regional Commission was established in 1964 to oversee economic development in a 205,000 square mile area from southern New York to northern Mississippi. Appalachian Regional Commission programs are still active today and frequently involve nutrition and farming initiatives.

The Midwest

The Midwest ranges from the Appalachian Mountains in the east to the Rocky Mountains in the west. It is often thought of as the "heart of America" or the "flyover states," and its culture is often held up as the norm for mainstream America. It is also characterized as bland, conservative, boring, conformist, family oriented, and farm based; however, it actually contains a great deal of variety, and there are enormous differences between rural and urban areas. The Midwest can be divided into overlapping subregions: eastern Midwest (Indiana, Michigan, Ohio), middle Midwest (Indiana, Missouri, Iowa, Illinois), upper Midwest (Michigan, Minnesota, and Wisconsin) and the Great Plains (North Dakota, South Dakota, Nebraska, Kansas, western Missouri, Iowa, Minnesota). The first three are discussed together, and the plains are treated separately.

Eastern, Upper, and Middle

Before European settlement, the Midwest's natural resources provided abundant hunting, fishing, and gathering for Native American cultures. Although the Woodland tribes were moved west of the Mississippi River after the Indian Removal Act of 1830, many of their traditions were adopted by early settlers. Hunting, fishing, and gathering wild foods (pawpaws, persimmon, berries, nuts, morels) became staples of pioneer foodways and have remained significant activities into the present. There were also pockets throughout the upper Midwest where tribes were able to remain and have kept their traditions somewhat intact. The Ojibwas in Minnesota, for example, stayed in their homelands, and their tradition of cultivating and gathering wild rice has become an iconic regional food.

The midwestern frontier began to be colonized by Europeans in the late 1700s and early 1800s, although states farther west did not see widespread settlement until the mid-1800s. Horses and wagon trains brought some settlers across the Cumberland Gap into Ohio, many of whom were British and German Americans looking for farmland and less populated areas. Others followed the Great Lakes and the many rivers crisscrossing the Midwest, such as the Ohio River (and the Erie Canal), the Maumee (which they hoped would connect Lake Erie with the Mississippi River at the port of Toledo), and the Mississippi River itself, which became a major thoroughfare of commerce and transportation.

The need for transportation systems brought numerous workers. The canals and trains were built largely by Irish and Chinese immigrants, some of whom then settled in the makeshift towns that sprung up alongside. (They were not always welcome, however. The town of Providence on the Maumee River in northwest Ohio banned Irish residents in the 1830s. Ten years later, the town was wiped out in a cholera epidemic.) The Homestead Act of 1862 encouraged settlement by offering 160 acres for five years of continuous habitation along with a small fee. The flat lands, rich soil, abundant water sources, and four seasons of the Midwest attracted numerous farmers.

The frontier offered hardship and deprivation as well as opportunity and abundance. Life there was oftentimes harsh, lonely, and unforgiving with unpredictable weather and natural disasters, from grasshopper plagues, hailstorms, and droughts to high winds that could wipe out the year's crops. Settlers were forced to rely on the local natural resources, which in good times were abundant—wild game (ducks, prairie chickens, turkeys, rabbits, squirrels, and the occasional deer), fish, and wild berries (plums, cranberries in Wisconsin, persimmons in Indiana, strawberries, raspberries, gooseberries). A distinctive regional tradition was ice fishing, in which holes are cut into the ice on lakes through which hooks and lines can be set. In places where the ice holds for an extended time, small shacks were built around these holes and frequently included heaters and other amenities for the comfort of those fishing.

Home gardens supplied much of the food—turnips, rutabagas, cabbages, carrots, tomatoes, squash, onions, melons—and were frequently cultivated from seeds sent from the East by relatives or carefully hoarded from one growing season to the next. During the winter months, fresh fruits and vegetables were not readily available, and families had to rely on what they had preserved through a variety of methods, including salting, pickling, smoking, drying, and later, canning. Family cows provided milk and beef, and a hog was usually butchered every fall to provide pork and lard throughout the year. Provisions that could not be home raised, such as flour, sugar, salt, and coffee, were obtained through the occasional trading post or merchants, and these were frequently not reliable providers, being subject to weather conditions. Johnny Appleseed, who in real life was John Chapman, a follower of the Swedenborgian church, planted apple trees throughout Indiana and Ohio in the first half of the 1800s.

Food was intertwined with every aspect of everyday life for pioneer women. Early cooking equipment was rudimentary, and open hearths limited cooking methods to boiling, frying, and roasting over an open flame. Cast iron stoves, introduced in the 1830s, improved conditions immensely, enabling bread making and baking, which soon were expected of every housewife. Food preservation was challenging; fresh produce and meat could be frozen during winter months, but in warm weather items needed to be smoked, dried, or canned. Many fruits and vegetables were preserved; frequently this involved their being boiled down in a large copper kettle over an open flame. Fruit butters, particularly apple but also pear and pumpkin, were made this way, and this was often a group activity lasting several days. A similar process was used for ketchups made of cucumbers, currants, gooseberries, and other vegetables as well as tomatoes. Cupboards and sinks were rare in pioneer homes, making storage and clean up difficult. Staples such as flour, salt, sugar, and coffee were stored in wooden barrels (many of which were produced in the oak forests of northwest Ohio) or metal tins in order to be kept dry, but produce was kept in cold storage in cellars or sheds. Rodents and insects were constant dangers to the stored food.

Midwestern pioneer foodways grew initially out of a British and German foundation. Northern European immigrants dominated the upper Midwest and Great Lakes, while Irish and Eastern Europeans shaped the urban centers. The early settlers farmed and established the hearty meat, bread, and potato diet needed to sustain agricultural activity. The Germans kept their traditions of the overladen "groaning board," tastes for pork and sausages, and a preference for frying, pickling (sauerkraut), and root vegetables. They relied heavily on vinegar, both as a flavoring and a preservative (particularly in pickling and sauerkraut); the melding of sweet and sour tastes in sauces (as in cabbage slaw and potato salad with vinegar and sugar dressing) and marinades for meat; varieties of sausages; a tradition of homemade noodles; a tendency toward heavy, rich desserts; and even the home brewing of beer. They also brought their ethos of orderly, practical, no-nonsense living, an underlying characteristic of midwestern culture and food. They preserved their homegrown produce by canning and pickling, and many German homes butchered their own meat and made their own sausage, often turning these skills into businesses. They also kept traditions of making cottage cheese and cheeses and, in the upper Midwest, collected wild horseradish to use as a condiment on meats and potatoes.

Germans settlers also brought long traditions of lager-style beer making, initially as a home tradition but also establishing commercial breweries throughout the Midwest in the 1800s. Ohio, for example, boasted numerous small home breweries before Prohibition. Wisconsin began brewing beer commercially in the 1830s, and Milwaukee soon became established as the center of beer making; Schlitz, Pabst, and Miller were all based there. These beers were wheat based, but newer varieties experimented with local ingredients. Wine, unexpectedly, was also produced in the Midwest. The Cincinnati area was the largest wine producer in the country until the Civil War, and afterward areas of Ohio and Michigan on Lake Erie, which have soil and climates similar to that found in northern Italy, developed a number of vineyards and wineries. These were stifled during Prohibition, but some survived as tourist sites as well as wine producers.

In the early 1900s, another wave of German immigration involved industrial workers who went to larger urban areas, often in the Midwest where there tended to be large German enclaves. German ethnicity became private and hidden, however, for approximately four decades encompassing the two world wars, during which time German culture was considered suspect in the United States. German names were not used for foods, and food that was obviously German was not offered publicly. German ethnic foodways also fell into disfavor toward the end of the 1900s, because it was thought to be too heavy and to contain too many starches and too few fresh fruits and vegetables.

Amish and Mennonite settlements in Ohio and Indiana keep alive an older, pre-electricity way of life. Both originated from the Anabaptist movement of the early 1500s in Switzerland, but the more strict Amish split off in 1693. The Amish first settled in 1730 in Lancaster County, Pennsylvania, and then spread to Ohio and Indiana. Today, the largest population is in central and northeast Ohio. The Amish maintain distinct and separate cultural traditions and communities. Known by their horse-drawn buggies, the Amish believe in strict social boundaries between believers and nonbelievers. Their food reflects their philosophy of family- and farm-based simplicity: it is home raised, closely tied to the seasons, and hearty and sustaining for the physical labor involved in farming. Meals emphasize meat with multiple carbohydrates. Homemade noodles, chicken and dumplings, mashed potatoes, cabbage, homemade pickles and jams, and rich desserts— pies, in particular—are among some of the dishes that have become iconic of the Amish. Restaurants and farm markets introduced their food to outsiders, and they became known for their chicken, homemade noodles, and pies.

Mennonites came originally to New Amsterdam in 1653, began settling in Philadelphia in 1683, and then moved further west, keeping to rural areas, particularly in Ohio and Indiana. In the 1800s, Russian Mennonites immigrated to the Pacific Northwest and western plains states. Mennonites do not maintain separate lifestyles, as do the Amish, and do not constitute a subculture; however, they frequently run food-related businesses that emphasize social and environmental responsibility in food choices. They were pioneers in the fair trade movement, and their stores are frequently the only source for alternative health foods and vegetarian items in the rural Midwest. Bluffton, Ohio, and Goshen, Indiana, are home to Mennonite colleges and offer such businesses as well as a supply of international foods (because of Mennonite missionary activities). Mennonites also frequently run fresh produce markets, and family-oriented restaurants.

The flat or rolling hills of much of the Midwest are also ideal for dairy cattle. Swiss immigrants to central Ohio in the mid-1800s brought a tradition of cheese making and dairying, and established small family-run cheese factories that still produce high-quality, specialty cheeses. Scandinavian immigrants further west established dairies, making Wisconsin the largest producer of milk and cheese. Cheese curds, ice cream, and other dairy products have become icons of that subregion of the Midwest. Welsh immigrants settled in west and central Ohio, often transplanting entire villages and maintaining a strong community surrounding a church and a tradition of communal singings.

The abundant farmland also attracted Scandinavian immigrants, who brought their food cultures to the northwestern and northern parts of the Midwest in the second half of the 1800s. The climate was similar to their homelands—short growing season, cold winters with abundant ice and snow—and they maintained many of their culinary traditions, emphasizing dairy products, root vegetables, soups, potatoes, fish, whole-grain breads, and porridge. These ingredients and cooking styles combined to make the hot-dish casseroles typical of the region.

The upper Midwest also had copper mining and lumbering industries. Immigrants from Cornwall, England, came to mines in the Upper Peninsula in the early 1800s, bringing their tradition of hearty potato and meat-filled turnovers. Finns also came to the region for the mining, and adopted these Cornish pasties, adding rutabagas to them. Scandinavians in general worked in forests, developing a distinctive lumberjack culture that gave such figures as Paul Bunyan to the American mainstream. Iron mines in the upper Midwest attracted numerous Slavic immigrants, particularly in Minnesota, in the early 1900s.

In the mid-1800s, the Midwest offered opportunities to numerous immigrant groups who found no place for themselves in the East. Newly developed transportation systems meant farm produce could be shipped to the more urban East, requiring not only more farmhands but also more work connected to loading, storing, and processing food. Cincinnati became the center for pork, and Chicago's stockyards were infamous. St. Louis, because of its location on the Mississippi River, became a gateway to and from the center of the country. French settlement was particularly strong there, and it was one of the more cosmopolitan midwestern cities. Industrialization offered more jobs and lead to urbanization, allowing immigrants to cluster in neighborhoods where they maintained their language and culture. Almost every city in the Midwest became a mosaic of ethnic enclaves— usually predominantly Irish, Italian, Hungarian, Polish, and Slavic. Chicago,

Cleveland, St. Louis, Milwaukee, and St. Paul-Minneapolis stood out as multiethnic cities.

The urban centers also drew southern blacks after the Civil War who looked to the North as a place of social freedom and opportunity. They tended to look for work in factories, far removed from their heritage as slaves working the soil. Chicago, in particular, was a beacon of a hopeful future, and racial interaction there was harmonious until poor and usually uneducated blacks from the South began flooding the city in the 1910s. Chicago and Detroit became famous for music as well as for commercial establishments serving soul food.

For a variety of reasons, industrial farming became the norm beginning in the 1930s, and the region shifted toward corporate farms rather than small family farms. Numerous food-processing factories were set up to be close to the crops, which in turn meant produce was also shipped in from other regions. Major companies—Heinz, Campbell's Soup, Gerber—established their production in the Midwest, so that close connections developed between food industries and farmers. The industrial farming also required migrant work forces, and the Tex-Mex food traditions brought by migrant workers beginning in the early 1910s introduced midwesterners to tacos, tortillas, rice and beans, and chili peppers used as a seasoning and a side dish. Partly because of the marginal social status of these migrants, their foods were viewed somewhat suspiciously, and Mexican food did not become widely popular outside the Hispanic population until blander versions were introduced by mainstream restaurants, such as Taco Bell or Chi Chi's.

In the 1920s, the emerging auto industries in Detroit and Toledo attracted migrant workers (mostly from the Appalachia). Immigrants from other countries, particularly the Middle East. Lebanese Christians began establishing communities there in the 1880s, and the auto industries drew two waves of immigration in the 1940s and 1960s from various Arab nations (primarily Muslims). Many of these newcomers also worked in food occupations—as peddlers or owners of small groceries and food stands—where they continued a strong tradition of hospitality and sharing of food. Middle Eastern food is now very popular in the eastern part of the Midwest, and can be purchased at diners, carry-outs, and fine restaurants.

Although the Midwest as a whole tends to be conservative about trying new ethnic foods and is known primarily for its meat-and-potatoes home cooking, it was also home to a number of food inventions that entered the American mainstream. Home delivery of pizza, for example, was introduced by Domino's Pizza in Detroit, and before long pizza became a staple, and there were pizza parlors in almost every town. The distinctive Chicago style of deep-dish pizza was invented in 1943.

Greek immigrants, who began settling the urban Midwest in the early 1900s, frequently opened small businesses around food, offering basic American fare of hamburgers and hot dogs, along with some Greek staples, such as gyros, lemon-flavored chicken and rice soup, Greek salad (greens with feta cheese, whole olives, and olive oil dressing), spinach and cheese pies, and baklava (walnut- and honey-filled phyllo dough). An important Greek contribution to midwestern foodways was Cincinnati chili, which was invented in the 1920s by a Macedonian immigrant. Cinnamon makes the meat sauce distinctive. Also, the idea of stacking toppings is found in other Greek-American creations, such as Coney hot dogs sold by Greeks in Detroit. Similarly, the first commercially processed Chinese food began in the Midwest: in 1922 a Detroit grocer and his former roommate from the University of Michigan, a Korean, started canning bean sprouts and founded La Choy. Their canned versions of Americanized Chinese dishes and ingredients defined Asian food for years for many midwesterners.

Appalachian culinary traditions are common throughout the southern parts of Ohio, Indiana, and Missouri. Industrial centers in the Midwest also drew migrants from the mountains in the first half of the 1900s, who often settled together into neighborhoods and continued their foodways traditions.

The Great Plains

Overlapping with the West, the Great Plains stretches between the woodlands along the Mississippi River to the mountains of the West. The extreme temperatures, meager water, and severe storms (especially in winter) of these grassy plains kept them largely uninhabited for many years. Nomadic Native Americans hunted bison (buffalo), particularly once Spanish explorers introduced horses. The first Europeans to the area were hunters and trappers in the early 1800s. With the Homestead Act of 1862, railroads brought homesteaders from the Northeast and from Europe (particularly central and northern Europe) who turned to farming, raising wheat and cattle. The vast herds of buffalo were decimated by the settlement, and the grasslands were opened to cattle and sheep grazing and to farming. Meanwhile, cowboys drove cattle from Texas to the railroads, establishing the ranching culture that characterized the West.

Laura Ingalls Wilder immortalized the life of the pioneers in the autobiographical novel *Little House on the Prairie* and other books. In these she described the late 1800s settlement period from a child's perspective, often including extensive descriptions of food and the activities surrounding growing, preserving, and preparing it. The plains and tornadoes of Kansas were made famous for many Americans through the classic film, *The Wizard of Oz*.

The overgrazing and poor soil management of the early settlers eventually led to erosion, turning the southern part of the region into the dust bowls of the mid-1930s, which included parts of Oklahoma, Colorado, Kansas, Texas, and New Mexico. Extensive irrigation systems were developed in the 1950s, leading to the plains producing vast fields of wheat and other grains. The Scandinavian and central European cultural influence remained strong.

The West

The West was a much later addition to the United States than the East and South, and it has always been something of its own country, less tied to the past and tradition, more independent, and often more innovative. Like the other regions, though, it contains widely varying subregions with distinctive mixtures of cultures: Mountain States, the Southwest, California, the Pacific Northwest, Alaska, and Hawaii. Its food similarly varies, ranging from traditional Asian, Hispanic, Russian, and American pioneer to the newest trends and cutting-edge culinary experiments.

Mountain States

The mountain states are Montana, Wyoming, Idaho, Nevada, Utah, Colorado, Arizona, and New Mexico. The Rocky Mountains run north and south, their jagged, windswept peaks forming a natural barrier to outside exploration or even travel. In 1540, the Spanish explorer Francisco Vásquez de Coronado made his way into the region, bringing diseases along with horses, guns, and Christianity. The Native American cultures were decimated, leaving the region open to further exploration and settlement, first by fur traders and miners in the 1740s who lived independently as "mountain men." The Lewis and Clark expedition explored the region from 1804 to 1806, and the Oregon Trail opened in 1842, bringing thousands of settlers to the arable valleys and mining towns. In 1847, the Mormons made their way across the plains and the mountains to Salt Lake City to escape religious persecution. They established a distinctive culture—with a strict adherence to church authority and bans against alcohol and caffeine—that is still thriving today. The completion of the Transcontinental Railroad in 1869 also enabled settlement. Immigrant groups from southern and eastern Europe established strong ethnic communities. Italians settled into farming and Basques became sheepherders. Although these ethnic groups retained many of their culinary traditions, the pioneer diet based on meat (beef), bread, and potatoes with dairy dominated.

Meanwhile, cattle herds thrived on the mountain pastures during the summers and spent winters in the more protected lower pastures. An extensive cowboy culture developed, in which masculinity and guns ruled. The Wild West was romanticized as a lawless region of saloons, ranches, and cowboys and Indians. That heritage is evoked today in the region's foodways of steaks, chuck-wagon suppers, Rocky Mountain oysters, and chili. Sometimes referred to as "Marlboro Country," after an advertising image of a lone cowboy seated on his horse and smoking a cigarette, the region's isolation allowed a social freedom that was not possible in more crowded regions. The beauty of the mountains had also long attracted notice, and in 1872, the first national park was established—Yellowstone National Park.

The Southwest

The Southwest comprises New Mexico, southwest Texas, Arizona, southern Colorado, southern California, southern Nevada, and southern Utah. The American Southwest was home to Native American cultures that had developed sophisticated systems of farming and irrigation in order to inhabit this arid land with extreme temperatures. These cultures established the three sisters as the foundation for the regional cuisine. A wide variety of corn was also grown, and kernels were frequently soaked in lye to make posole (hominy), which was often stewed with onions, garlic, oregano, red pepper, and a little bit of meat (pork, lamb). The Navajo adopted sheepherding from the Spanish settlers, and mutton became common meat.

Spanish explorers first entered the area through Mexico and began establishing churches and missions in the late 1500s, often planting vineyards in order to have wine for mass. They also introduced Spanish culinary traditions of sweets, cheese making, custards, rice, and spices. They also imported the Spanish Inquisition to the New World in 1626, a move that invoked extreme hostility from the Native Americans.

Mexican independence in 1821 established Mexican foodways as the dominant culinary culture of the Southwest. Mexican traditions of corn tortillas and tamales, refried beans, and tomato and chili sauces became a standard part of the regional cuisine, as did oregano, cilantro, and cumin as the main spices. Settlers in this region cultivated a wide variety of chilies, consuming them fresh, dried, roasted (as chipotle peppers) and mixed with other ingredients into sauces (salsas). Ground pumpkin seeds were used to thicken stews, while green and toasted seeds were part of many dishes. A soft cheese (*queso fresco*) was made from a combination of cow and goat milk. It could then be dried (*queso anejo*) and crumbled over various foods.

In 1821, the opening of the Santa Fe Trail in New Mexico allowed trade with France as well as Americans, and in 1823, Anglo-Americans began moving into Texas with land grants from the Mexican government. Mexico closed the Southwest to American immigrants in 1830, but Anglo settlements were already expanding. In 1836, Texas was declared independent from Mexico, and although the Americans lost the famous Battle of the Alamo in San Antonio that year, the state was annexed by the United States. The rest of the Southwest similarly came under American jurisdiction in 1846. The discovery of gold, first in New Mexico in 1828 and then in California in 1848, brought more Americans and Europeans, and the opening of the Transcontinental Railroad in 1869 and its various connecting lines not only brought settlers into the Southwest but also stimulated the development of eateries for travelers. A chain of Harvey House restaurants developed in response, offering clean, reliable service and home style food based on the pioneer food traditions (meat and potatoes). Immigration in the later 1800s often included immigrants from central and Eastern Europe who added their own traditions to the mix. German immigrants to west Texas, for example, brought sausages and potato dishes as well as the accordion. Chili con carne developed in Texas, and German-Texans invented commercially processed chili powders. (Nachos, tortilla chips covered with cheese and salsa, were invented at the Dallas state fair in 1964.) These immigrant cultures mixed with the Mexican traditions, particularly in west Texas and southern California, to form Tex-Mex and Cal-Mex cuisines.

Hispanic peoples in the Southwest have also maintained their own traditions. Frequently relegated to the lower economic and social classes, their food used inexpensive ingredients, such as beans and corn. In some cases, discarded items were turned into delicacies—tripe was the basis for menudo stew, and fajita, a tough cut of beef, was marinated and grilled. Tex-Mex cuisine developed out of these conditions. Mexican food in New Mexico and Arizona developed into distinctive traditions of roasted chilies, varieties of salsa, and distinctive dishes, while Southern California kept a strong Mexican food presence. Cal-Mex food emphasized fresh flavors, fish, avocados, and citrus.

These regional styles of Mexican-American foods were homogenized (and sanitized) and introduced to Americans outside the Southwest through the commercial food industries. The popular fast-food company Taco Bell was started by California resident Glen Bell as Taco Tia in San Bernardino, California, in 1954. In 1962, he opened Taco Bell in Downey, California, and it is largely responsible for tacos (both hard shell, an American invention, and soft tortilla tacos), burritos, and nachos becoming icons misrepresenting Mexican food. These foods have become popular meal items in homes across the United States and, as a measure of their acceptance into American culture, are even frequently served in school cafeterias. It can be argued that Taco Bell opened the taste buds of the American mainstream for more authentic presentations of Southwestern and Mexican cuisine.

Although margaritas and platters of rice, beans, and guacamole accompanying standard tacos, burritos, enchiladas, or fajitas define many Mexican restaurants throughout the country, even those establishments now offer more variety. Mexican fried ice cream is a popular birthday treat, and salsa has become as American as ketchup—even more so, because it is eaten as a dip for snacks as well as used as a condiment.

Two other cultures dominated the Southwest. Cattle handlers were needed to herd the longhorn cattle distinctive of the region, and cowboys developed their own culinary culture. Based on the need to carry supplies on the trail and the abundance of cows at hand, their cuisine featured beans, cornmeal, and beef. Large populations of Native Americans also remained in the Southwest, although they were forced to live on federal reservations. Government rations of wheat flour, salt, cornmeal, dried beans, and salted meat were adapted into native cooking. Fry bread, similar to a thick tortilla or pancake, was one result, and has since been used for "Indian tacos."

California

The many abundant wild foods (fish, game, berries, nuts, edible plants) offered a cornucopia to the Native Americans who originally lived in California. They used acorns as their basic starch, washing and drying them to leech the tannic acid from them, and then grinding them into flour for mush. This acorn mush was then dried into cakes in the sun. These could also be mixed with wild berries—blackberries and raspberries grew especially well—wild mushrooms, game meats (deer, bear), and shellfish and fish, particularly salmon.

The influence of Mexican cooking is particularly prevalent in Southern California. Spanish missionaries from Mexico came into the area beginning in 1769 in San Diego. They brought with them chili peppers, olives, figs, grape vines, fruit trees, dates, and nuts. They also planted corn and wheat fields, and they later introduced chocolate, ginger, brown sugar, and coffee. The grapes were used to make wine for the mass but were the beginning of a major industry for the state. In the early 1800s, ranchos, private land grants under Mexican rule, were established to began a cattle industry. Cowhide and tallow were very valuable, and the vaqueros, cowboys, ate the beef—frequently charred over embers. They also ate beans and used a sauce of chopped onion, tomato, and green pepper with vinegar, salt, and olive oil. These foods carried over, as did *carne seca*, beef cut into long strips, dipped into chili sauce, dried, and then shredded for *carne con chile* or enchiladas.

The annexation of California by the United States in 1847, and the discovery of gold the following year, brought fortune hunters from everywhere in Europe and United States. The plain but hearty fare of pioneer America (primarily Midwestern) is still the foundation of Anglo-California cooking. San Francisco even offers a breakfast dish from the Gold Rush: the Hangtown fry—a plate of fried oysters, bacon, and scrambled eggs. Sourdough bread was a staple of western pioneers and was brought in with Gold Rush. It is now associated with San Francisco, where a French baker started offering it in 1849. The original business, the Boudin Bakery, is still in business today.

The Gold Rush and the railroads brought numerous Chinese laborers. They not only established Chinatowns in San Francisco and Los Angeles, but they also followed the railway lines to other parts of the country. Some of the most famous Chinese-American foods today come from that era— chop suey (possibly from the Chinese for "miscellaneous scraps") and Americanized chow mein (stewed vegetables on fried noodles); both were probably created in San Francisco. Los Angeles claims fortune cookies (1918), although San Francisco is home to the Lotus Fortune Cookie Company, which invented the machine that folds the cookies. Egg rolls were possibly invented there as well.

Japanese and Filipino immigrants also came to California in the late 1800s as agricultural workers and established communities and restaurants. Japanese Americans were put in internment camps during World War II, and their food remained primarily a private ethnic tradition until Californian restaurateurs introduced sushi to mainstream America in the 1990s. They even added avocado and crabmeat to create a regional version, the California roll.

Numerous other ethnicities also settled in the state and maintained strong identities and food traditions. Los Angeles has a large Eastern European and Jewish population, and Russian culture is strong in the north. A town near Santa Barbara, Solvang, was settled by Danes in 1911 and is now a living history town with restaurants serving traditional foods, including iconic *ebleskiver* dumplings.

In the late 1800s, California developed an extensive agriculture industry that has continued to thrive. Luther Burbank, the famous plant breeder who developed numerous crops and sold seeds nationally through catalogs, worked in Santa Rosa north of San Francisco. The Santa Rosa plum was only one of his many creations. The wine industry began in California at the beginning of the 1900s, and California quickly became established as the center for grape and wine production in the country.

In 1911, a film studio was built in Hollywood, a community annexed by Los Angeles, and a distinctive culture of stardom and glamour developed around the burgeoning movie industry. Although that industry has expanded to other cities and countries, Hollywood still retains an aura of make-believe. In the 1930s, California also developed an extensive "car culture" that lead to the development of suburban drive-throughs and fast-food restaurants.

California early developed a reputation for being progressive and cutting edge. That included its approach to food, so that a number of trends in American culinary culture developed there. California cuisine developed in the 1960s and introduced exotic and fresh vegetables, cooking techniques that emphasized natural taste of a food, and unusual combinations of textures and flavors. This fusion cooking then led to American nouveau cuisine with its emphasis on innovation, originality, and freshness. One of the leaders of California cuisine was Alice Waters, owner of the Berkeley restaurant Chez Panisse. Waters insisted on fresh, locally grown produce and led the way in establishing gardening programs in schools and communities. California was also at the forefront of vegetarian cooking in the United States, partly as an offshoot of the counterculture of the 1960s. Similarly, organic farming was established in California communes and then within the agricultural industry, so that some of the most successful organic farm today are in California. These trends resulted in new foods, new cooking styles, and even new approaches to food and eating.

Pacific Northwest

The Pacific Northwest includes northern California, Oregon, and Washington as well as southern Alaska, western Idaho, Montana, and Wyoming. In some ways, its food shares more in common with Canadian British Columbia than the rest of the United States. Native Americans in the region depended on the sea and forests for sustenance and have continued many of their food traditions, particularly smoked salmon and grilling fish on cedar planks.

The first European settlers in the area were trappers and explorers. Farms and communities began to be established along with the Oregon Trail. Starting in Missouri between the 1840s and 1860s, the trail brought pioneers from the Northeast and the Midwest, who in turn brought their food traditions, which were based largely on Yankee (based on British) and German traditions of heavy reliance on meat, bread (cornbread), and dairy products. They also brought apple and pear orchards. Washington apples are now shipped all over the country.

These settlers also adapted Native American hunting and gathering traditions, particularly with seafood and the plentiful berries, especially blackberries and huckleberries. The berry cobblers popular today are a remnant of that heritage. Atlantic salmon quickly became a staple of both everyday and celebratory meals, and a common dish was whole salmon, baked (usually stuffed with herbs or vegetables) or grilled (in foil over alder chip coals).

Salmon steaks were common, long before they became popular for health reasons elsewhere. Other seafood was also plentiful: at least five different types of oysters, pink scallops (also called "scooter" or "singing" scallops because they scoot along the sand), mussels, and the famous giant geoduck. Dungeness crabs are unique to the West Coast; these large, meaty crabs were often served at crab boils. Halibut was also distinctive to the Pacific Northwest, coming from the Gulf of Alaska. Related to flounder, a halibut can reach over a hundred pounds. Sturgeon, a bottom feeder, was also popular; its taste is compared to pork or chicken. A thriving commercial fishing industry started in the late 1800s and has continued into the present.

The California Gold Rush in the mid-1800s also spread to the Pacific Northwest, bringing numerous Scandinavian and Russian immigrants in the latter 1800s. Scandinavians introduced their techniques of preserving fish by smoking, and Russians brought salmon *pirogs*, a large turnover filled with salmon, rice, cabbage, and mushrooms, served with sour cream and dill. Chinese came to California originally to work on the railroad. The line terminated in Seattle, so many settled there, establishing a large community with restaurants and groceries. Japanese immigrants settled in Puget Sound before World War II, and waves of other Asian immigrants have created a mix of cuisines available: Koreans in the 1950s; Filipino and Hong Kong Chinese starting in the 1960s, and Southeast Asian (Lao, Vietnamese, and Thai) in the 1970s and 1980s. Some of these Asian immigrants brought strong farming traditions and have continued that occupation, offering fresh produce to the numerous specialty ethnic groceries and restaurants.

The Northwest has long been rich in produce, both for national distribution and for sale locally in the many farmers' markets, particularly at the Pike Place Market in Seattle (one of the oldest in the country, established in 1907) and the Farmers' Market in Portland, Oregon. "Back to the land" farms flourished there in the 1960s, and the region is still a leader in organic farming and community-based agriculture.

Alaska

Although Alaska is part of the Pacific Northwest and shares much of that region's foodways, it is also a land and culture quite distinct in itself, still strongly Native American. European explorers entered Alaska in the 1700s, bringing their own foodways as well as adapting Inuit foods. Russian fur traders and settlers introduced flour for bread and pastries, tea and sugar, pea soup, and hearty crops, such as cabbage, radish, turnip, and potato. The Gold Rush brought in people from throughout the United States as well as the Scandinavian countries, particularly Finns. Alaska was made a state in 1959, and since then, its fisheries and oil industries have been steadily developed. Game hunting and fishing were also developed into major tourist industries.

Hawaii

Hawaiians have maintained their culinary culture through years of colonizers and immigrants to these islands that stretch 1,500 miles in the Pacific Ocean. Captain Cook reached the islands in 1778, and in the early 1800s, Hawaii was a British protectorate, which allowed for the establishment of rice, sugar cane, coffee, and pineapple plantations. These industries attracted workers from Asian countries (Japan, China, Korea, the Philippines), and they brought their own food traditions. Hawaii was annexed by the United States in 1898 and became the 50th state in 1959. It continues to be a prime producer of coffee (Kona coffee from the Big Island); tropical fruits, such as bananas, pineapples, coconuts; and newer exotic fruits such as star fruit, sour sops, mangoes, and baby bananas.

Hawaiian food historically mixed Native, Asian, and Anglo traditions, using ingredients such as raw fish, seaweed, poi, tropical fruits, and Spam to create some of the most distinctive cuisine in the United States. This cuisine ranged from traditional foods, such as Kalua pork, *poke* salad, poi, and *lomi* salmon; to dishes using the imported plantation crops, such as Macadamia nut pie or the Mai Tai drink; to new dishes incorporating national, processed foods, such as "spam *musabi*" (pressed rice with Spam) or *saimen* (noodle soup with fish cakes). Much of its food reflected its multicultural heritage: *manapua* (Chinese buns), chicken long-rice (Japanese rice and chicken), *loco-moco* (two scoops of rice topped with a choice of spam, hamburger patty, or grilled Portuguese sausage, then covered with a fried egg and brown gravy). A standard meal today is a "plate lunch," with rice, macaroni salad, and a meat entrée (usually an American or Asian food). Spam was embraced in Hawaiian foodways after World War II, and many residents joke that it is "Hawaiian steak." The traditional luau feast has been transformed from a religious feast to a social one (and oftentimes a tourist event), and often includes contemporary American favorites along with selected traditional Native foods.

NOTES

1. Linda Murray Berzok. *American Indian Food* (Westport, CT: Greenwood Press, 2005).

2. The melting pot and salad bowl are popular but simplistic metaphors for describing the immigrant nature of American identity. The melting pot refers to the idea that immigrants blend into one generic but harmonious American culture that unifies

all citizens. The salad bowl refers to a more realistic view that immigrants retain their own cultures but also add to and become part of the larger American culture. Both metaphors ignore the fact that the United States has been shaped primarily by western European immigrants who historically had the power to define what characterizes Americans. For more on theories of ethnicity in the United States as it relates to food, see Susan Kalcik, "Ethnic Fooways in America: Symbol and Perofrmance of Identity," in *Ethnic and Regional Foodways in the United States: The Performance of Group Identity*, eds. Linda Keller Brown and Kay Mussell, 37-65 (Knoxville, TN: The University of Tennessee Press, 1984). An excellent summary is also found in Anne R. Kaplan, Marjorie A. Hoover, and Willard B. Moore, "Introduction: On Ethnic Foodways," in *The Taste of American Place: A Reader on Regional and Ethnic Foods*, 121-134 (New York: Rowman & Littlefield Publishers, 1998).

3. Numerous scholars have recently examined the complexity of immigrant foodways and the various roles they play in the larger cultural context. For overviews see, Joel Denker, *The World on a Plate: A Tour through the History of America's Ethnic Cuisine* (Lincoln: University of Nebraska Press, 2007), Donna R. Gabaccia, *We Are What We Eat: Ethnic Food and the Making of Americans* (Cambridge, MA: Harvard University Press, 1998), and Richard Pillsbury, *No Foreign Food: The American Diet in Time and Place* (Boulder, CO: Westview Press, 1998). Excellent studies of how food is used by specific ethnic groups in the United States can be found in the edited collections by Shortridge and Shortridge, and Brown and Mussell. Also see Krishnendu Ray, *The Migrant's Table: Meals and Memories in Bengali-American Households* (Philadelphia: Temple University Press, 2004).

4. Angus K. Gillespie, "A Wilderness in the Meglopolis: Foodways in the Pine Barrens of New Jersey," in *Ethnic and Regional Foodways in the United States: The Performance of Group Identity*, ed. Linday Keller Brown and Kay Mussell, 145–168 (Knoxville: The University of Tennessee Press, 1984).

2

Major Foods and Ingredients

The United States produces much of the food Americans consume, but it also imports ingredients and food products from all over the world. Foods eaten are mixture of native culinary traditions, ingredients, and recipes transplanted from other cultures, as well as newly arrived foods. The United States encompasses diverse physical environments and has widely varying natural resources, so although many foods are nationally known and consumed, each region has variations in eating habits, specialized dishes, and variations on national dishes.

This chapter identifies major ingredients and foods within the various regions as well as regional variations on national foods. Selected information is offered on the origin, preparation, importance, and social function of American foods from a regional perspective.

GRAINS

Most American meals contain some sort of starchy carbohydrate, such as bread, pasta or noodles, dumplings, rice, or potatoes. These are usually accompaniments to a main dish of meat but can also be the primary food in the meal. The forms they take tend to have regional associations. Various grains can be used to make these dishes. Corn and wheat are the primary grains, although rice, wild rice, barley, rye, and oats also have a place in regional cuisines.

Corn

Corn is native to the United States and was introduced to European settlers by Native Americans. Several kinds of corn are now common in the United States, but sweet corn eaten off the cob as a vegetable is distinctive to American foodways. Corn on the cob and buttered kernels of corn are considered all-American foods. Other types of corn are turned into popcorn or crushed and ground as a grain. Indian corn—dried ears of colorful kernels—is associated with New England, the Pilgrims, and the first Thanksgiving.

The Midwest Corn Belt, which stretches more than 350,000 miles from Ohio to Nebraska, produces 80 percent of the corn grown in the United States. Much of this is used as feed for cattle, pigs, and poultry, but much is also used industrially, either in food production (including high-fructose corn syrup) or other industries. Popcorn is still grown on family farms, particularly by the Amish in Ohio and Indiana, and roasted ears of corn are common at festivals and fairs throughout the Midwest.

Historically, corn was the major grain in the American colonies and the basic staple of pioneers settling the West. Corn was used to make an unleavened bread similar to a pancake that usually was simply cornmeal mixed with water or milk, some salt, and a little bit of fat (lard, bacon grease, butter). This was known by a variety of names: johnnycakes or bannocks in New England; corn pone, hoecakes, or ashcakes in the South; and corn dodgers on the western frontier. Corn bread made with baking soda and baking powder so that it rises is a staple of southern food and soul food today. Recipes and cooking methods differ cook to cook; generally, southern cooks do not put sugar in the batter, but northern ones do. Southern cooks also make spoon bread, a form of corn bread that has more milk, butter, and egg and has more of a pudding consistency so it has to be eaten with a spoon.

Sweet corn grew well all along the East Coast, but it was particularly well suited to the southern Appalachians, where it was a major source of food for humans and animals throughout the 1800 and 1900s. It was also distilled into moonshine, which could then be transported more easily down the mountains to sell at markets. Anti-liquor laws did away with most locally run stills, but home production is still legal if done for medicinal purposes. Cornmeal boiled with water as a hot cereal is called "mush" and was a basic pioneer food as well. Today, cornmeal mush is generally found in the Mid-Atlantic, particularly among the Pennsylvania Dutch, where it is eaten as a breakfast cereal, usually topped with sugar or syrup. In the Northeast, it is made into Indian pudding. Cornmeal is also the prime ingredient in Italian polenta, grilled or fried slices of chilled mush found in Italian American areas in the Northeast, Midwest, and West Coast.

Corn is also used to make hominy and grits, iconic foods of the South. Hominy is corn that has been soaked in lye to remove the hull. It is then washed and boiled or fried with bacon grease and salt. In the Southwest, hominy is called by the Spanish word posole and is used in soups and stews. Grits—ground, dried hominy—are so integral to southern foodways that people refer to the "grits line" instead of the "Mason-Dixon line" dividing the North and the South. They are used in a meal in place of potatoes or rice and are frequently eaten the same way, with butter, salt, and gravy. Sugar is rarely used and is seen as a northern taste. A standard part of breakfast with eggs, gravy, or salted country ham, grits can be eaten for other meals as well. Shrimp and grits are a dish of Charleston, South Carolina, and Louisiana offers "grillade and grits"—braised beef or veal with buttered grits. Grits are also mixed with cheese, milk, and eggs and baked as a savory pudding, and leftover grits in the South are often chilled, sliced into half-inch pieces, dipped into flour, and fried.

In the Southwest, corn is finely ground into *masa* and mixed with water to make a round, thin flatbread called tortilla. Commercial *masa harina* can be bought throughout the Southwest and in Hispanic groceries across the United States. This flour is also used to make tamales. The Southwest also grows blue corn, a type that has a soft starch and can easily be crushed into flour. Both white and blue corns are used to make tortilla chips, a specialty of the Southwest that has been anglicized and popularized across the United States.

Finally, corn is also used to make popular snack foods, such as corn nuts and corn chips, as well as corn flakes, a cold cereal invented in Battle Creek, Michigan, in 1894 as a health food.

Wheat

Wheat is now the primary grain used for bread, cereal, and pasta in the United States. It was brought by the Spanish to what later became Mexico and California and by the English to their colonies, beginning with one of the earliest settlements, Jamestown. Although wheat grew well in Virginia, tobacco took over as the cash crop there, so it was grown in the Mid-Atlantic colonies. New York, New Jersey, Pennsylvania, Delaware, and Maryland exported wheat to New England, the West Indies, and England and were known as the "bread colonies." Today, the wheat belt extends from Texas across the Great Plains through Kansas, Montana, and Washington. Kansas is the largest commercial producer of wheat. The line, "for amber waves of grain," in the patriotic song, "America the Beautiful," celebrates the fields of wheat stretching mile after mile across the plains.

There are several types of wheat, categorized by growing season and the strength of gluten, a substance that helps bread to rise and hold together so that it can be shaped. Soft wheats have weak gluten and work well for cakes and crackers. Hard wheat has a stronger gluten and is used for bread. "Common" or "bread wheat" is most prevalent and is grown on both winter and spring on the midwestern prairies. Durum wheat is produced in Minnesota and North and South Dakota and is used for pasta. Club wheat is grown in the Pacific Northwest. Wheat can be processed into a number of types of flour, including whole wheat, cracked wheat, refined or white flour, and cake flour. Graham flour is a uniquely American flour in which the bran and germ are coarsely ground, and the endosperm is finely ground. It is named after a Presbyterian minister, Sylvester Graham, who promoted it in the mid-1800s as a way to curb lust.

Although wheat is the basic grain for Americans, it is rarely eaten on its own, except as a sweetened, hot cereal. Wheat berries and wheat germ can be mixed into breads and cereals and were originally associated with the West Coast alternative lifestyle diets of the 1960s and 1970s. Couscous, coarsely ground durum wheat from North Africa and the Middle East, has entered American foodways, primarily in urban areas, particularly along the East Coast. Similarly, bulgur wheat (parboiled, dried, and de-branned wheat) is often used for tabbouleh, a Middle Eastern salad with parsley and tomatoes.

Wheat flour is often mixed with other grains, such as cornmeal, barley, rice, and oats, to make bread. Pumpernickel is a mixture of rye and wheat flour common among German immigrants in the Mid-Atlantic and throughout the Midwest. Today, it is still found in those areas and is also associated with Jewish delicatessens.

OTHER GRAINS

Barley

The United States is the fourth largest producer of barley, yet the grain does not figure largely in contemporary American foodways. Historically, it was used in the Mid-Atlantic colonies to make whiskey or malt for beer, and beef and barley soup was considered a healthy strengthening soup. Eastern European immigrants in the Midwest and Mid-Atlantic have a barley and mushroom soup for ritual dinners. The grain has been reintroduced to mainstream United States through the health food movements coming out of the West Coast. Barley salad—boiled barley, chopped vegetables, usually dressed with an olive oil and herbs—is a standard way to serve this grain.

Oats

Oats are frequently associated with Scotland and with Scottish immigrants to the United States, but hot oatmeal is a popular breakfast dish throughout the United States. The Quaker Mill Company, established in the late 1800s, is the largest processor of oats and the pioneer of food advertising, ironically attaching old-fashioned images to the grain. Today, the United States is one of the leaders in oats production, primarily in Minnesota, North and South Dakota, Wisconsin, and Iowa.

Rye

Rye is closely related to barley and wheat. It is perhaps best known in the United States as the base for rye whiskey, which is made primarily in the Mid-Atlantic and the Northeast. It is also found in the crisp flat breads made by Scandinavian and northern European immigrants to the upper Midwest, and in the pumpernickel bread of Eastern European immigrants to the industrial areas of the Midwest and the Mid-Atlantic.

Wild Rice

Wild rice is actually the seed of a grass that is so closely associated with Minnesota that it is the official state grain. It was originally cultivated by the Ojibwa Indians of the upper Midwest but is now considered a gourmet and health food.

Rice

Rice has both regional and ethnic associations. Arkansas is now the largest producer of rice in the United States, followed by Louisiana, California, Mississippi, Missouri, and Texas, but Indica types (long or medium grain) were grown for export in the southern colonies beginning in the mid-1600s. The Low Country areas of South Carolina and Georgia were the origin of a high-quality long-grain rice known as "Carolina gold." Although rice production ended in South Carolina by the 1920s, rice is still associated with the area, partly through Charleston cuisine, which frequently uses rice. Carolina rice pudding, a sweet dessert of rice, raisins, and milk, flavored with nutmeg, is now found throughout the Midwest as an old-fashioned dessert, but it seems to have a longer history of family recipes in the South. Rice pudding is popular in New England, where it is prepared as custard with eggs and milk. Today, rice is eaten in the South as an accompaniment to meat, particularly fried chicken, and is usually covered with butter and gravy. Rice is also mixed with black-eyed peas and ham to make hopping

John, a Southern New Year's dish that is eaten for good luck. New Orleans offers red beans and rice, and Cajun Louisiana has "dirty rice," which is rice mixed with sausage and spices.

Rice is also associated with southern soul food. Originally, rice production depended on slaves from western Africa where there was a long tradition of rice cultivation. In the 1940s, a rice company in Texas reflected that heritage when it began featuring "Uncle Ben," an elegant, older, African American gentleman, as its brand image.

The Hispanic influence in the Southwest is seen in rice dishes, such as arroz con pollo and rice and beans, as well as in Tex-Mex Mexican rice (rice flavored with chili peppers) and Americanized Spanish rice (flavored with tomato and sweet pepper).

California offers Hispanic-influenced rice dishes but also began growing Japonica, the short-grain rice that is central to Asian cuisines, in the 1900s. Because of the Asian immigration to California starting in the mid-1800s, California is still associated with Americanized Asian foods—fried rice and sushi, for example. California is also home to Rice-A-Roni, created in 1958 by a company in San Francisco. This mixture of "minute rice" (a process of drying precooked rice developed by an Afghan), pasta, and seasoning is sold throughout the United States but is associated with San Francisco. California is also home to various health food movements and alternative lifestyles that introduced brown rice to Americans.

The incorporation of ethnic and immigrant cuisines into mainstream American cooking has doubled rice consumption in the United States, and most supermarkets now carry a wide variety of rice. American producers have also started growing some of the more exotic types—Calmati and Texmati are adaptations of the fragrant Indian basmati rice, which, along with Italian Arborio rice and Indian basmati rice, is often imported by immigrant groups and gourmet cooks throughout the United States.

BREAD

Bread is traditionally a basic staple at almost every meal across the United States, so much so that a common blessing before meals is "give us this day our daily bread." People talk about jobs as providing "bread and butter," and at meals, people "break bread" together. Bread comes in many forms: loaf, flat, rolls, crackers, and specialized forms such as bagels. Historically, corn was the basic grain for bread, but it was overshadowed by wheat as soon as wheat was available. Today corn bread is found primarily in the South, and the stereotypical American bread is a loaf of store-bought, sliced, soft, white bread made with refined wheat. Often known by the brand name Wonder Bread, it is associated with the working classes in the South and with general Midwestern eating. Whole wheat bread is now nationally available commercially, but the better-quality breads tend to be associated with the West Coast and upscale urban centers throughout the nation. Artisan breads, those made by small bakeries often using local and organic ingredients, are produced nationally but again are most associated with California, the Northwest, and certain Northeast states, such as Vermont and New Hampshire. Other ingredients are sometimes added to wheat flour bread to make a sweet, cake-like bread. Pumpkin and cranberry bread is particularly popular in New England; raisin, banana, and zucchini in the Southern states; and zucchini, pumpkin, and banana breads in the Midwest.

Certain varieties of bread are associated with regions and, in some cases, cities. San Francisco, for example, is famous for sourdough bread, a kind of wheat bread that has a slightly sour taste. The South boasts of corn bread, preferably unsweetened and baked in a cast-iron skillet, although African American recipes often call for a bit of sugar. Corn bread, frequently with a cake-like texture, is a staple of African American cooking and can be found in urban centers, particularly throughout the eastern Midwest (notably Chicago and Detroit). New England claims several special breads. Anadama bread, a wheat loaf that includes cornmeal and molasses, has been carried over from colonial times. It is supposedly named after a woman named Anna whose bread was either so good or so bad that her husband responded with a curse. Boston brown bread is a distinctive round bread that is a rich, dark brown color. A batter of whole-wheat flour, cornmeal, molasses, baking powder, baking soda, salt, and optional raisins or nuts is poured into a can and steamed in a kettle. Today, it might be steamed in a Crock-Pot. The Irish American population in New England brought soda bread with them. Leavened with bicarbonate of soda, it is often sweetened with raisins and sugar and is closer to a dessert bread than to the traditional soda breads of Ireland. Irish American communities in urban centers, particularly in the Midwest (Cleveland, Chicago, Detroit, St. Louis), usually include it in public celebrations of Irish culture. It has also become common on St. Patrick's' Day throughout the country, along with green beer and shamrock-shaped cookies.

Bread also comes in smaller portion sizes and shapes. Parker House rolls came from Boston's Parker House Hotel in the 1880s and are now a national favorite. Biscuits, preferably made with buttermilk, are almost icons of southern cooking and are also common in Midwest Amish cooking. Hot dog buns, which began to be produced commercially in 1870s, are national, but New England uses hot dog rolls, which look like a small loaf of white bread split down the middle. These are also used for lobster rolls (lobster meat with mayonnaise and chopped celery), scallop or clam rolls (made with deep fried scallops and clams), and seafood salad rolls. Also associated with New England are muffins, particularly those flavored with New England fruits—cranberries, blueberries, and apples. These are a standard mid-morning snack with coffee.

Flatbreads are a historical food dating to times when cooks had to make do with griddles or iron pots over an open fire. They can be made with corn-meal or wheat flour—originally, whatever grain was available was used (oats, rye, rice). The names tend to be regional: johnnycakes, also known as journey cakes, and Shawnee cakes, are the names used in New England, par-ticularly Rhode Island, which holds an annual johnnycake festival. Some parts of the upper Midwest also use that term. Southerners usually use the names ashcake (because it is baked in the ashes of the fire), hoecake (pos-sibly because tradition claims they were baked on the blade of a hoe), and cornpone.

Another kind of flatbread is pancakes, also known as flapjacks, hotcakes, and other names. They are usually eaten with butter and syrup—maple sy-rup in New England, corn syrup in the South, sorghum or molasses in the southern mountains, and commercially produced sugar-based maple syrups nationally. Whipped cream, sour cream, and jam or fruit preserves are also used as toppings, particularly in regions settled by Eastern Europeans. In the British American version of pancakes, lemon juice and sugar are sprinkled on large thin cakes and then rolled up. These are similar to thin crepes, which are associated with French cooking and often filled with meat, fish, vegetables, and/or cheese. Pancakes can be made by adding any grain added to the basic mixture of wheat flour, baking soda, baking powder, salt, and a liquid—buckwheat is common among the areas settled by Russian and East-ern European immigrants, such as the upper Midwest (where they are some-times referred to as blini).

Unleavened flat breads are found in the Southwest in the form of the tor-tilla. Drawing from Mexican tradition, these are made from cornmeal or wheat flour and cooked quickly on a special griddle, called a *comal*. In the Southwest, tortillas accompany most meals that have a Hispanic flavor but are also used as wraps around any variety of meats, beans, and vegetables, a tradition that has spread throughout the United States. Similarly, tortilla chips have a southwestern association, and in that region come in more va-riety—blue corn chips, coarser ground cornmeal—and more variety in the salsas served with them.

Also associated with the Southwest, and probably a variation on tortillas, is Indian fry bread, an invention dating to the Navajo reservations in New Mexico in the 1860s, when displaced Native Americans found ways to use the government rations of white flour and lard. Fry bread was adopted by other Native Americans and became a tradition in Arizona and New

Mexico. New Mexico has a version of fry bread with honey butter (similar to Mexican sopapillas). Fry bread is also used in another invented dish, Indian tacos. These consist of fry bread covered by beans or ground beef, chopped lettuce and tomato, shredded cheddar cheese, chopped onions, and chili peppers. Indian tacos are very popular at fairs in the Southwest, and Arizona newspapers even called it the state dish. Indian tacos are also common at Native American powwows across the nation, particularly in midwestern and western states.

Crackers are crisp, baked flat breads. Soda crackers are eaten everywhere but tend to have a special place in the South, where they are still a common staple of snacks and a soup accompaniment. Graham crackers, made with graham flour and slightly sweetened, were invented in Michigan but are not associated with the state. Oyster crackers are small hexagonal-shaped crackers that were invented in 1847 in Trenton, New Jersey, to accompany oyster stew. They are still associated with New England and chowders but have expanded to the rest of the country, particularly the Midwest, where they accompany chili.

Bagels are another form of bread that still has regional associations, even though they are popular nationally. Bagels were introduced to the United States by European Jewish immigrants in late 1800s, and the technique of boiling them before baking was a way to get around Jewish dietary laws requiring that bread not be eaten until hands have been washed. Because bagels were not technically bread, hand washing was not required, so they were convenient for traveling and people on the go. They developed in the Lower East Side of New York and were sold on streets and in small family-run bakeries. In 1950s, new toppings were introduced—cream cheese, sweet butter, smoked salmon. Although they have been assimilated everywhere and come in every flavor possible, bagels are still associated with Jewish culture, Jewish delis, and New York City.

PASTA

Noodles, strips of flattened dough, were likely introduced to the United States by German immigrants (who called them spaetzle). Homemade noodles (made of flour and egg) are still common today in German areas of the Midwest and Pennsylvania as well as parts of the southern Appalachians. A cousin to noodles, pasta was brought by Italian immigrants in late 1800s. Now a staple throughout the United States, it still has Italian associations, and freshly made pasta in a variety of shapes is available primarily in the Northeast and in urban centers with Italian neighborhoods in the Midwest and West. Rice noodles come from Asian cuisines and are found in the

United States where Asian immigrants have historically settled, particularly the East Coast, California, and Hawaii.

Dumplings are bits of dough, usually boiled in a broth. New Englanders, Midwesterners, and Southerners have dropped dumplings, which are large dumplings made of flour, eggs, butter, and herbs. Maine offers Joe Booker stew, which is made of beef, vegetables, and dumplings with parsley. Residents of Appalachia have several variations of dumplings, including some called "slickers."

PULSES/LEGUMES

Legumes in the United States are usually referred to as dried beans. They were one of the three sisters of Native American foodways and are still central to Native American cultures in the Southwest. New Mexican beans tend to be black or even mottled pink.

One of the most popular beans today is the small white bean known as a navy bean (because of their use by the U.S. Navy in the early 1900s) or pea beans. Navy beans are also used in commercial, canned baked beans (with a sauce of mustard, tomato, and sugar) and are a standard accompaniment for picnics, barbecues, and hamburger or hot dog meals. They still have a strong association with New England, where Native Americans taught colonists to bake beans with maple sugar and bear fat in a pit filled with hot stones. Anglo colonists replaced the bear fat with lard and added or substituted molasses with maple syrup. This became a specialty in Boston, where laws banned cooking on Sundays in the early 1700s. Pots of beans would be baked on Saturday for Sunday meals, and thus Boston became known as Beantown. To this day, Boston baked beans are a favorite and are offered as souvenirs in Boston eateries. In the South and Midwest, barbecue sauce is often added to the beans. Navy beans are also used in Senate bean soup, a daily item at the Senate Building cafeteria in Washington, D.C.

Kidney beans have also become popular nationally, primarily through their addition to chili. In this way, they have become associated with cowboys, cattle drives, and the West. Pioneers often took dried beans with them, and their legacy continues today in bean soups. Kidney beans are also common in bean salads in the South and Midwest. Pinto beans, which sometimes substitute for kidney beans, have a strong tie to the Southwest, where they are central to Hispanic cooking. They are often used for refried beans (*frijoles refritos*), in which the cooked beans are mashed and then fried with onion, garlic, and spices. This mixture is then used as a side dish; as an ingredient in seven-layer dip, an Anglo dish; in nachos; or in a tortilla for a bean burrito. Small black beans, sometimes called turtle beans, are also refried in this way and are commonly associated with Latin American cuisine. Cuban and Caribbean restaurants in Florida frequently serve black beans and rice. Pinto beans are also a staple food in the southern Appalachian Mountains, where they are referred to as "soup beans" and where a bowl accompanied by corn bread is a traditional meal.

A large white kidney bean called "cannelloni" is common in traditional Italian cooking and is found in the United States in Italian immigrant communities, particularly in the Northeast, Midwest, and Far West. Great Northern white beans can substitute for cannelloni but tend to be shaped more like a lima bean. They are often used in soups and chowders throughout the Northeast and northern Midwest. (Lima beans are eaten as vegetables and in dishes such as succotash.) Dried split peas, similarly, are most often used to make soups with ham or bacon. Coming from Dutch, English, and German tradition, split pea soup is eaten throughout the country. Because the peas do not require as much cooking time, this soup tends to be favored over other bean soups in hotter climates as well as in New York, where the Dutch heritage lingers. German areas in the Mid-Atlantic also have traditions of split pea soup.

Small red beans (or kidney beans) are used in Cajun red beans and rice. Louisiana claims a dish called "limpin' Susan" that uses red beans and rice and is traditional on Mondays, using the bone left over from the Sunday dinner ham.

Black-eyed peas or African cowpeas are common throughout the South. Also known as bird peas, cornfield peas, conch peas, Congo peas, crowder peas, pigeon peas, red peas, or southern peas, they were brought from Africa with the slave trade and were a basic staple for southern blacks and whites. Mixed with rice and ham hocks, black-eyed peas make a dish called hopping John. Cowpea cakes, fried cakes of ground beans, are popular among Caribbean immigrant communities in Florida. Bean cakes or bean patties are also found in the southern Appalachian Mountains and are currently being reinvented as a regional delicacy. Field peas tend to be a staple food there, often accompanying corn bread.

Chickpeas or garbanzo beans (the Spanish term) come originally from the Middle East and are now common wherever Middle Eastern immigrants have settled, but particularly along the East Coast and urban centers in the Midwest, such as Detroit. Chickpeas are the basis of hummus, which has also recently become popular nationally. Southwestern cooking also uses chickpeas, but Spanish colonists introduced them initially.

Soybeans are grown extensively in the Midwest but are generally not eaten there. Tofu or bean curd made from soybeans can now be found everywhere, but for a long time tofu was only available on the coasts and in Asian groceries.

Lentils, a quick-cooking dried pea, were initially introduced to the United States on the East Coast as a French-style soup. Lentil soup with rice and vegetables has become a mainstay for vegetarians. Lentils are also used in Middle Eastern salads and in an Indian dish called *dahl*.

VEGETABLES

Many vegetables are available year round throughout the United States and have lost their historical connections to regions with specific growing conditions. Furthermore, most vegetable varieties today have been cultivated or are hybrids with imported varieties. Corn, squash, and beans—the three sisters of Native American foodways—are native to the United States and are now national foods. Similarly, tomatoes and potatoes came originally from Peru, spread to Central America where they became part of the Columbian exchange, then were taken to Europe, and finally introduced to North America by European colonists.

California is one of the largest commercial growers of produce in the United States and the home of a trend of eating fresh, locally grown vegetables and cooking them in a way that emphasizes the quality of those vegetables. San Francisco chef Alice Waters is largely responsible for this trend and is also credited with popularizing heirloom vegetables—older, historical varieties that have been ignored by the industry growers. In the late 1700s, Thomas Jefferson also collected varieties of vegetables, and his gardens at Monticello in central Virginia are a contemporary museum of vegetables. A number of vegetables are nationally standard and have no regional associations: broccoli, carrots, cucumbers, cauliflower, green beans, peas, lettuce, and more.

Artichokes

Now grown primarily in California, artichokes were popular in the early colonies. They are still popular, particularly in urban areas in the Mid-Atlantic, Northeast, and West Coast where artichoke hearts are frequently a gourmet touch to salads, and steamed fresh artichokes served with melted butter are a romantic meal. They were also popular among Italian immigrants, so they are prevalent in Italian communities in the Northeast.

Asparagus

Asparagus was brought to New England by the English and Dutch in the 1700s and is still common throughout the East Coast, served as an accompaniment to ham or on toast with melted butter or a hollandaise sauce.

California is the leading grower of asparagus and popularized its use in cold salads and quiches. The cultivation of asparagus in home gardens is not as widespread as other vegetables because it takes several years to develop.

Avocado

Avocados are associated with California and southwestern cuisine. A popular way to eat them is mashed and seasoned with lemon juice and cilantro for guacamole, which is then used as a dip for tortilla chips or as a side dish with Mexican and Mexican-American dishes. A grapefruit and avocado salad is popular in the South, and residents of the southeast historically called them "alligator pears."

Beans and Peas

Numerous varieties of beans are found in the United States, but the type used most often as a vegetable is the whole-pod green bean, which is actually the unripe fruit of the bean vine. These are usually boiled or steamed and eaten plain, with butter, or with a cheese sauce. A favorite Midwest dish for potlucks and Thanksgiving is green bean casserole, which was invented by the Campbell Soup Company. In the Northeast and the Southeast, green beans are frequently called "string beans," because of the stringy vein that runs along the edges.

A common image of the South and the southern Appalachians is the woman of the house sitting on the front porch stringing beans or shelling peas. Another Appalachian tradition is "leather britches," green beans strung together and hung up to dry, a technique probably borrowed from the Cherokee. French-style beans are slender green beans, usually cut into long thin strips. Louisiana's French heritage appears in the transformation of the French word for green beans, *haricots verts*, to *zydeco* to refer to a regional style of traditional music. Unripened bean pods actually come in other colors as well, including yellow (called wax beans), purple, and speckled.

Lima beans are the large seed of a bean plant that was originally imported to the United States from Lima, Peru (hence the name). They are a traditional part of New England succotash (lima beans, corn, diced carrots). They are frequently called butter beans in the South, and southern succotash is frequently only corn and butter beans.

Peas are the seeds of an annual, *Pisum sativum*. An integral part of contemporary British and Irish cooking, they are also a national standard in the United States, possibly because Thomas Jefferson cultivated them. In home gardens throughout the United States, new young peas are a sign of spring. Sugar peas (the pod along with the peas) are a favorite in the upland South and the Mid-Atlantic, and the similar snow peas are used in Chinese American cooking.

Root Vegetables

Potatoes

Although potatoes originated in Peru, were taken to Spain by Columbus, spread throughout Europe, and then brought to North America, they are now considered an all-American vegetable. They play a large role in the agricultural economy of Idaho, Maine, and North Dakota but are cultivated throughout the United States. Russet potatoes are good for baking and are frequently called Idaho potatoes.

Potatoes are frequently associated with the traditional meat-and-potatoes diet of Middle America. In reality, they are eaten throughout the United States in a variety of forms. Fried potatoes (usually pre-boiled and sliced before frying) are a standard breakfast dish in southern Appalachia and the Midwest, and they often accompany hamburgers or sandwiches as home fries, country fries, or cottage fries. Texas fries are thick, cut long ways, and sprinkled with paprika, black pepper, and salt or chili peppers to be mildly spicy.

Deep-fried, long, rectangular-cut strips of potato have been called "french fries" since the late 1910s, and although they have been popularized into a national food by fast-food chain restaurants since the 1940s, the dips and sauces for them are often regional: fry sauce in Utah, melted cheese and chili sauce (boiled ground meat with tomato and spices) in the Midwest, and salsa in the Southwest.

Potatoes baked in a cheese sauce are a popular dish but are known by different names regionally: cheesy potatoes in the Midwest (which also boasts tater tot casseroles), scalloped potatoes in the Northeast, and potatoes au gratin in parts of the Southeast. New England has a variety of mashed potatoes called "smashed potatoes," which includes the potato peel. Salt potatoes are a specialty of central New York. These are small, new potatoes boiled in salty water so that they develop a salt crust, and are then served with melted butter. Potato chips were invented in a restaurant in Saratoga Springs, New York, in the 1850s. They are now one of the most popular American snack foods and have lost any regional associations, except sometimes in the flavorings. In the first three-quarters of the 20th century, many potato-producing areas had small, local factories that made chips. In northwest Ohio, for example, each neighborhood was loyal to a different maker, and it was a common family ritual to buy potato chips.

Sweet potatoes, a root vegetable, are frequently called yams in the South and the West. True yams grow on a vine and are found primarily in West

Africa, where they are a staple food. Sweet potatoes are associated with southern cooking and are often eaten baked in the skins and topped with brown sugar and butter, or boiled and mashed. They are also made into a casserole that is actually more like a pudding, with pecans, pineapple or orange slices, and a topping of brown sugar crust. Marshmallows are sometimes melted over the casserole, although that might be more of a midwestern tradition, where sweet potato casserole is a standard part of Thanksgiving. Sweet potatoes are also associated with African American cooking; in particular, they are used in pie as an alternative to pumpkin. Sweet potato fries (strips of sweet potato either baked or deep-fried) and chips (deep-fried thinly-cut rounds) have replaced French fries and potato chips as a healthy alternative in numerous restaurants. Even fairs and carnivals offer them, emphasizing their newness on the American culinary scene.

Carrots

Originally from Afghanistan, carrots were brought to the United States by English colonists and soon became popular with most farmers. Mennonites introduced larger, oranger varieties of carrots, but the carrot capital of the world is now Holtville, California, which holds a festival every year.

Beets

Beets, a colorful root vegetable, were important in Colonial America and are still part of many New England boiled dinners. They also lend the distinctive color to red flannel hash, another classic New England dish in which cooked and cubed corned beef or bacon, potatoes, beets, and onions are fried together. Also from New England are Harvard beets, which are cooked with a thick sweet and sour sauce. The Pennsylvania Dutch, as well as the Amish and Mennonites in Ohio and Indiana, pickle red beets and hard-boiled eggs.

Beets are also the basis for borscht, a staple soup brought by Eastern European and Russian immigrants to the Northeast and to urban centers in the Midwest. The Catskill Mountains in upstate New York are referred to as the borscht belt because of their summer resorts, which are popular with Jewish vacationers from New York City. Sour cream and dill usually flavor the soup, and thick dark bread accompanies it. Variations in borscht occur according to ethnic group.

Turnips

Turnips grow easily in temperate climates and are often used as animal feed. They are a staple part of New England boiled dinners and are frequently served boiled and mashed (with maybe a sprinkling of nutmeg) for Thanksgiving. Westport, Massachusetts, boasts a historic marker for the Macomber turnip, which it developed.

Considered something of a "poor man's food," sliced raw turnips and cooked turnip greens are eaten in southern Appalachia and in southern African American cultures. Turnips are also important in Irish folklore and culture, where they were said to be the original jack-o'-lantern. The turnips used, however, were winter turnips, or rutabagas.

Rutabagas

Rutabagas are a variety of yellow turnips. These large, dense vegetables are also called swedes because of the association with Swedish immigrants in the upper Midwest. Rutabagas are hard to cut, but they are sweet and crunchy eaten raw and are used in cooking similar to carrots. They are included in the meat pasties of the Upper Peninsula of Michigan, as a marker of Cornish heritage. (Finnish American pasties tend to use carrots instead.)[1]

Radishes

Most Americans know the radish as the small, red, somewhat hot root vegetable that is usually used as a salad ingredient or a garnish. The town of McClure in northwest Ohio was for years a leading processor of radishes and held an annual radish festival with contests for new recipes for the vegetable. An Asian variety of radish—the long, white, daikon radish—is now raised in California and the Mid-Atlantic for Oriental groceries.

Parsnips

Parsnips are related to carrots but are eaten cooked. A part of British tradition, they show up mashed or roasted for meals in parts of New England and in Irish-American communities in New England and the Midwest.

Kohlrabi

Sometimes confused with turnips, kohlrabi, a mild aboveground tuber, is common in German and Scandinavian areas of the upper Midwest. It is usually boiled or roasted, and served like other root vegetables.

Onions

Onions (one of the three basic European vegetables, along with beans and cabbage) were brought to America by Pilgrims on the Mayflower. The bulb type of onion is still featured in American cooking today, but they are produced primarily in the Pacific Northwest. A number of specialty, sweet onion varieties are also grown and are named after their geographic location: Grand Canyon sweets in Arizona, Maui sweets and Hawaiian hula sweets in Hawaii, Nu-Mex sweets in New Mexico, Texas spring sweets in Texas, Walla Walla sweets in Washington, and, probably the best known, Vidalia sweets, which were first grown in the 1930s near Vidalia, Georgia, and are now the official state vegetable.

Scallions

Scallions or green onions have a small bulb and tender, edible leaves. They are traditionally eaten raw with soup beans and corn bread in the South, where they are sometimes called "green shallots" or "spring onion." Leeks, similar to an overgrown scallion, have a mild flavor, but are grown primarily in the northern Midwest and East Coast. Ramps are a wild leek native to Appalachian region, where they are considered a sign of spring. Also called "bear's garlic," "hill onion," "wood leek," and "Tennessee truffle," they have an extremely intense flavor that is unpleasant to many. Ramps are celebrated at many festivals in West Virginia, Tennessee, and North Carolina, and ramp dinners are a common springtime community fundraiser.

Garlic

Garlic is usually treated as a spice rather than a vegetable. Long associated with immigrant Italian cultures in the Northeast and once considered to be a sign of coarseness, garlic has only recently emerged as a vegetable in its own right, primarily through Californian cuisine but also through a growing interest in regional Italian cuisines. Garlic is often roasted and spread onto toast, or included with other vegetables in a roast or stew.

Cabbage

Because cabbage is hearty, can withstand cool weather, and lasts longer than other greens, it was an ideal pioneer vegetable. Most commercial cabbage is now grown in Wisconsin. It is often a part of New England boiled dinner as well as part of the stereotypical Irish dish, corned beef and cabbage, which is found in Irish enclaves in New England and the Midwest (and everywhere on St. Patrick's Day). German immigrants introduced sauerkraut, and homemade sauerkraut is still a common family tradition in the German heritage areas of the Mid-Atlantic and the Midwest. It also shows up with the Thanksgiving turkey in those areas as well as Baltimore.

Sauerkraut is also a traditional southern Appalachian food. Eastern European immigrant communities often use stuffed cabbage or cabbage rolls (cabbage leaves wrapped around a mixture of ground meat and rice) as one of their heritage dishes. Red cabbage is also popular among these groups and is used for salads and pickles. The Amish and Pennsylvania Dutch are famous for sweet-and-sour red cabbage.

Sauerkraut Balls

1 pound bulk sausage (or mixture of minced pork, ham or hamburger)
2 tablespoons chopped sweet onion
1 cup (4 ounces) sauerkraut, drained
4 ounces cream cheese (optional)
1 egg, slightly beaten
1 tablespoon flour

Seasoning (1 teaspoon dry mustard, 1/4 teaspoon thyme, 1 clove garlic, 1 tablespoon parsley)
Salt
Pepper
2 cups milk
3 eggs, slightly beaten
2 cups dry, unseasoned bread crumbs
Vegetable oil for frying

1. Fry the meat and onions over medium heat until the meat is done. Remove from pan and mix with sauerkraut, egg, flour, and cream cheese. Add seasonings to taste—dry mustard, salt, and pepper.
2. Roll the meat mixture into 1-inch balls, place on wax paper, and refrigerate or partially freeze.
3. Combine milk and eggs in a bowl and blend. Place bread crumbs in a bowl or plate.
4. Dip balls into milk and egg mixture, then roll in bread crumbs.
5. Fry sauerkraut balls in hot oil until golden brown (about 5 minutes). Drain on paper towel.

Serve with mustard, sour cream, or other dips of your choice.

Cactus

Cactus plants are used as food in the Southwest and reflect the Native American and Mexican heritage of the region. Their fruit, prickly pears or cactus pears, are eaten fresh or made into a paste (*queso de tuna*). Cactus pads are called *nopalitos* and are used as a vegetable. Cut into thin strips,

Sauerkraut balls are an appetizer in some German heritage areas of the Midwest. Made from sauerkraut and ground meat (usually pork or sausage) and deep fried, they are usually dipped in mustard or other sauces. Courtesy of Nathan Crook.

they resemble French-cut green beans; they can be cooked in the same way and then served as a side dish or made into a salad.

Cucumbers

The common American cucumber is raised by many home gardeners throughout the country, but the Southeast, California, and Michigan are the biggest commercial growers. Cucumbers are usually eaten raw throughout the United States and are a standard part of salads. A favorite southern salad is sliced cucumbers, tomatoes, and onions sprinkled with oil, vinegar, salt, and pepper. In the German heritage areas of the Midwest and Pennsylvania, cucumbers are often prepared in a sweet-and-sour dressing, while areas of the Midwest that were settled by Eastern Europeans, they are thinly sliced and covered in sour cream. Cucumber pickles are popular throughout the United States in a variety of forms.

Corn

One of the three sisters of Native American cultures, corn has become one of the driving forces of American food.[2] It touches everything—it is used as feed for livestock and poultry, as corn oil, as syrup, as starch in everything, and now it is even used as fuel. Along with being used as the primary grain for breads and cereals in the South, it is eaten as a vegetable throughout the country. Fresh green corn is frequently eaten raw off the stalk in the southern Appalachians as well as lightly boiled and slathered with salt and butter to be eaten off the cob. Southerners also cut the kernels away from the cob and fry them in milk or use them to make a pickled corn relish, corn fritters, or corn pudding. Corn is also notorious in the region for being distilled into moonshine.

Corn on the cob is also part of New England clambakes, and corn kernels are essential to succotash. Maine has traditional corn chowder—with fried bacon, onions, potatoes, and milk or chicken broth. The Native American cultures of the Southwest cultivated numerous varieties of corn, including a blue corn, and held corn sacred in their religious beliefs and ceremonies. The Pueblos still conduct a ritual Green Corn Dance.

The Midwest, however, is called the "Corn Belt" of the country, because it is the primary commercial producer, and midwesterners are often referred to as corn-fed. The Midwest celebrates corn at county fairs and town festivals featuring corn-shucking contests, corn queens, and roasted corn (roasted in the husk over an outdoor grill). Midwestern corn pudding is a custard-like pudding containing corn kernels, and it is very different from the southern version, which frequently uses cornmeal to thicken it.

Native Americans taught New England colonists to make popcorn, and strings of popcorn are still traditional for New England Christmases. The eastern Midwest, however, leads in popcorn production with its numerous family farm producers and popcorn festivals. Although they are no longer associated with the Midwest, two corn products originated there: cracker-jack was introduced at the Chicago World's Fair in 1893, and cornflakes were invented in Battle Creek, Michigan.

Eggplant

Eggplants, also known by the French name *aubergine*, need hot nights in order to do well, so they are more common in southern regions. In the South, they are sliced, breaded, and fried (similar to fried green tomatoes and fried squash). California cuisine introduced the concept of grilling young eggplants. Eggplants are also found in signature dishes of several ethnic groups and are available along the coasts and in urban centers—Middle Eastern baba ghanoush (a dip made of roasted eggplant), Italian eggplant parmesan, Greek moussaka (casserole of eggplant slices, ground lamb, cheese, and egg sauce), and French ratatouille.

Greens

Greens, also called "potherbs," are the leaves of root vegetables or flowering plants. Spinach is considered the all-American green, partly because of its place in popular culture as Popeye's secret for strength. California is the primary commercial producer of spinach, although an outbreak of *Escherichia coli* in the fall of 2006 and a salmonella scare in the summer of 2007 in southern California have made the public suspicious of nationally distributed spinach.

Cooked greens are a staple of southern cooking. Often cooked with ham hocks or bacon, collards and turnip greens are particularly associated with African American soul food but are also staples in southern Appalachia. Kale, beet greens, mustard greens, and Swiss chard are cooked the same way into a "mess of greens." The cooking water of the greens is called "pot liquor" and is used like gravy on meat or sopped up with cornbread.

Salad greens

Salad greens are leaves eaten raw and fresh. Iceberg lettuce is the most common and has become associated with the blander regional cooking of the Midwest. Other raw salad greens (romaine, spinach) are commonly used in more upscale restaurants, by cooks with more sophisticated palates, and in areas that have a history of attention to fresh vegetables, such as California. Boston lettuce is a sweet, buttery-flavored lettuce, and romaine, with its darker color and slightly bitter taste, is the standard ingredient in Caesar salad (invented in Tijuana, Mexico, and San Diego, California) as well as for Passover seders as the bitter herb symbolizing the bitterness of slavery. Endive, a winter green with a strong, bitter taste, was introduced by German and Dutch immigrants to the Northeast and Mid-Atlantic. Escarole, a less bitter, broad-leaf endive, is a popular addition to salads. Chicory, related to endive, is associated with French cooking, and dried, ground chicory root is a distinctive ingredient in New Orleans coffee.

Wild greens

Wild greens are picked throughout the country, although they are frequently considered weeds and have disappeared in some places because the heavy use of lawn chemicals has pushed many wild greens out of common use. Pokeweed, also called "poke sallet" (the old English term for cooked greens) and "inkberry" (because the toxic berries were used as ink during the Civil War), is a hardywild green perennial that grows in the South and the lower Midwest. The leaves are a traditional food gathered in the spring in southern Appalachia, and Harlan, Kentucky, boasts an annual poke sallet festival. Like many wild greens, poke needs to be cooked and rinsed several times to get rid of the bitterness. Ham hocks are usually tossed in while the greens cook. An alternative in the mountains is to dip them in cornmeal and fry them.

Another wild green is Lamb's quarter, also called "pigweed," which grows in colder climates as well as in the South and can be eaten raw or cooked. It tends to be favored in the Midwest, particularly Illinois and Wisconsin. The ubiquitous dandelion was historically used as a food by pioneers and still appears in a number of ethnic cuisines. Northerners tend to pick dandelion leaves and flowers, sometimes using them to make wine and beer. A Pennsylvania Dutch recipe calls for pouring warm bacon dressing over the young leaves, and dried, ground roots can be a coffee substitute. Dandelion leaves are cooked and flavored for a popular Middle Eastern salad sold in ethnic groceries. Italian Americans dip the flowers in batter and fry them for a seasonal treat. Many Asian immigrants also consume the leaves, often stir-frying them and seasoning them with sesame oil.

Also wild, nettles grow east of the Rocky Mountains and are traditional in French, Irish, and Scottish American cooking, and are sometimes used to make beer. Wood sorrel, which has a sour seedpod, also grows east of the Rockies but is more common in southern states. Purslane grows wild, frequently along roadsides, throughout the South, including the drier Southwest. The young leaves can be eaten in salads, and older leaves are added to soups as a thickener.

Watercress grows in and around water in temperate climates. The peppery leaves are added to salads and to British tea sandwiches, and the sprouts are eaten as well. The plant is now widely cultivated. New Market, Alabama claims to be the watercress capital of the world.

Hearts of Palm

Looking somewhat like white asparagus and used in salads and main dishes, hearts of palm are the core of the palmetto tree or cabbage palm. They are only available fresh in Florida, where they are known as swamp cabbage.

Mushrooms and Morels

White button mushrooms are the most common type eaten in the United States. Almost every state has some commercial cultivation of mushrooms, but Pennsylvania leads in production, followed by California. Wild mushrooms grow particularly well in the Northeast and Pacific Northwest and are frequently gathered and sold.

Morels, which are likened to French truffles, grow wild across the upper Midwest and are celebrated at festivals in Minnesota, Illinois, and Michigan, although local residents frequently do not advertise the morel hunting grounds. Morels are called "molly moochers" in Appalachia. Because morels tend to grow well in areas that have been burned, mushroom enthusiasts look for them after forest fires, particularly in western states, such as Montana and Colorado.

Okra

Okra was brought from Africa during the slave trade. It is still found primarily in the South, where it is eaten by white and black southerners, frequently sliced, breaded in cornmeal, and fried. It is a major ingredient in southern vegetable soups and stew, particularly Brunswick stew and Louisiana gumbo. When boiled, it tends to have a viscous (slimy) quality that can be off-putting to many people.

Peppers

Until the 1960s, only the sweet green variety of pepper was readily available. Red, yellow, and orange sweet peppers are now also cultivated throughout the country and are often eaten raw either as an appetizer, dipped in dressing, or as part of a salad. They are a common ingredient in standard American cooking and are sometimes called "mangos" in parts of Ohio and Indiana. Stuffed peppers (with a ground meat and rice mixture baked in a tomato sauce) are a Hungarian dish, which has been Americanized into mainstream home-cooking.

Chili Peppers

Chili peppers are associated with the Southwest, where Latino and Native American peoples cultivated them. Strings of dried chilies, called *ristras*, are considered a symbol of good luck and are frequently a tourist image of the states growing them. These hot and spicy peppers come in numerous varieties. Jalapeños are the most popular, and pickled jalapeños are common now on pizza or as an accompaniment to Latino dishes in restaurants. Orange-colored *habaneroes* are extremely hot.

Cayennes are usually dried and ground and provide the red pepper flakes used to sprinkle on pizza. *Anaheims* is the California name for red and green chilies. These are the types used for salsa and sauces in much commercial Mexican American cooking. Peppers stuffed with cheese or meat, chile relleno, is a popular southwestern dish.

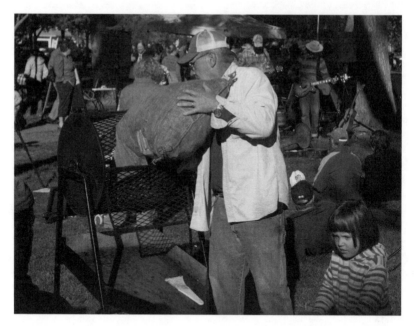

A common site in the fall throughout New Mexico is chili peppers being poured into roasters, as in this roaster at the Albuquerque farmers' market. The smell of roasted chilies wafts through the air, giving a distinctive aroma to the region. Courtesy of Nathan Crook.

Distinctive to New Mexico and Arizona are chilies that are roasted, dried, ground, and pressed into bricks for making chili. Commercial chili powder was actually invented by a German American Willie Gebhardt, in New Braunfels, Texas, in the 1890s, and numerous brands and variations are now available nationally. In these powders garlic, oregano, cumin, cayenne, and paprika are added to ground Anaheim red peppers, but the fresh cilantro that makes Southwestern salsas so fresh tasting is usually left out.

Chili peppers are also used in Tabasco sauce, a standard ingredient in Cajun and Mexican American cooking. Hot pepper sauce is common in southern African American eating, especially on greens and beans, and it is frequently added to barbecue sauces. The upland South uses pickled hot peppers to spice up traditional corn bread and beans, while hot pepper chowchow is popular throughout the South. Chili peppers are associated with a number of ethnic cuisines and are found in restaurants in immigrant communities, particularly Central American, Chinese, Thai, Indian, and Ethiopian.

Squash

Squash, one of the Native American three sisters, is another all-American vegetable. Summer squash grow easily in home gardens, ripening at the end of the summer. The yellow summer squash is more traditional in the South, although zucchini are as common there now as they are everywhere. Both types of squash are frequently sliced into rounds, breaded, and fried; stewed lightly with nutmeg; or made into a casserole with eggs and cheese. Squash blossoms are also sometimes breaded and fried. Zucchini are often associated with Italian cooking in the Northeast and stewed with tomatoes and Italian seasonings. In California cooking, both types are often grilled.

Winter squash ripens in the fall and can be stored over the winter. Varieties such as acorn and butternut, boiled and mashed with butter and salt, are considered a requirement for a traditional New England Thanksgiving. The Midwest offers a wide range of varieties, such as hubbard, buttercup, delicata, and more, but the West Coast (California) has introduced innovative ways of grilling these sweet and filling vegetables.

Tomatoes

Tomatoes were brought from South America to Europe by Christopher Columbus, where they first became part of Mediterranean cuisines but were not accepted by northern Europeans until the mid- or even late-1700s. They may have been introduced into coastal southern states from the Caribbean, but only slowly became part of mainstream diets. They now grow easily in backyards everywhere and are produced commercially in numerous states, particularly California. Tomatoes are celebrated at festivals around the country, including Pittston, Pennsylvania; Rutledge, Tennessee; Carmel and Fairfield, California; and Reynoldsburg, Ohio, which claims to be the birthplace of the industrial tomato. Northwest Ohio hosts a tomato institute, where new tomatoes are developed for the food industry (the square tomato, for example), and tomato juice is the state beverage of Ohio. Heinz ketchup is used the world over but is based in Pittsburgh, Pennsylvania.

Tomatoes are sliced and used in sandwiches throughout the country, but the South has a special place in its everyday foodways for tomato sandwiches. Thick slices of freshly picked garden tomato are placed on white bread slathered with mayonnaise, salted and peppered, and eaten with plenty of napkins to wipe up the juice. Fresh tomato, mozzarella cheese, and basil salad has been introduced nationally through Italian cuisine and through California cooking. Tomatoes are also used for puddings, and different recipes are found regionally. The South tends to make their tomato puddings with whole or sliced tomatoes topped with breadcrumbs and cheese, and the Southwest adds chili peppers. Tomato pudding in parts of the Midwest, however, is actually a bread pudding with tomato juice and brown sugar.

FRUITS

Even though many fruits are available throughout the year around the country, they are still closely associated with the climate and season needed for the growing. Temperate fruits, such as apples, pears, and peaches, grow throughout the United States; subtropical fruits, such as citrus, olives, avocado, and cactus, are grown in the Southwest and the Southeast; and tropical fruits, such as banana and pineapple, are grown in Hawaii. A number of fruits are native to the United States and tend to grow in the more temperate zones—berries, grapes, cranberries, persimmons, and plums.

Apples

Apples were established in the United States by the mid-1600s and are still grown in the regions of the early colonies. Early on they were used more for cider than for eating, however. By 1820, cider was the unofficial national beverage and could even be used as currency.

Apples for eating and cooking were developed by mid-1800s. Historically, there were thousands of apple orchards and as many as 17,000 varieties of apples, but the numbers have declined so that now Red Delicious is the standard variety for commercial production with Golden Delicious a second commercial variety. Most apples are grown in six states—Washington, New York, Michigan, California, Pennsylvania, and Virginia—and are identified by state. Also, some varieties are closely associated with regions—New England McIntosh, Northern Spy, Arkansas Black, for example—and other regional varieties are currently being developed or revived.

Apple pie is considered a national dish, but it is particularly associated with New England, where it is traditionally eaten for breakfast as well as for dessert. Ice cream or whipped cream is a common national topping, but cheddar cheese slices are an option in the South. Apple pie with a crumb topping is favored in Pennsylvania and the German parts of the Midwest, but the South prefers apple crisp, apples tossed with sugar and cinnamon, covered with a brown sugar, oatmeal, and flour mixture, and baked. Apple brown betty, favored in the Midwest and West, is similar, but the topping tends to be more like a biscuit. Apple dumplings, in which cored and peeled apples are wrapped in their own pastry shell, are popular in Midwest and probably reflect the German heritage. Fried apples are a common breakfast item in southern Appalachia, and homemade applesauce is a tradition wherever apples are grown. Apple butter, a thick preserve, comes from a German tradition of boiling down plums to make plum butter, and is found in strongly German areas in the Mid-Atlantic, the Midwest, and southern Appalachia. Traditionally, apple butter was made in large copper kettles over open fires and involved a 2- to 3-day process of chopping and stirring. This process is still used, but Mid-Atlantic makers tend to boil down cider and apples together, whereas the Midwest boils cider first. Midwesterners also pride themselves on not adding anything to the butter, whereas Pennsylvanians usually flavor it with cinnamon and cloves and add sugar. The southern Appalachian process is more like making a thick and sweet applesauce.

Bananas

Although bananas were originally grown commercially in Florida, they are now primarily imported from Central America and are only grown in Florida backyards for family consumption. One of the most popular fruits in the United States, bananas are celebrated at the International Banana Festival in Fulton, Kentucky. Called the banana capital of the world, Fulton was the distribution center for the railroads transporting bananas for more than 70 years until 1963. Fulton now holds the record for the world's largest banana pudding, a layered dessert of vanilla wafers, custard or pudding, sliced bananas, and whipped cream or meringue. Although banana pudding is a national dish, it also tends to be a favorite among African Americans and southerners. Bananas, and their cousin the plantain, are commonly fried or made into fritters in Costa Rican and Puerto Rican foodways, and those dishes can be found in immigrant communities in Florida and in New York. Banana and peanut butter sandwiches (sliced bananas on peanut butter on white bread) are also popular in the South.

Berries

Most varieties of berries are native to the United States and still grow wild in temperate zones, although cultivated berries are grown commercially in parts of the South, Michigan, and the Pacific Coast. Berries are used primarily for jams or preserves and desserts—cobblers and crisps in the South, pies and muffins in the Northeast, and pies in the Midwest and Northwest.

Blackberries

Blackberries come in two types. Upright ones grow east of the Rocky Mountains. These bushes can grow up to seven feet tall and tend to be very dense and thorny. Running blackberries (known as dewberries in the South) grow wild along the Pacific Coast and are grown commercially in the West and lower South, particularly Arkansas. They are good for cooking because they retain their form. Blackberry cobbler and jam are southern specialties.

Blueberries

Blueberries (which are not botanically a berry but are related to apples and pears) are also native to the United States, but were not domesticated until the early 20th century. Michigan and the Northeast have lowbush blueberries, which have a small and sweet berry, and the Mid-Atlantic coast has highbush blueberries, which grow to ten feet tall. The native variety in the Southeast, rabbit eyes or southern highbush, can grow even taller. Blueberries require very acidic and moist soil, and most commercial production now is New Jersey, North Carolina, Michigan, and Maine. Blueberry pie is a specialty of Maine, and blueberry muffins are traditional to New England. Michigan advertises chocolate-covered blueberries and dried blueberries.

Raspberries

Hopkins, Minnesota, outside of Minneapolis, is hailed as the raspberry capital of the country and has been hosting a festival since the Depression era. Lynden, Washington, also hosts a raspberry festival and claims that local growers produce 65 percent of red raspberries in the United States. Thimbleberries found in the Upper Peninsula of Michigan, among other places, is a variety of raspberry.

Strawberries

Strawberries are one of the most popular berries in the United States and are grown both in home gardens and commercially throughout the country. Strawberry festivals appear across the country, from Florida to California, as far north as Maine, Minnesota, and Wisconsin, and south to Louisiana and Texas. Strawberry shortcake is a national dessert but can differ by region. Southerners traditionally use a biscuit as the base, northeasterners seem to prefer a slice of pound cake, and midwesterners often use the commercially-produced sweet cakes made especially for individual servings. Ice cream is the topping of choice in the South, but whipped cream is popular elsewhere. Strawberry wine is a southern delicacy.

Boysenberries

Boysenberries are actually a hybrid of loganberry and dewberry that was developed at Knott's Berry Farm in Buena Park, California, in the 1920s. They were marketed as especially good for making jam.

Serviceberries

Serviceberries are a small, dark berry found in the eastern Midwest (Ohio and Indiana). They were so named because they were used in pies that were brought to dinners at funeral services in the spring after the winter thaw since they ripened early.

Juniper berries

Juniper berries are native to the Northwest coast and were central to Native American foods throughout the West. They were often dried and used in pemmican. Today they are often used as garnishes and flavorings for meat dishes in the Northwest.

Cranberries

Cranberries are considered a national icon of Thanksgiving and are a significant part of New England lore and culture. The early pilgrims used them as food and medicine and called them bearberries. Cranberry drinks, including a cocktail and ocean cooler, are a New England specialty. Indigenous to the United States, cranberries grow in bogs and wetlands and are difficult to cultivate commercially. They were taken to Wisconsin by an English settler from Massachusetts in 1828, and that state now produces most of the U.S. crop. The southern part of New Jersey, known as the Pine Barrens, is the second-largest producer. Numerous festivals celebrate cranberries in those two states, and chocolate-covered cranberries are marketed as a regional specialty by both. Dried, sweetened cranberries are now marketed nationally and are frequently added to salads that are given local or regional names.

Cherries

Cherries were brought by settlers to the Northeast but are often associated with the colonial Mid-Atlantic region because of the legend of George Washington chopping down a cherry tree as a boy. The modern sweet bing cherry originated in Oregon, and New York and Pennsylvania, along with northern California and the Northwest, are now the biggest commercial producers of sweet cherries. Michigan also produces cherries, but these tend to be the sour or tart variety, which are often used for pies and preserves. Michigan also offers a distinctive cherry wine, dried cherries, and chocolate-covered dried cherries.

Also found in the eastern and upper Midwest are ground cherries, a large yellow berry covered by a thin, paperlike husk. They tend to be used more as a garnish and decoration than as a food, although they can be eaten fresh and are quite sweet. Mennonite farmers in Pennsylvania and Ohio have helped preserve ground cherries and often use them for pies and preserves.

Grapes

Some grape varieties are native to the Americas. The Southeast and upland South are home to the muscadine, which has a thick inedible skin, a sweet flesh, and a strong aroma that makes a sweet wine. Scuppernongs, a variety of muscadine, are used for wine and jam. Most grapes cultivated today, including those for wine, were developed in Europe. Hybrids were established first in the late 1700s in the Ohio Valley near Cincinnati. This area was the largest wine-producer until after the Civil War, when growing and production shifted to Lake Erie and upstate New York. Catawba and Concord grapes, grown in the Eastern seaboard and the eastern Midwest, are the kind most used for commercial juice and jelly. New York's Niagara grapes, a yellow, sweet dessert grape, are another popular variety.

Today, California leads the United States in vineyards and wineries, and the region produces the bulk of the table grapes sold. California also has a thriving raisin industry and boasts a distinctive grape syrup.

Citrus

Citrus fruits require subtropical climates, so they are associated only with the southernmost portions of the United States, particularly Florida, Arizona, Texas, and California.

Oranges were first planted in Florida by Spanish explorers Pánfilo de Narvaez in 1538 and Hernando de Soto in 1539, but these were the sour, bitter oranges of North Africa and Spain. Commercial orange growing in Florida began when the United States acquired Florida in 1821. Indian River citrus, a variety still used today, was a hybrid of sweet buds grafted onto sour wild roots. It was established in 1830 on Merritt Island (between the Indian River and the Atlantic Ocean). The dominant variety today, the Valencia, was introduced in 1870 and enabled Florida to become known as "the sunshine state" producer of oranges.

Historically, oranges were associated with the railroads, but that association only appears now in the fiddle tune, "Orange Blossom Special." Florida is still connected to oranges. It offers the Orange Blossom Trail tourist association, the Orange Bowl football playoffs at the University of Miami, fresh-squeezed orange juice, Grand Marnier liquor, and fresh orange slices as a common garnish for meat and poultry dishes.

Southern California also claims a historical connection to oranges. Franciscan missions cultivated oranges beginning in 1769, and the first commercial grove appeared in 1841. Navel oranges (seedless, thick skinned, and easy to peel) were brought to Riverside, California, in 1870 and from there spread to other areas, namely Arizona and Florida. Southern California has a chain of fresh-squeezed orange juice stands, identified by a giant orange.

Tangerines, mandarins, tangelos, and clementines are also cultivated in the same areas as oranges, but are more recently developed crops.

Grapefruit were brought to Florida from Barbados in 1823 and were established in citrus-growing states in the late 1800s. The Red Ruby variety was created in south Texas in 1929.

Lemons and limes were brought to the Caribbean by Christopher Columbus and other Spanish colonists in the New World. They were established in St. Augustine, Florida, and coastal South Carolina in the mid 1500s. Both fruits are used for juice, and southerners claim a number of specialty drinks using them—lemonade with mint and strawberries and lemonade and limeade with gin. Florida also produces the distinctive key lime, which is smaller and tarter than the standard lime. Key lime pie is a regional specialty.

Pawpaws

Pawpaws, also known as the "American custard apple," grow wild in the eastern United States, and were historically common enough to be mentioned in the children's song, "Picking up Pawpaws." Now rare, they are used for desserts and jams in a few areas around the Ohio River Valley, particularly in West Virginia, Indiana, and southern Ohio. They are also referred to as "Hoosier bananas" in Indiana, possibly because of the similarities in color and texture of the two fruits.

Persimmons

The persimmon, a small orange fruit that is unpleasantly tart until it ripens, is native to the eastern United States and used to be common in the same areas. Stringy fibers must be separated from the sweet flesh before it can be used to make puddings or bar cookies. Persimmon trees still grow wild in some parts of Indiana, and persimmon pudding is a popular heritage dish there. An Asian persimmon has been recently introduced to California, and this bright orange, sweet fruit is growing in popularity.

Peaches

Native to Persia, peaches were brought to the Americas by the Spanish, where they then grew wild in the South. A hybrid was cultivated in Georgia and South Carolina, and both states now produce renowned sweet peaches. These peaches are eaten raw, dripping with sweet juice; canned in syrup; or used for baking in peach cobblers and pies. A southern specialty is pickled peaches, spiced with cinnamon and cloves.

Michigan also produces peaches commercially and boasts a number of peach festivals. California growers produce cling peaches that are particularly good for canning. California also produces nectarines, which are actually a smooth-skinned peach, and apricots.

Melons

A variety of melons grow throughout the United States, although cantaloupe, honeydew, and watermelon tend to be the national favorites. The orange-fleshed cantaloupe is frequently called "muskmelon" in the Midwest, where several varieties, such as Crenshaw's, Santa Clauses, and Persian melons, are commercially raised. Numerous festivals across the Midwest and Northwest celebrate melons, notably in Howell, Minnesota, Milan, Ohio, and Winston, Oregon.

Watermelons are also raised throughout the United States, but they are closely associated with the South, so much so that watermelon motifs are a frequent symbol for parts of the Deep South. Numerous southern states host watermelon festivals or include watermelon-eating contests, seed-spitting contests, and ice-cold, sliced watermelon at family and community gatherings. Southerners also like to pickle the otherwise uneaten rind, and southern cookbooks often include variations on fruit salads with min, or a liquor poured over it. Watermelon was also historically used as a condescending stereotype of African American culture and is still problematic for many African Americans, reminding them of that history.

Melon seeds are roasted and salted—similar to pumpkin and squash seeds—as a treat in many Asian cultures, and are found in Middle Eastern and Asian groceries throughout the country.

Tropical fruits

Tropical fruits have long been grown in Hawaii and Florida. Pineapples are one of the mainstays of Hawaiian agriculture, but the state also produces fruits such as jackfruit, lychee, longan, mango, mangosteen, and rambutan, which come from Southeast Asia.

South Florida has traditionally grown avocado, lime, and mango and has recently cultivated many fruits that come from Southeast Asia and from Central America, including papayas and passion fruit. Kiwi fruits, originally from New Zealand, are being cultivated commercially in California, and cold-weather varieties are grown in South Carolina, Georgia, and Alabama.

SPICES, HERBS, AND CONDIMENTS

American food tends to be a "cool cuisine," using few spices other than salt and black pepper to enhance food. Although tastes began to change in the last decades of the 20th century, spices tend to be found in sauces or condiments that can be added to the food rather than cooked into the dish itself. Individual eaters, then, can enhance their food according to their own region, taste, or mood—scrambled eggs, for example, can be doctored with tomato ketchup (Midwest), salsa (Southwest), chowchow (Appalachians), hot sauce (New Orleans), and so on.

Salt generally refers to basic table salt; however, variations are common: celery salt and garlic salt are probably the most popular. Sea salt is often used in gourmet recipes. Similarly, black pepper usually appears pre-ground, but freshly ground at the table is becoming more common, particularly along the coasts and in urban areas. An unusual regional dish emphasizing pepper is Philadelphia pepper pot, a stew of tripe, vegetables, and black peppercorns.

Herbs are usually the flower or leaf of a plant, and spices are the seeds, bark, or roots. Condiments are sauces and mixtures used to enhance the flavor of food (or, perhaps, disguise it). Many spices are tropical and require climates only found outside the United States; others are associated with specific ethnic cuisines. Although most spices are available nationwide, many are connected to regional cooking.

Some all-American spices are featured in traditional New England cooking, with its solid British heritage and mythic Thanksgiving dinner. These include bay leaves, used as part of Yankee pot roast; sage, used particularly for poultry stuffing; parsley, dried or used fresh as a garnish; thyme, used to season poultry, fish, sauces, and soups; dill, often used to flavor meat, poultry, and pickles. Fresh dill is also common in Eastern European cooking. Caraway seeds are often found in rye bread and dishes of Eastern European immigrants in the Northeast. Rosemary oftentimes accompanies pork. A southern Appalachian variant is Cumberland rosemary, which is not related to true rosemary but was used as a substitute.

Dried basil, fennel (also known as anise), garlic, flat-leaf parsley (often called "Italian parsley"), and oregano were popularized by Italian immigrants, and although they have become nationalized, they are expected in Italian neighborhoods in the Northeast and Midwest. Oregano is also associated with Tex-Mex cooking, where it is sometimes called Mexican sage.

Fresh basil features in California where it is used to make pesto with pine nuts (originally found in Italian cooking). Tarragon is a delicate and sweet addition to French-influenced cooking in the Southeast and Mexican cooking in the Southwest, especially with tomatoes. And, of course, dried and fresh chilies are an integral part of Southwestern cooking. Saffron is an extremely expensive spice used in Indian rice dishes and in some Mediterranean dishes, particularly with fish and tomatoes. In the upper Midwest, it is used in Scandinavian American baking, and in the Mid-Atlantic it is used by the Pennsylvania Dutch. Lemongrass is an essential part of Thai and Vietnamese cooking and is now available in groceries where those populations live as well as in cities along the coasts and in the Midwest and South. Tamarind is popular among Southeast Asian and Mexican immigrant groups, who often make it into a refreshing sour drink (similar to lemonade). A distinctive regional spice is filé, which is made from sassafras bark or leaves, a tree indigenous to the eastern United States. Filé is a necessity to the gumbo stews found in the Deep South, particularly along the Gulf Coast.

A number of spices are used with sweet foods or sauces. Allspice is grown in southern Florida and is common in Caribbean cooking as well as in ketchup and other sauces. Nutmeg, the nut or seed of a tropical fruit, is common in New England and the South on top of custards and other milk dishes. Mace, the covering around the nutmeg nut, is a standard spice in New England pumpkin bread and pie, as are cloves and ginger. Southern tradition calls for sticking whole cloves into oranges and hams, imparting a sweet, hot flavor. Ginger is now grown in Hawaii and southern Florida, and dried ginger is used to make ginger ale and ginger beer, historically a New England favorite. Cinnamon is often used in baking and in New England–style hot cider and mulled wine. It also appears in Greek and Balkan American meat sauces, including the distinctive regional Cincinnati chili developed in that city by Macedonian immigrants. Sweet-smelling cardamom seeds are common in the upper Midwest in Scandinavian and Dutch pastries and cookies.

The all-American condiments are ketchup, mustard, and mayonnaise. Ketchups can be made of any vegetable—not just the standard tomato—and are still made by the traditional method in parts of the Midwest, in which tomato juice and crushed tomatoes are boiled down in a large copper kettle over an open fire. It is generally assumed though that ketchup refers to tomato ketchup. Salsa has grown in popularity since the 1990s and now tends to replace ketchup as a condiment in the Southwest as well as other parts of the United States. Mustard comes in several varieties. The brown, spicy mustards tend to be more popular in cities and on the East Coast. The standard commercial American mustard includes turmeric, which colors it bright yellow. Mayonnaise is still frequently homemade in the South, and commercial mayonnaise is the basis for many salads in the Midwest. Horse-radish is most often found where there are large Eastern European immi-grant communities, particular in the Mid-Atlantic, Midwest, and Pacific Northwest. It is also used in traditional Irish meals, particularly as an ac-companiment to corned beef.

NUTS AND SEEDS

Americans today usually treat nuts and seeds as a snack food, but they actually play a significant role in several regional food traditions. Edible chestnuts, for instance, used to grow wild throughout the Eastern half of the United States, but Asian chestnuts brought to the United States in early 20th century brought a blight that killed most of the native chestnuts. A few still bear nuts; several parks in Washington, D.C., have healthy chest-nut trees, and knowledgeable residents (usually southerners, African Ameri-cans, or Korean immigrants) gather the chestnuts for their private use. Heritage dinners frequently revive earlier traditions, using chestnut flour for bread, making poultry stuffing out of chestnuts, and roasting whole chest-nuts. Philadelphia was famous for roasted chestnut vendors, and Appala-chian mountain residents often gathered the wild nuts to sell. Today, chestnuts in the shell are sold during the Thanksgiving and Christmas holi-days but are something of a decorative novelty.

The southern Appalachian Mountains are host to a number of nut-bear-ing trees, and these were a traditional source of food in the region. Examples include hickory nuts and black walnuts, both of which have extremely hard shells and require a great deal of effort to extract the meat but were popular additions to cakes and cookies.

Pecans are iconic of the South, and they give a distinctive southern flavor to numerous dishes, including pecan pie, corn bread pecan dressing for tur-key, pralines, cakes, and salads.

Peanuts are also integral to southern foodways. Although technically a legume, peanuts are considered a nut in the United States. Originally from South America, peanuts were taken by Portuguese explorers to Africa. They then entered North America with the slave trade from Africa. Peanuts are sometimes called "goobers" or "goober peas" in the South, and boiled pea-nuts are a traditional snack in Georgia and South Carolina. The African American inventor George Washington Carver is credited with developing peanut butter in the late 1800s, and it has since become a national all-American food. Peanut butter and jelly sandwiches are a quintessential lunch or snack. Sandwiches of peanut butter and banana tend to be a

Southern specialty, and fried peanut butter and banana sandwiches were a favorite of Elvis Presley at his home in Memphis, Tennessee.

Acorns, the nut of the oak tree, are not usually considered edible today, but they were the basic starch for Native Americans in the Pacific Northwest as well as a grain substitute for western pioneers and Appalachian settlers. They must be soaked to get rid of the bitter tannin, but can then be eaten like other nuts or ground into flour. Acorns are also a coffee substitute. They commonly appear now only in heritage reenactments or in wild foods dinners.

Pine nuts (*piñons*) are a specialty of the Southwest, where they are traditionally harvested by Native American cultures. In New Mexico they are used to make a special coffee called *pignon* after the Spanish name for pine nut. They have gained national popularity partly through their use in pesto, an Italian sauce of ground pine nuts, fresh basil, and olive oil. Pine nuts are also common in Middle Eastern cooking and are frequently used as a garnish for these dishes in the United States.

Almonds are commercially produced in California, and although they are now considered an all-American snack food, they are still ground into marzipan for use in pastries in German immigrant communities in the Mid-Atlantic and Midwest.

Coconuts are associated with beaches, palm trees, and tropically flavored food in Florida, Southern California, and Hawaii.

Sunflower seeds are historically a popular snack among Americans of Russian and Central European descent in the western plains and upper Midwest, and they are now eaten nationally, both shelled and in the shell. Their oil is often added to other cooking oils. Native to the Americas, sunflower seeds are produced primarily in the Dakotas and the Texas panhandle, although Kansas is known as "the Sunflower State."

Sesame seeds were introduced into the southern United States by slaves from Africa who called them by the African word, *benne*. Although now associated with Asian and Middle Eastern cuisines, they are used primarily in the United States as a topping on breads (hamburger buns, bagels) and in crackers. They are also ground into tahini paste and used as a base for the Middle Eastern staple, hummus, made with ground chickpeas.

DAIRY PRODUCTS

Dairy products are a mainstay in the American diet, consumed in a variety of forms and frequently appearing at every meal and for snacks. Dairy in the United States generally refers to milk from cows rather than sheep or goats.

Milk

Cow's milk is the national drink. It was promoted over the last century and a half as "the perfect food," and children and adults are encouraged to drink milk on a daily basis for "strong bones." Goat, buffalo, and sheep milk are associated with certain ethnic groups (Italians and Middle Easterners, particularly on the West and East coasts), persons with health concerns, or specialized, artisan cheese makers, particularly in New England (Vermont and New Hampshire) and the Pacific Northwest.

Today, the largest milk-producing states are California, Wisconsin, New York, Pennsylvania, and Minnesota. The Upper Midwest is particularly known for its dairy industry. Milk is a major part of midwestern cooking as a result of German and Swiss influence in cheeses, milk-based dishes, and cream sauces. New England has a long history of dairying, and this heritage shows up now in ice cream production and consumption. The Midwest also has strong associations with ice cream and still boasts many small family-run ice cream producers.

Buttermilk

Sweet milk that has been allowed to sour slightly was historically a farmer's drink throughout pioneer America. Today, it is still drunk in the southern Appalachians and the Midwest, particularly where small family dairies are still in operation. It is still a favorite of the Pennsylvania Dutch and Amish as well. Buttermilk is used mostly as a cooking ingredient in pancakes, biscuits, Irish soda bread, and the famous Amish buttermilk pie.

Butter

Butter was historically a basic staple of the European American diet and is still eaten in abundance, spread onto breads and melted over cooked vegetables, particularly in the South and the Midwest. One of the largest commercial manufacturers of butter, Land O'Lakes, started in 1920s in Minnesota and uses images and the nickname of the state for its marketing.

Cheese

The process for making cheese was brought to the United States by European colonists, particularly the English and Dutch, and it is still a tradition in those areas they settled—New York, Pennsylvania, and New England. Swiss immigrants to central Ohio in the late 1800s established cheese production there, which is still ongoing, and Spanish colonists also brought cheese making to the Southwest. Mexican cheeses, particularly *queso blanco*,

a mild, crumbly cheese, are central to Mexican American cooking throughout New Mexico, Texas, and Southern California. Goat's milk is frequently
used for these cheeses as well. Cheddar, now the most common cheese in
the United States, was a favorite in New England and New York, and Vermont and upstate New York starting factory production of cheddar cheese
in the mid-1800s. Wisconsin, however, is now considered "America's Dairy-
land," with its master cheese makers and invention of brick and Colby
cheeses. Brick actually refers to the process of making the cheese—using
bricks on the cheese curds to squeeze out the liquid—and Colby is named
after the city it comes from. Wisconsin is also famous for its squeaky cheese,
cheese fudge, and deep-fried cheese curds. The latter are often served as a
side dish in fast-food establishments and are eaten with ketchup.

American cheese is actually a processed cheese product, and although it
is mass marketed nationally, it tends to be associated with the South and
the eastern Midwest as well as with working classes in general. The Kraft
Company, which began producing processed and canned cheeses in the
early 1910s, also developed Velveeta in 1928 and Cheez Whiz in 1952. Velveeta is commonly used for macaroni and cheese in southern and African
American cooking, and authentic Philadelphia cheesesteaks require either
Cheez Whiz (Pat's Steaks) or American cheese slices (Geno's).

Italian immigrants introduced a variety of cheeses—many of which are
common throughout the country as processed, commercial cheeses. Traditional forms of parmesan, provolone, ricotta, and mozzarella are generally
associated with New York City or ethnic Italian neighborhoods in larger
industrial cities, such as Boston, Cleveland, or Chicago.

California actually has more dairy farms than other states, but it is better
known for artisan farmstead cheeses. Interior New England also boasts similar cheeses.

Cream cheese was developed in the Mid-Atlantic and is still associated
by brand name with Philadelphia, but it was Jewish restaurants in New York
that popularized cream cheese on bagels in the mid-1940s. New York Jewish
restaurants also introduced cheese blintzes, sour cream, and cottage cheese
(a farmer's cheese common in Eastern Europe but made without animal
rennet).

Yogurt is now a commonplace dairy product throughout the United
States. It is eaten on its own (often with fruit and sweeteners) as a snack or
meal, mixed with other ingredients for health drinks, and used as a condiment on items ranging from breakfast cereal to supper dishes. Originally
associated in the United States with the 1960s counterculture and California alternative lifestyles, it is now considered all-American and sold in
supermarkets and school cafeterias everywhere. A number of ethnic culinary
traditions make frequent use of yogurt—primarily Middle Eastern, Indian,

and Greek—and establishments offering these foods often include their own versions of yogurt.

Milk is used to make a dessert that is now a favorite throughout the United States: cheesecake. Introduced by English colonists, who used cream thickened with eggs and butter, cheesecake now has regional and ethnic varieties. Italians use ricotta cheese, Russians use sweetened creamy cheese (and make Russian *pashka* for Easter). New York style uses cream cheese and was made famous by restaurants in New York City such as Lindy's and Junior's.

Milk is also used for savory custards with a vegetable or meat filling. Some corn puddings in the Midwest, particularly in Ohio and Indiana, where Amish and Mennonites have settled, are actually a custard with sweet corn. Quiche is a form of savory custard pie and was originally popularized in California.

MEAT AND POULTRY

The United States is a nation of meat eaters—not just bits of meat mixed with vegetables or grains, but whole distinct portions of meat, slabs of steak, patties of ground meats, and whole parts of poultry. Most meals have meat as the centerpiece and everything else is an accompaniment as represented by the quintessential midwestern meat-and-potatoes daily meal.

Beef

Beef is considered the national meat and is used for such iconic American dishes as steak, meatloaf, pot roast, barbecued ribs, and hamburgers. Although cattle are raised throughout the country, beef is definitely associated with Texas and the West, where cowboys, cattle drives, and cattle ranches are central to the culture and landscape. Fresh steaks, thick cut and cooked rare, are an icon of the Anglo West. Chicken-fried steak seems to have come from the West, and refers to a thin cut of poor-quality steak that is battered and fried.

Veal, the meat of a calf, is associated with ethnic cuisines, particularly Italian, French, and German. Although it is available throughout the United States, it tends to be consumed more in the Northeast and Midwest, where ethnic Italian and German heritage is strong, and in metropolitan areas, particularly on the West Coast, where it is associated with refined Continental cuisine.

Corned beef refers to salt-cured beef soaked in a brine of sugar, saltpeter, and spices. Simmered with onions, potatoes, carrots, cabbage, and seasonings, it is often a part of a New England boiled dinner or an Irish American meal. Corned beef is now served nationally on Saint Patrick's Day, and in the Midwest a meal of corned beef boiled with potatoes, carrots, and cabbage is referred to as a "Jigg's dinner." It is also used in a Reuben sandwich—a deli sandwich of sliced corned beef on rye bread with sauerkraut and Thousand Island dressing that originated in either New York or Nebraska (both claim it). Corned beef hash is also a traditional New England dish—with beets, it becomes red flannel hash.

Pork and Ham

Although pigs were one of the first animals brought to the New World by the first settlers, beef tended to be much preferred, and cattle were favored over pigs in New England, the Mid-Atlantic, and most of the Midwest and far West, leaving pigs for the South. German immigrants also favored pork products, and there are still pockets of strong pork traditions in German-settled areas of the Mid-Atlantic and Midwest. The South definitely reigns, though, as the producer of fine hams. Virginia is famous for its smoked hams made from pigs fattened on peanuts and cured in a solution of sugar or salt. Many families throughout the upper South and lower southern Appalachians—North Carolina, Virginia, Tennessee, Kentucky, Georgia, and Virginia—still butcher their own hogs and cure their own hams. A thick ham steak is a common part of breakfast and dinner in the South, where the ham's saltiness is countered by bland grits, fried potatoes, or mashed sweet potatoes. Another Southern tradition is ham hocks cooked with beans or greens; in fact, bacon grease is used as a flavoring in many southern dishes. Southerners like to say they use everything in the pig except the squeal. Pig's knuckles, pig's tails, and pig's feet are often pickled and eaten as a snack, and the first two might be used for sausage. Pork chops are a southern standard, particularly chicken-fried pork chops. Pork chops are also favored in parts of the Midwest along with strong German-based traditions of pork sausages.

Chicken

Chicken is another national favorite. It is frequently associated with the South and with African Americans. Southern fried chicken, with its crispy coating, is an iconic southern dish, partly because of restaurants such as Kentucky Fried Chicken that affirm the association. Other areas claim fried chicken, also. Maryland fried chicken features cream gravy poured over the chicken (it is called "smothered fried chicken" in the South), and Amish meals throughout Ohio and Indiana advertise fried chicken dinners, probably reflecting the Germanic origins of frying meat dipped in batter. Amish chicken, in general, is considered healthier and tastier because it is raised free range. Cajun chicken, which is probably more a marketing invention than a regional tradition, is chicken in a spicy batter.

Battered, deep-fried chicken wings, called "buffalo wings," have become a national snack recently and named for Buffalo, New York, where they originated. New Englanders tend to roast or bake their chicken whole (similar to turkey), and Californians substitute chicken for beef in numerous dishes (such as chili) as a health measure.

Stewed chicken is traditional throughout the Midwest and South. Appalachian residents like theirs with dumplings, and midwesterners put thick, homemade noodles in theirs. Chicken noodle soup is a national favorite, but a version found in urban centers along the East and West coasts is Jewish matzo ball soup.

Eggs, specifically chicken eggs, are eaten nationally. They are particularly ubiquitous in the South and Midwest. "Egg money" made from selling eggs was historically one of the few sources of income for women. Although eggs are standard breakfast items, they appear in a variety of forms at other meals, both formal and informal, including picnics. Pickled hard-boiled eggs are a southern snack; and the Pennsylvania Dutch pickle eggs with beets, which turns them pink. Deviled eggs (hard-boiled eggs with the yolks taken out, mixed with mayonnaise, mustard, and relish and then used as a filling) are a standard dish at every southern gathering and are also popular in the eastern Midwest. Eggs are also a basic ingredient in many breads and baked goods, and hard-boiled ones are mixed into casseroles and salads.

Turkey

Turkeys are native to the United States (by way of Central America) and still live in the wild in rural areas of New England, the Midwest, and the upland South. Smoked turkey legs are often offered as a pioneer food at fairs and historical reenactments in the Midwest. A specialty dish of the Southwest is turkey molè, turkey cooked in a bitter chocolate and chili sauce.

Whole turkeys are featured in the quintessential American Thanksgiving meal, where they are traditionally roasted. A Deep South variation is to deep fry the whole turkey, and a West Coast variation is smoking the turkey in a barbecue-type covered grill. The filling used to "stuff" the turkey for Thanksgiving is called "stuffing" in New England, where it is usually made of white bread crumbs, onions, sage, and sausage. The South uses cornbread dressing (often with pecans, onions, celery, and cooked turkey innards). The Mid-Atlantic and parts of Midwest put oysters in their white-bread stuffing, as does the Gulf Coast of Louisiana. Minnesota offers wild rice stuffing.

Rabbit

Although wild rabbits and hares were a standard part of pioneer diets, they do not tend to be considered true game animals today. They are still eaten in the rural South (particularly the Appalachians) and Midwest. Domestic rabbits are raised for their meat in a number of areas including the rural Midwest, Hispanic food cultures in the Southwest, and central and eastern European immigrant populations along the Mid-Atlantic and Northeast. Restaurants featuring Continental cuisines (particularly French, Spanish, and German) also frequently offer rabbit.

Iconic foods are often stereotypes of regions. This can of possum is a joke, playing on the backward and backwoods image of Appalachian culture. Courtesy of the author.

Game and Exotic Meats

The most popular large game animal is deer, still found abundantly throughout the rural (and even suburban) Midwest and Northeast. Local butcher shops in those areas often offer venison steaks, venison sausage, and ground or cubed venison (a favorite for chili). Antelope and elk are favored large game in the western plains and mountain states, caribou in the upper Pacific Northwest, and Maine hunters produce moose steaks. Black bears are prevalent throughout the Appalachian Mountains, although bear hunting is restricted. Wild boars are hunted in the mid-South.

Small game—squirrel, raccoon, groundhog, and possum—are hunted in the southern Mountains and the Midwest, although they are not usually available commercially. Oregon is famous for its jackrabbit stew. Rattlesnake is a delicacy in the Southwest, as is the occasional armadillo. Turtle is eaten in southern Indiana and other pockets of tradition in the Midwest and Mid-Atlantic. Snapper soup, made from snapping turtles, is an iconic food of the Philadelphia area. Similarly, frogs are hunted in the Midwest and South for their meaty legs, which are usually battered and fried and said to taste like chicken.

There is a small commercial industry for duck, primarily in Wisconsin, Indiana, and Illinois. They are usually sold for holidays or special occasions. Wild duck is still popular among hunters, particularly in the Midwest and East. Canada geese are popular in the northern parts of the eastern United States, but their populations have declined dramatically in recent years.

Ring-necked pheasant, grouse, and quail are some of the most popular game birds in the United States. Northwest Ohio was made famous in the 1930s and 1940s for its feral pheasant populations as a favorite hunting ground of movie star Clark Gable. Quail are native to the United States and range from the Southwest across the South into the upper Midwest and Northeast. The northern bobwhite is a type of quail that is particularly popular in Virginia and the rest of the South. Sharp-tailed grouse and ruffed grouse, on the other hand, are more common in the upper Midwest (Minnesota has the largest population), and sage grouse are found in the far western region. Smaller game birds, such as doves, are eaten in the Midwest and far West.

Ostrich meat is being marketed as a healthy substitute for red meat, and ostrich farms have sprung up throughout the South and on the West Coast.

Organ Meats

Organ meats tend to not be as large a part of the American diet as they were in the past, partly because of health concerns, but also because of their association with poverty and lower-class status. Livers, kidneys, and hearts used to be standard dinner fare and are still eaten in more rural areas of the Midwest and as old-fashioned or ethnic foods. Chicken livers, breaded and fried, can actually be purchased at fast-food outlets, but few other organ meats have such national acceptance. Chicken livers also play a part in Jewish food traditions and are sold frequently at Jewish delis. Calf's liver is often fried and served with fried onions (similar to steak) and is available at many family-style and upscale restaurants. Pig liver and head parts are ground and mixed with cornmeal to make liver pudding in the South. North Carolinians fry thin slices of liver until they are crisp; the dish, called "livermush," is considered an icon. Similar foods are found around the country: Pennsylvanians call it scrapple; Cincinnati residents have a distinctive version using pork, beef, and pinhead oats, called *goetta*. Head cheese is made from chopped pieces of meat from the head or feet, set in aspic from the gelatin from the foot. It is particularly popular in Louisiana Cajun food and is called "souse." Tripe is a basic ingredient of Philadelphia pepper pot soup and Southwestern menudo, and intestines are still used as sausage casings in many German and Eastern European heritage areas. They are also stewed into chitlins throughout the African American South and have become an iconic soul food. Squirrel brains are a stereotype of Appalachian foodways.

FISH/SEAFOOD

Although refrigerated transportation and flash freezing make fish and seafood available throughout the country, there are vast differences between regions in the types of fish that can be freshly caught. Saltwater fish are obviously found along the coasts, and each region tends to have its specialty: salmon (along with herring) in the Pacific Northwest; cod, haddock, flounder, and sole in New England; and red snapper, grouper, and large swordfish and tuna off the Florida and Gulf Coast. Deep-sea fishing is a major draw in the warmer climates. Similarly, salmon fishing is a tourist sport (as well as a necessity) in Alaska, and farm-raised salmon is offered as an alternative to overfishing and depleting the wild population.

Freshwater fish, similarly, thrive in different regions of the country. The Great Lakes bordering the midwestern states to the north offer abundant fishing, both commercial and recreational. Lake perch and bass are two favorites, and walleye is found in the tributaries of the lakes as well as in the lakes themselves. Lake Erie still has a thriving fishing industry, and restaurants along the shore offer fried perch sandwiches. The mountain streams of the Appalachian region and the far West are home to trout, and an entire culture of fly-fishing has developed around them. Catfish are found in the

Mississippi River and muddy streams throughout the South. These distinctive white-fleshed fish tend to be associated with African American foodways, partly because they are bottom-feeders and therefore not considered highly desirable. Carp, similarly, have been disdained, but are widely used by Asian and Eastern European immigrant groups.

CLAMS

Native to the U.S. coasts, clams are associated with Native Americans, New England, the Mid-Atlantic, and the mythic American past. There are several species of clams, and each is harvested differently. Surf clams and ocean quahogs come from the ocean bed. Hard-shell clams are either dug by hand or by dredging, and soft-shell clams are gathered at low tide. The hard-shell clams are called littleneck, cherrystone, or chowder and are eaten raw or used in chowder. Soft-shell clams are frequently fried and are sometimes called "fried clam bellies." Ipswich Bay in Massachusetts is famous for its clams. Clam shacks, serving soft-shell clams, are common along the coast from Boston to Maine, and clambakes are popular social food events and fund-raisers. Similarly, the coastal Mid-Atlantic is famous for its steamed clams. Rhode Island produces a quarter of the quahogs in the United States. The Pacific Northwest now cultivates some of these Atlantic Coast varieties of clams, as well as its own distinctive geoduck, the largest clam in the world, which grows up to seven pounds and lives to be more than 100 years old. They are found in the Puget Sound off the coast of Washington State.

Other bivalve mollusks are also cultivated on both coasts. Mussels tend to thrive in colder waters (the many freshwater varieties are generally not consumed) and tend to be associated with more ethnic or Continental cuisines, although they are included in clambakes. Oysters, on the other hand, have long been a part of mainstream American foodways, eaten raw on the half shell, smoked, deep fried, as oysters Rockefeller, and used in turkey stuffing along the Mid-Atlantic and parts of the Midwest. They were one of the first coastal foods transported inland before refrigeration, because they could be stored in barrels up to two weeks. (Oysters must be eaten live; otherwise, they are toxic.) Oyster farming is a major industry in the Mid-Atlantic and spread to California when the eastern oyster was introduced there in 1875 and the Pacific oyster in 1929.

The Atlantic sea scallop is harvested by divers from the ocean floor of the Northeast Coast. Bay scallop populations in the Northeast have dwindled, however, so most of the scallops consumed in the United States actually come from China. Scallops are a popular item in American cuisine and are oftentimes associated with festive or upscale dining. They are also available, however, at many family-style and Americanized Italian restaurants.

Crustaceans include lobster, crawfish, shrimp, and prawns. Shrimp thrive in warmer waters and are integral to cuisines along the southeastern coast (shrimp and grits from Charleston, South Carolina, for example), the Gulf Coast (Louisiana's jambalaya and gumbo) and Southern California (shrimp tacos). They are also standard in Mediterranean dishes popular in the United States (shrimp scampi), and cold shrimp (with tails on, but heads off) are commonly served as an appetizer with cocktail sauce. Prawns are a different species from shrimp, but the term is frequently used interchangeable, especially for larger jumbo shrimp.

Crabs are also popular in mainstream American cuisine and come in several varieties according to region: golden crabs are available in the south Atlantic; Florida waters offer stone crabs; California, the Dungeness crab; and Alaska, the Pacific king crab. Blue crabs are especially associated with the Chesapeake Bay area and are sold at crab shacks throughout the Mid-Atlantic. They are frequently served on tables covered with paper so that the shells and remains can be easily gathered up and thrown out. Plastic bibs protect the eaters, who break the shells with mallets at the table. These crabs are also integral ingredients in crab cakes and the Maryland crab boil. Soft-shell crabs are blue crabs that have shed their hard shell. These are fried whole and usually eaten between two slices of soft white bread. The large king crabs of the Pacific Northwest are especially prized, and their claws alone are a delicacy.

Lobster is considered a delicacy and a gourmet food, although it is now available throughout the United States in chain restaurants. Live lobsters, however, are still associated with coastal New England, particularly Maine, where they are one of the state symbols. Crawfish live throughout the South but are usually considered edible only in Louisiana, where they are traditionally part of Cajun "poor man's" cuisine. They are now considered upscale and are used frequently in Creole cooking. Lobster is often used as an icon of Cajun and Louisiana culture.

BEVERAGES—ALCOHOLIC

Beer

Beer is considered an all-American alcoholic drink with a long history in the United States. Legend has it that it was even the reason behind the Pilgrims landing at Plymouth Rock off of Cape Cod rather than further south as planned. The *Mayflower* was running out of beer, and the crew threatened to mutiny if they continued. The Virginia colonists used corn to brew a beer that was recognized by the English for its quality. The first commercial brewery in the United States was established by Adrian Block and Hans Christiansen in 1612 in New Amsterdam. New England had its first breweries in the 1630s in Boston. This early beer was very different from modern beer. It was only slightly alcoholic, was made from malt, and was often a daily staple considered healthier than plain water. It was thought to be such a necessity that the president of Harvard University was dismissed in 1639 because he allowed the student beer supply to run out. During the American Revolution, taverns were meeting places for organizers, and it is interesting that the centers for beer production coincided with those cities central to the birth of the nation—Philadelphia, New York, and Boston.

In the early 1800s, German and central European immigrants introduced beers made from lager yeast. They established breweries in Philadelphia in the 1840s as well as in the central Midwest, particularly Milwaukee. These names of these breweries are still synonymous with American beer—Pabst, Schlitz, Miller, and Blatz. St. Louis, Missouri, is home to Anheuser-Busch, which started in the 1850s and produces two of the top-selling beers in the United States—Budweiser and Bud Light.

Prohibition was instituted shortly after World War I, and beer suffered as a result, partly because of the association of beer with Germany. Some of the major breweries shifted to "near beers" and gave them Italian-sounding names. Bottled beer was introduced in 1935, closing down many local breweries but allowing for national distribution.

An interest in more localized production, better-quality beers, and varieties of tastes led to a trend toward microbreweries (by definition those producing 15,000 or less barrels a year) beginning in the 1980s. Also called "craft breweries," these often use regional names and references and promote their ties to place—even though many brands are now available nationally. The story of the most successful microbrew, Samuel Adams Boston Lager, reflects the complexity of defining region in today's world. Now based in Boston, the beer was originally developed in St. Louis, was later brewed in Cincinnati, and is now produced in Milwaukee.

Certain regions of the country are more active in microbrewing—Maine, Vermont, upstate New York and New York City, California, the Pacific Northwest, and the western plains states (other than Utah, whose population is heavily Mormon, which prohibits alcohol consumption). The upper Midwest, particularly Wisconsin, also boasts numerous microbreweries. Similarly, home brewing is now a frequent hobby that does not seem to be tied to region, although individuals living in "dry" areas in the South may practice it out of necessity.

Wine

Wine has generally been considered a more respectable and formal drink than beer; however, it also tends to have associations with European lifestyles and sophistication. In conservative parts of the South, it tends to be looked on with suspicion, and in parts of the rural Midwest and western plains wine tends to be seen as effeminate and inappropriate for an all-American meat-and-potatoes eating culture. Be that as it may, Ohio was central in the history of wine production in the United States. The Cincinnati area boasted the largest wine industry until the Civil War, after which wine production moved to the south shore of Lake Erie. Many of the vineyards and wineries had to go underground during Prohibition, but they are active today and are frequently connected to fine restaurants. California took over the nation's wine production after Prohibition, and today the San Joaquin Valley accounts for almost 90 percent of all American wines. The Sonoma and Napa valleys are known as wine country and are famous for their beauty and hospitality. The private, family business run by Ernest and Julio Gallo is America's largest wine producer, selling one of every four bottles purchased in the United States. Inexpensive, fruity wines are associated with the South (and with high school or college students).

Much of the United States is now developing wineries, and regional varieties can be found almost everywhere that has the right climate and soil. One Web site lists more than 3,200 wineries, and every state has at least one: California has 1,333; Washington, 325; Oregon, 290; New York, 233; Virginia, 145; Pennsylvania, 112; North Carolina, 107; Texas, 103; Ohio, 78; and New Jersey, 34. Even Alaska has 7 and Hawaii 2. Some are surprising—Arizona has 30.[3] Many of these specialize in wines made from local produce—Michigan, cherries; Ohio, concord grapes; North Carolina, scupperdines and Muscatine grapes. Many wineries include a restaurant or offer tours and tastings.

Ice wine is made from grapes that have been left on the vine to freeze, giving them an intensity of flavor. Ice wines are something of a novelty drink that is currently being produced in the colder, northern states.

Other Alcoholic Drinks

Bourbon is a style of whiskey made from a mash of at least 51 percent corn and aged for at least two years. Originally named after Bourbon, Kentucky, it is still associated with Kentucky through the nine makers in that state, including the most famous—Maker's Mark, Jim Beam, and Wild Turkey. It is also associated with the Kentucky Derby and is used to make the mint juleps that are traditional for its celebration.

Brandy uses fruit—usually grapes, apples, and berries—as its base. Originally a European tradition, it is often used in cocktails, such as New Orleans' *café brulot*, coffee with spiced brandy. California has the only brandy industry in the nation, although homemade varieties can be found throughout the country.

Champagne is a sparkling wine that takes its name from a region in France. It is distinctive in that it is fermented a second time in the bottle in which it is sold, and this second fermentation produces the bubbles. France and the European Union agreed that the term champagne was a protected designation of origin so that only wines from that region could be called by that name. The United States, however, does not recognize French control of champagne, so American "champagne" is any bubbly wine. American versions were first made in New York's Finger Lakes region and Ohio in the mid-1800s. The drink champagne now comes primarily from California's north coast and Napa Valley. Champagne is associated throughout the country with celebrations and festivities.

Hard cider is the fermented pressings (juice and pulp) from apples. Although no longer common or easily available, it has a long illustrious history in the United States, where it was frequently the drink of choice for Americans; it was even a significant political icon in the 1800s, being used in the 1840 presidential campaign to represent the down-to-earth, pioneer character of William Henry Harrison.[4] Today it evokes its British roots, and is often sold in pubs and upscale bars offering ales and microbrews. It is produced primarily in New England and upstate New York, and Vermont's Woodchuck Cider is one of the most successful commercial brands. A number of apple-producing states are now looking at hard cider as a way to promote local, regional products.

Hard cider can also be made from pears, and a number of hard ciders have cranberry, grape, raspberry, or cherry pulp added as flavoring. Applejack brandy in New England is made by freezing hard cider in wooden barrels, removing the frozen water, and distilling. It is still commercially produced in New Jersey

Rum is distilled molasses or sugarcane juice. Very popular in colonial America, it was imported from the Caribbean islands where its production was tied to the slave trade.[5] It is still associated today with tropical islands, pirates, and Florida. It is often mixed with colas or other ingredients for piña coladas or rum toddies (also called hot buttered rum).

Tequila is distilled from cactus pulp. It is strongly associated with the Mexican-influenced culture of the Southwest. It is used for margaritas, a flavored mixed drink made using finely crushed ice that is sold at Mexican restaurants throughout the United States.

Whiskey is distilled from fermented grain mash and aged in wooden (preferably oak) barrels. The whiskey-making tradition was brought to the United States by the earliest Scots and Scots-Irish immigrants. Barley, malted barley, rye, corn, and wheat can be used for the mash, and corn whiskey (at least 80 percent corn) is famous in the upland South as moonshine. Although a license can be obtained to distill corn liquor at home for medicinal uses, illegal stills can still be found tucked away in isolated "hollers" of the mountains. Rye whiskey (51 percent rye) is also notorious as a southern drink. Two Tennessee whiskeys (Jack Daniels and George Dickel) are sometimes confused with bourbon, but these are filtered through sugar-maple charcoal. Blended whiskeys are combinations of straight whiskey with unaged whiskey, flavorings, and neutral spirits. Whiskey is also associated with the Wild West and saloons.

Cherry bounce is a historical specialty drink of cherries mixed with alcohol. Regional variations are found in New England and Virginia, where it is mixed with rum or brandy; southerners prefer whiskey; Cajuns, bourbon; and midwesterners, vodka.

Of English heritage, eggnog is usually a cold drink of cream, sugar, and eggs flavored with nutmeg. Various alcohols can be added—brandy, rum, bourbon, or sherry. The southern preference is peach brandy, rum, and whiskey. Eggnog is common for Christmas and New Year's, and it is usually sold commercially only during that season.

Hot toddies—a mixture of whiskey, hot water, lemon, sugar, and spices—were adopted from Scotland by colonial America. New Englanders replaced the whiskey with rum or brandy. They are still popular today as a way to treat colds.

BEVERAGES—NONALCOHOLIC

The United States is fortunate in its resources for clean potable water. Some regions boast of the purity and taste of their water—the Appalachian Mountains from the north to the south, the western mountain areas, and the Pacific Northwest. California and the urban East Coast were the first to produce bottled waters, such as Perrier, but these are common throughout the country now.

Milk

Milk is promoted as the standard the all-American drink (especially for children, even though African Americans and Asian Americans tend to be lactose intolerant). Its highest consumption is in New England and the Midwest. The upland South also has a high milk consumption.

Milk is used as the basis for numerous dessert-type drinks. Egg cream is a New York City specialty. A combination of milk, seltzer, and chocolate syrup, it was probably introduced by Jewish immigrants. Originally served in soda fountains and ice cream parlors, egg creams are popular again in New York as part of the nostalgia of the past.

Milkshakes are usually a mixture of milk and ice cream. In New England, however, a milkshake is milk literally shaken until frothy. Flavorings are added, but there is no ice cream. In that region, a drink made of ice cream, milk, and flavorings is called a "frappe." An ice cream soda is ice cream with a carbonated soft drink added to it. These were popularized in the 1950s youth culture as all-American, and they are still common in Midwest.

Milk with coffee syrup, called "coffee milk," is popular in Rhode Island. If ice cream is added, it becomes a "coffee cabinet." Commercially processed coffee syrup is sold in Rhode Island, and coffee milk was proclaimed the official state drink in 1993.

Fruit Juice and Cider

Fruit juice is common throughout the United States, particularly for breakfast, and it is promoted as a healthy way to get vitamin C. Freshly squeezed orange juice evokes visions of sunny Florida. Grapefruit, grape, tomato, and apple are also standard juices. Lemonade and limeade are summertime favorites. Fruits are also turned into slushies by combining them with finely ground ice. These concoctions vary in name and ingredients by region—shaved ice is used in Hawaii and California, for example.

Cider refers to the pressings (juice and pulp) from apples, although pears can be used also. It tends to have old-fashioned, pioneer, and seasonal associations, and it is usually available fresh in the fall wherever apples are grown. Many commercial and locally run apple orchards have cider presses; however, laws prohibiting the sale of unpasteurized cider have closed down many of them. Some still offer samples of cider along with apple-picking and heritage celebrations, particular in the Midwest and the Appalachian Mountains where a strong antigovernment sentiment is played out in the operation of cider mills. Hot cider, either simply heated or mulled with cinnamon and other spices, is a popular fall drink.

Soft Drinks

Artificially flavored noncarbonated soft drinks are quintessentially American and represent the prevalent industrial, scientific approach to food. Kool-Aid is the most famous of these powdered mixtures that are simply added to water. It was invented in Hastings, Nebraska, in 1927, and a Kool-Aid festival is held in Hastings every year. Now infamous from Tom Wolfe's 1968 account of Ken Kesey and the Merry Pranksters in his book, *The Electric Kool-Aid Acid Test*, as well as the mass suicide of Jim Jones's followers in Jonesboro, Guyana, by drinking grape Kool-Aid laced with cyanide, Kool-Aid tends to be associated with working-class middle America and African-Americans.

Carbonated soft drinks are called by different names in different regions: tonic in New England, soda pop in the Mid-Atlantic, and pop in the Midwest. In the South, the term "coke" is used generically to refer to all carbonated soft drinks. Some flavors and brands are regional or have regional associations as well. Vanilla-flavored cream soda, invented in Wisconsin in 1856, is still associated with the Midwest. Coca-Cola is now quintessentially American, but it was started in Atlanta in 1886 by a pharmacist, John S. Pemberton, and still has strong ties to that city. Waco, Texas, boasts of Dr. Pepper (invented in 1885); New Bern, North Carolina of Pepsi (invented in 1894); and Massachusetts of Moxie. RC (Royal Crown) cola is an icon of the Deep South. Mountain Dew has southern associations to moonshine, and ginger ale is more northern.

Birch beer is made from the yeast-fermented sap of birch trees. (Birch wine could be made from the boiled down sap.) The drink, which became popular in the 1880s and 1890s, was sold as an alternative to alcohol and was said to have medicinal properties. Now a piece of old-fashioned Americana, it is mostly found in the Mid-Atlantic and New England, especially in Pennsylvania Dutch country. Two commercial producers are Kutztown Soda Co. in Pennsylvania and Boylan's in New Jersey.

Root beer is made of made of sassafras and is also called sarsaparilla. It has old-fashioned, all-American associations, and because it usually lacks caffeine, it tends to appear at family and child-friendly events and venues. It is often still made at home and in small-scale operations, such as Zemer's Rootbeer, which started as a family business in Michigan and is now based in Texas. The drink is also commercially produced throughout the United States. Hire's, Dad's, and A&W are popular nationally, although the popularity tends to reflect regional preferences. A&W root beer, for example, was invented in California in 1919 and is still most popular in that state as well as Texas and Utah. Barq's contains caffeine, and Abita is a Louisiana version of root beer, produced with cane sugar, as is the root beer of the Saint Arnold Brewing Company in Texas.

Ginger beer, made of ginger, lemon, and sugar, was very popular in the United States in the early 1900s. Today, it has associations with Great Britain and the Caribbean Islands.

Coffee

Coffee, served hot, is considered an all-American beverage, partly because it was the alternative to tea during the Revolutionary War.[6] Coffee itself does not have regional associations, but some of the companies producing it do. Starbucks from Seattle, founded in 1971, is the most famous. Since the 1980s, numerous smaller companies, many of which are locally owned and run, have developed special roasts and serve their own coffee. Specialty coffees—variations of coffee, milk, and flavorings—are now popular, as are varieties of grades of coffee beans. Familiarity with all this variety is often considered a badge of social standing,[7] and the fair trade movement attempts to remind coffee consumers of their social responsibilities to coffee growers.[8] Some ethnic variations on coffee can be found regionally: Scandinavians in the upper Midwest have a traditional egg coffee, made with an egg in it to hold the grounds.

Iced coffee and cold coffee drinks have a different tradition from hot coffee. Some areas of the South have long served iced coffee as an alternative to iced tea, but the Northeast has several coffee drinks that are only known regionally. Rhode Island coffee milk is one example and is served with varying recipes in the state. Manhattan Special is a commercially produced coffee milk available in the New York City area. The proliferation of coffee businesses and coffee houses has stimulated the invention of more varieties of iced coffee drinks. Thai iced coffee was introduced by immigrants to the West Coast in the 1970s and 1980s and is increasingly popular, particularly in urban areas that have Thai restaurants.

Postum is an alternative to coffee invented in 1895 by W.W. Post in Battle Creek, Michigan, because he believed caffeine was unhealthy (actually poisonous to the body). Popular among Seventh Day Adventists and others eschewing caffeine, it was made from roasted wheat and wheat bran with molasses. Postum was discontinued in 2007.

Hot Chocolate

Also called hot cocoa, hot chocolate is a cold-weather comfort drink throughout the country. The first powdered mix for it was offered in 1935 by Carnation Milk, and today varieties of mixes are available, many of them containing powdered milk so that hot water is all that is needed. Hot chocolate can also be made from scratch with cocoa powder, sugar, and milk. Marshmallows are often added, and many coffee shops now offer hot chocolate with whipped cream. A regional type of hot chocolate is found in the Southwest where it is made Mexican style, from blocks of semi-sweet chocolate with cinnamon, sugar, and vanilla blended in. The blocks are dissolved in hot water or milk for a frothy drink. Some traditionalists also add chilies, which reflects the Aztec origins of chocolate.

Tea

Historically, tea represented the British political and cultural hold on the colonies (as in the Boston Tea Party), and it still has British associations.

American tea is historically black tea, as opposed to the green teas more common in Asia. Black tea refers to green tea leaves that have been fermented; oolong tea is lightly fermented. In the United States, tea usually comes in tea bags, and it is frequently drunk hot with lemon or milk and sugar. Herbal teas, which actually have a long tradition in the United States, began to be produced commercially in the late 1960s by Celestial Seasonings in Boulder, Colorado. Associated initially with eastern religions and countercultural values, herbal teas have been mainstreamed and are a frequent alternative to caffeinated drinks. Chai, a hot sweetened and spiced black tea with milk from India and the Himalayan region, was initially only found in the United States in immigrant communities and underground coffee houses. It is now sold at numerous coffee shops, frequently iced as well as hot.

Iced tea (sometimes called "ice tea") is very American, and sweet tea (iced tea brewed with sugar, saccharin, and/or honey) is iconic of the South. Lemon slices are often added, as is mint. Long Island iced tea has any variety of spirits (gin, rum, vodka) added.

Bubble tea is a drink from Southeast Asia and southern China consisting of tapioca pearls, fruit, and gelatin squares in various fruit juices. It was introduced into Chinatowns in the United States and became popular on the West Coast in the 1990s. It can now be found as a novelty drink in most urban centers throughout the United States.

SWEETENERS

Americans tend to have sweet tooths, although recent health and diet concerns have made some change their habits. Vast amounts of candy, soft drinks, coffees, and numerous desserts and sweet snacks are consumed in the United States.

Cane sugar is the most common at-home sweetener, though high-fructose corn syrup is used commercially. Powdered sugar and brown sugar are frequently used in baking. Brown sugar is an ingredient, along with corn syrup, in pecan and chess pies. Christmas cookies from Central and Eastern European traditions are frequently rolled in powdered sugar.

Molasses and sorghum tend to be regional to the upland South, even though molasses is usually an ingredient in Boston baked beans, rum, and Pennsylvania Dutch shoofly pie. Traditional "stirrings," in which the cane or grain is boiled down to the thick syrup, are still held, frequently as historical reenactments or festive events.

Similarly, maple syrup and maple sugar are associated with New England, although syrups from tree saps are produced throughout the eastern part of the Midwest. Birch, poplar, and oak are also tapped. The trees are tapped with a shunt inserted in late winter when the trees are coming back to life, and the sap starts to run. The sap is gathered in buckets attached to the shunts, producing a clear, sweet liquid that can be drunk as "maple water." It is then slowly boiled down into syrup. The long boiling process requires constant vigilance; it is oftentimes treated as a social event and is usually done in sugar shacks built for that purpose. Maple syrup and maple candy are sold as iconic foods of interior New England as well as Ohio, Michigan, and Indiana, and maple syrup is often featured at tourist sites in small souvenir jugs.

Honey, the liquid produced by honeybees digesting and regurgitating flower nectar, is a traditional sweetener and food throughout the United States. Its flavor depends on the vegetation in the bees' territory, and it is often identified according to the primary flower. Honey is used today as a sweetener in hot tea, as a spread on bread, and in baking. It is particularly popular in the South. Honey tends to be a home industry in the Upper South, the eastern Midwest, and interior New England, and the latter is the largest commercial producer of honey in the United States. Stevia, an herb native to Central and South America, is legally considered a dietary supplement rather than a sweetener, although it is considerably sweeter than sugar. Its juice and leaves are sold primarily in health food stores, on the coasts, and in urban areas.

Artificial sweeteners are popular diet aids, but their use raises a number of health concerns because of possible links to cancer. Saccharin, invented in the late 1800s, was used as a commercial additive, particularly during World War I when there were sugar shortages. Believed to be a diet aid, it became popular in the 1960s and 1970s as a calorie-free sugar substitute. It is still available, usually as "Sweet'N Low," which is found in restaurants in single-serving pink packets. Saccharin is used to sweeten the diet drink Tab and is often used in southern sweet tea. Aspartame was developed in the 1960s, partly as an alternative to saccharin. It is a frequent additive to soft drinks and processed foods, especially those being sold as low fat or low calorie. Concerns about its long-term health impacts have decreased its use among many health-conscious individuals. It is frequently sold under the brand name NutraSweet.

CHOCOLATE

Chocolate, originally extracted from the beans of the cacao tree in Central America, is one of the most popular flavorings for desserts and sweets in the United States. It is also eaten as a candy and served as a drink, usually hot. Chocolate is used for cake icing; as the main ingredient in fudge, brownies, and many candy bars, cookies, and cakes; and as a dip or sauce for nuts, fruit, and other foods. European traditions of candy making were brought to the United States in the second half of the 1800s, and numerous businesses developed, often where there was access to dairy production. The oldest producer, Hershey Chocolate Company in Pennsylvania, began in 1894. The town of Hershey, with its chocolate factory, is a favorite tourist site for chocolate lovers.

American chocolate tends to be mild and sweet milk chocolate. In the 1970s, however, Americans started developing an interest in the European darker chocolates. These expensive "fancy" chocolates were generally available in urban areas, but now a wide variety can be purchased almost everywhere in the country.

Hot chocolate has a long history. It was originally consumed in Central America, where it was typically flavored with chilies and other spices. Christopher Columbus took the bean to Spain, and by the end of the 1500s, Spanish royalty were enjoying drinking chocolate. From there chocolate spread to Europe and then to the American colonies, where it was a popular drink by the late 1600s. The Spanish colonies (California, Louisiana, and Florida and the Southwest) also borrowed the Mexican tradition of chocolate drinking, but usually added cinnamon, cloves, and chilies to the chocolate, a style that is still practiced in areas with a Mexican influence.

NOTES

1. Yvonne R. Lockwood and William G. Lockwood, "Pasties in Michigan's Upper Peninsula: Foodways, Interethnic Relations, and Regionalism," in *The Taste of American Place*, eds. Barbara G. Shortridge and James R. Shortridge, 21–36 (New York: Rowman and Littlefield, 1998).

2. Margaret Visser. *Much Depends on Dinner: The Extraordinary History and Mythology, Allure and Obsessions, Perils and Taboos of an Ordinary Meal* (New York: Collier Books, 1986), 22–55.

3. Wines and Times, www.winesandtimes.com/wnt/index.php.

4. Boria Sax, "Apples," in *Rooted in America: Foodlore of Popular Fruits and Vegetables*, ed. David S. Wilson and Angus K. Gillespie, 11–13 (Knoxville: University of Tennessee Press, 1999).

5. Sidney Mintz, *Sweetness and Power: The Place of Sugar in Modern History* (New York: Penguin Press, 1985).

6. Mark Pendergrast. *Uncommon Grounds: The History of Coffee and How It Transformed Our World* (New York: Perseus Books Group, 1999).

7. William Roseberry, "The Rise of Yuppie Coffees and the Reimagination of Class in the United States," in *Food in the USA: A Reader*, ed. Carole M. Counihan, 149–168 (New York: Routledge, 2002).

8. Daniel Jaffee. *Brewing Justice: Fair Trade Coffee, Sustainability, and Survival* (Los Angeles: University of California Press, 2007).

3

Cooking

Cooking involves much more than simply placing ingredients in a pan and putting the pan on the stove. It requires a variety of activities and material objects as well as a complex set of knowledge and skills ranging from where to obtain ingredients to how to read recipes and how to set the table to create a desired atmosphere. All the components of foodways—procurement, preservation, preparation, presentation, and clean up—are bound up in cooking.

Adding to the complexity are issues of who cooks and when, how people learn to cook, and what dishes are considered socially appropriate to cook, all of which are further complicated by gender, class, age, and ethnicity. In recent years, the mass media has had a huge effect on cooking in the United States, and televised cooking shows now promote cooking as an artistic and profitable endeavor. This, along with other social movements, has elevated cooking so that it is no longer strictly relegated to the domestic and female sphere. Contemporary practices, however, differ according to region and often reflect the values of that regional culture.

Other mass media forms, such as printed cookbooks, popular periodicals (particularly women's magazines), and now the Internet, have introduced regional cooking to a national audience and constructed a sense of a national cuisine. That national cuisine has then in turn been localized by regional cooks using regional resources and practices. Although all Americans now have access to various regional cooking traditions, some of these are still strongly associated with specific regions. This chapter describes some of these traditions, using the foodways framework to describe the cooking process in all its complexity.

WHO COOKS: SOCIAL ROLES

Contemporary American cooking practices reflect broad national patterns but also vary somewhat by region. To further complicate matters, the question of who does the cooking also differs within regions depending on the context: urban versus rural, everyday versus special occasions, domestic versus commercial.

The overall historical pattern in the United States was that women did the domestic cooking and men did the commercial, public cooking. Women did cook commercially in boarding houses in the western frontier and urban centers, but these were considered a matter of extreme economic necessity, not a career choice. In the Far West, cooks were often Chinese men, and the South and Mid-Atlantic had a long tradition of African American women who ran the home kitchen and supplied sumptuous southern fare. The Northeast was more likely to have Irish women cooks in the home. In the 1950s, television shows like *Ozzie and Harriet* and *Leave it to Beaver* reflected the standard for many Americans: the husband "brought home the bacon," and the wife cooked it. Generally, women were expected to do the private, everyday cooking for the family, and men did the public, celebratory, and communal cooking. Professionally, cooking was more open to men than women; however, it generally was not seen as a high-status, mainstream, or masculine occupation.

These attitudes went further than social roles: women's cooking was perceived as functional, a natural aspect of being female and a part of a woman's nurturing nature, but men's cooking was seen as artistic and technically demanding, deserving of pay and recognition. Today, there is debate over the role of sexism in the world of the professional chef, which tends to be very male dominated. Culinary schools tend to admit more men than women. Some see this as the nature of the occupation, which demands physical stamina and strength, but the field is also highly competitive. Starting in the late 1990s, however, this pattern changed radically for a variety of reasons. An increased interest in cooking as recreation and art has attracted more people to the cooking profession in general, and it is now commonplace to see men cooking family meals as well as women working in the professional cooking world. Yet some regional patterns still exist. The East and West coasts tend to be more progressive and not as tied to traditional social roles—partly because so many women have entered professional culinary positions in those regions, but also partly because of more progressive values. Urban areas tend to be more willing to break the mold than rural areas. The Midwest and the South tend to be more conservative, so that it is still the woman's role to do the domestic cooking in those regions. Furthermore, it is still common in the South for black women to be hired and celebrated as cooks.

LEARNING TO COOK

There are several formal routes for training in cooking. Numerous vocational and community colleges offer degrees or diplomas in culinary arts, and numerous four-year universities offer degrees in restaurant and hospitality management, which can include an applied skills component. The International Culinary School at the Art Institutes offers programs in 40 states.[1] These programs differ from culinary schools in which students receive a full course of classes on all aspects of cooking. These schools feed directly into professional careers. The Culinary Institute of America, in Hyde Park, New York, is one of the most respected schools and offers students a foundation in international cuisines and food as a cultural and social phenomenon. The school has branches in Napa Valley, California, and San Antonio, Texas. Admission is highly competitive and tuition is high, but graduates are generally sought after in the food industry.

Training in domestic cooking, meanwhile, generally occurs informally in the home or formally in classes in public schools. Now referred to as "family and consumer science," home economics is usually taught in junior high and high school, where it often alternates with shop classes. Originally segregated by gender, home economics classes are now optional for any student, but tend to be primarily taken by girls and taught by women. Such classes are a legacy of the home economics movement, a social and political movement of the Progressive Era (1890–1913) that promoted college for women, claiming that university training would make them better domestic managers: more efficient in the kitchen, aware of the need for more sanitary practices, and more up-to-date with scientific developments in nutrition and cooking. Although such classes are now considered unnecessary for college-bound students, they are still popular in rural areas of the Midwest and South, the same areas where the 4-H farm youth organization is active. Also, numerous urban schools are trying to revitalize these classes and tie them to other subjects or to a school garden.

A current trend in learning to cook is formal cooking classes that are taken sporadically and for personal enhancement. Famous chefs and restaurants sometimes offer classes, and numerous cruises and tours combine cooking classes with eating food prepared by star professionals. These are more likely to occur in urban centers and on the coasts. Stores specializing in kitchenware, cookbooks, or specific food items often offer cooking classes as well, and other businesses and organizations, such as gardening clubs, bakeries, coffee shops, chocolate shops, and community centers often include cooking demonstrations and tastings as part of their outreach or marketing.

Today, many people are learning to cook or refining their skills and expanding their repertoire through the numerous food and cooking shows available on television and the Internet. Julia Child is credited with the first American televised cooking show, *The French Chef*, in 1963, and such shows have grown into a major form of entertainment and socializing for Americans of all ages and genders.[2] The Food Network is a television network and Web site that offers cooking shows as well as shows about all aspects of food. The network is distributed to more than 90 million households a year. Their Web site claims 5.5 million viewers a month and includes recipes, chat rooms, food news, celebrity chef gossip, and more.[3] Although the Food Network is based in New York City and is popular nationally, it often includes regional dishes and chefs. Other television shows, such as *Iron Chef*, feature star chefs, many of whom have regional and ethnic affiliations. These include New Orleans–based Emeril Lagasse, who is known for Creole and Cajun cooking, although he was born in Massachusetts and is of Portuguese and French Canadian descent; Paula Deen, who is based in Savannah, Georgia, and is known as the "queen of southern cuisine and home cooking"; Austrian-born and French-trained Wolfgang Puck, who is credited as a founder of California cuisine, which blends French techniques with California's abundant resources; and Rachael Ray, famous for her 30-minute budget meals and celebration of her family's Massachusetts and New York home cooking.

Ironically, at the same time cooking shows are growing in popularity, many critics bemoan the lack of cooking skills and time spent cooking among the general American population. Class differences seem to come into play, in which the working poor are less likely to have the resources (equipment, space, ingredients) to cook and instead rely on fast-food outlets and expensive neighborhood stores. Middle-class families, meanwhile, are often caught between busy work schedules and children's extracurricular activities that leave little time for cooking or family meals. The current interest in cooking as an artistic activity, though, is attracting more and more middle- and upper-class persons, and families are encouraged to use food preparation as a time for bonding. Food preparation and appreciation are also being pushed as a life skill for young people. Interestingly, this trend is even more evident on the coasts and in urban areas. The Midwest and the South have generally maintained the older traditions of home cooking longer than other regions.

COOKBOOKS

Cookbooks and published recipes (in newspapers, magazine, Web sites) play a major role in defining different food regions in the United States. By identifying certain dishes as representing a region and characterizing the foodways of that area, they make readers aware that a region exists. In doing so, they actually help to create a sense of a regional cuisine.

Not all cookbooks are the same, however. Some attempt to be ethnographic by describing dishes that people in a region actually cook and the ways they eat them. Others are historical, giving the history of a region and its food along with sample recipes from the past. Still others are cultural in that they explore the meanings and uses of food and its connections to local culture.

Many contemporary cookbooks blend a little of each of these approaches, while focusing more on creative cooking using local resources or simply the imaginations of local cooks. These sometimes assume that a dish found in one community or family is common throughout the region. They also frequently include favorite recipes of local cooks, regardless of where those recipes—or cooks—originated. It is difficult, then, to know whether a regional cookbook gives an accurate portrait of a region. Even though many authors have done careful historical or ethnographic research, and many have excellent cooking skills, the complexity of the idea of region and the varied uses of the word complicate the subject. For purposes here, regional recipes and cookbooks are those that draw on the natural resources and cultural history of a specific, defined geographic area. Given that understanding of the term, there are several types of cookbooks relevant to regional food cultures, although categories may overlap within one cookbook.

General Cookbooks

General cookbooks tend to focus on cooking techniques and recipes that are commonly used in the United States, but they do not claim to present specifically American food. They might identify the region, nationality, or ethnicity of a particular dish, but the intent is to pass along cooking skills. Two prime examples of favorite classic general cookbooks for many Americans are *The Joy of Cooking* and *Betty Crocker*.[4] General cookbooks promoting natural or seasonal foods tend to recognize regional dishes and ingredients. Similarly, a group of cookbooks may include social justice and concern for the environment as an "ingredient" in good food. Frances Moore Lappè's *Diet for a Small Planet*, published in 1971, was the first of these; it encouraged readers to look for local wild foods and those grown without chemicals.[5] Although *Diet for a Small Planet* was available nationally, it was most popular on the coasts, where people tended to more readily connect food choices with ethics. Those areas that relied heavily on red meat in their diets (as well as livelihoods) were particularly unreceptive to the book as it advocates eating less meat. In contrast, the eastern part of the Midwest was home to a series of cookbooks sponsored by the Mennonite Central Committee, based in Pennsylvania (and Ontario, Canada), advocating a grain- and legume-based diet. The first one, the *More-with-Less Cookbook*, was published in 1976 and contained "suggestions . . . on how to eat better and consume less of the world's limited food resources." Recipes were collected from Mennonite women from around the world; however, many of them were residents of Ohio and Indiana (where two Mennonite colleges are—Goshen and Bluffton), and their recipes were adaptations of basic midwestern dishes, with lots of casseroles, noodles, and dairy-based foods.

Cookbooks on American Food

These cookbooks present foods that are considered all-American or simply the foods eaten by Americans, emphasizing national identity. These tend to include dishes that are known throughout the country and are often made of nationally available ingredients. Such cookbooks sometimes divide the recipes by ethnicity or region but more often recipes are divided by their place within the meal (e.g., main course, dessert). The first of these types of cookbooks was published in 1796, *American Cooking* by Amelia Simmons. Although Simmons does not specify regional recipes, she uses ingredients distinctive to colonial America—such as pumpkin, cornmeal, sweet corn, and cranberries.

Regional Cookbooks

Regional cookbooks either focus on a specific region or give samplings of different regional dishes throughout the country. A 1970s series from Time-Life, for example, gave thorough cultural histories of the different regions and provided recipes of distinctive and representative dishes. With its extensive photography and accessible writing style, this series is still a basic resource in libraries.

The recent wave of interest in cooking and a search for local cultures has meant a surge in the publication of regional cookbooks. Some regional cuisines have long been recognized as distinctive—Southern, New England, eastern shore of Maryland, and Louisiana Creole and Cajun, for example. Others cuisines have likely become known because of cookbooks. Tex-Mex, for example, has gained status as a cuisine separate from Mexican food partly because of cookbooks.

Cookbooks also highlight specific cities that are well known for having a distinctive culinary culture. New Orleans, Charleston (South Carolina), New York, Chicago, and San Francisco are among the best known. Some books also highlight a subculture of a particular region, such as the Amish of the Midwest, the Pennsylvania Dutch of the Mid-Atlantic, the Cajuns of Louisiana, or the Creoles of New Orleans. Some regional cookbooks take the approach of presenting all the various ethnic groups in a particular area. *The Minnesota Ethnic Food Book*, for example, includes a discussion and recipes for a number of ethnic groups residing in Minnesota, including Hmong, Swedes, and Mexicans.[6]

Tourist Cookbooks

These cookbooks are specifically marketed to tourists, oftentimes as souvenirs. As such, they tend to play up the stereotypes of a region and present caricatures of the food and culture. Oftentimes, the recipes are not meant to be used for cooking, but are a parody of a real recipe. For example, Appalachian tourist cookbooks offer "hillbilly victuals" with recipes for moonshine, road-kill opossum, and the like.

Ethnic Cookbooks

These cookbooks present dishes of various ethnic and immigrant communities in the United States. They frequently, but not always, tie those communities to the region in which they have settled. Some were actually books historically used within an ethnic group, written in their own language, and served to both preserve traditional dishes from the home country and introduce American ingredients, menus, and cooking styles to immigrants. An example is a German-language cookbook published first in Germany (1844) and then in Milwaukee (1879), *Practical Cook Book*, by Henriette Davidis.[7] Other ethnic cookbooks are contemporary collections of dishes representing an ethnic group or group of ethnicities. These frequently select dishes thought to appeal to mainstream American tastes and adapt recipes to American ingredients and cooking habits. Some give historical background for the cultures featured so that the food is a way to learn about the people—for example, Jeff Smith's *The Frugal gourmet On Our Immigrant Ancestors: Recipes You Should Have Gotten from Your Grandmother* (New York: WIlliam Morrow and Company, Inc, 1990).

Ethnic cookbooks should not be confused with "international" cookbooks that present cuisines from outside the United States.

Community Cookbooks

Community cookbooks feature recipes from local community organizations, such as churches, schools, women's clubs, local history societies, and other civic groups. Local chapters of the Junior League, for example, have a tradition of publishing cookbook collections. Community cookbooks are oftentimes produced as fund-raisers and contain a sampling of recipes used by members of the organization. The recipes may or may not be regional or traditional; oftentimes, they are simply the favorite dishes of respected cooks within the group. Contributors might not even know the origin of a recipe, or they may have gotten it from a friend or a magazine. Although these cookbooks do not usually focus on regional or local foods, they frequently offer authentic representations of what people in a particular region actually eat.

Single-ingredient or Genre Cookbooks

These focus on one item, giving a wide range of recipes for variations with that item. Regional recipes are often included. Common examples of ingredients are corn, apples, pumpkins, beef, and fish. Categories of food may also be featured, such as bread, cookies, pies, or barbecue.

Cookbooks on Specific Cooking Techniques or Equipment

These cookbooks provide a variety of recipes using one particular cooking technique, such as grilling, baking, or deep frying. Some of these techniques are associated with regions (e.g., grilling with the West Coast, deep frying with the South, and baking with traditional cooks throughout the country). A similar type of cookbook focuses on a cooking implement, such as woks, Crock-Pots, microwave ovens, Dutch ovens, or newer inventions like the Foreman grill. Both types of books might include regional recipes, but their focus is generally not regional. Their popularity, however, is often regional since some of these implements tend to be favored in different regions.

Restaurant or "Star Chef" Cookbooks

Because restaurants are in specific locations, the cookbooks featuring their signature dishes can be considered regional, even though the restaurants might not focus on local resources or foodways. Sometimes, though, an eating establishment comes to define or reflect the image of a region. The 1977 *Moosewood Cookbook*, for example, presents recipes from the vegetarian Moosewood Restaurant in Ithaca, New York, a university town representing the back-to-the-land, counterculture communities scattered throughout the Northeast.[8] Similarly, Alice Waters based her cookbook on her restaurant, Chez Panisse, in Berkeley.[9] Her approach to using the freshest local and seasonal ingredients has come to define California cuisine.

Many of the chefs featured on television cooking shows have their own cookbooks. Similarly, chefs who have made a name for themselves at a particular restaurant or with a particular cooking style or dish (for example, grilling or pizza) often publish cookbooks.

FOOD PROCUREMENT

Procuring or obtaining foods and ingredients can differ between regions as well as within a region. There tend to be dramatic contrasts between rural and urban areas over the processes of procurement.

Grocery Stores

A variety of types of stores carry food, ranging from small corner stores to superstores that carry every item imaginable along with food. Most urban centers along the Mid-Atlantic and Northeast still have neighborhood delicatessens, bakeries, small green grocers, and butchers. These tend to be most vibrant in ethnic enclaves, while more artisan stores (cheese, baked goods) and specialty food stores (coffee, tea, chocolate) tend to be found in more upscale neighborhoods. Major midwestern cities with either strong ethnic populations (such as Cleveland, Ohio; Milwaukee, Wisconsin; and St. Paul, Minnesota) or universities (Ann Arbor, Michigan; Madison, Wisconsin) tend to have these small neighborly types of food stores. On the whole, however, American food shopping is characterized by weekly trips to a grocery store or supermarket where national brands for everything needed can be purchased under one roof.

Within this national pattern, different chains tend to be associated with different regions. The most famous, the A&P, started in 1859 in New York City as the Great American Tea Company, selling tea, coffee, and spices. The A&P extended to the West Coast in 1870 and established its own brand-name products. It also originated programs to reward customer loyalty with stamps and coupon books. Today, A&Ps are found along the eastern Mid-Atlantic and in the Northeast (from Massachusetts to Virginia).

Another national concept for food shopping is self-serve, pre-pricing. Set prices started in the early 1900s. Housewives loved them because they took away the guesswork and personal agendas of bargaining—they could shop where they wanted for the best price and quality rather than out of loyalty to a person.[10] Self-service food stores started in 1916 with the Piggly Wiggly

in Memphis, Tennessee, which allowed customers to choose their own mer-
chandise rather than waiting for the grocer pick it out. The concept quickly
spread through the country. In the 1930s, Kroger stores, started in 1883 in
Cincinnati, introduced the idea of surrounding the store with a parking lot,
which joined grocery shopping with the emerging car culture of the contemporary United States. Kroger stores are now found throughout the eastern
Midwest and the Southeast.

There are now both national chains and smaller regional grocery stores
throughout the nation, although in some areas, superstores, such as Wal-
Mart, also carry food. Critics are concerned that superstores destroy smaller
and more local businesses. There also are more specialized supermarkets that
tend to be found by region. Asian supermarkets flourish on the East and
West coasts, where Asian populations cluster, as well as in select midwestern and southern cities, Minneapolis and Atlanta, for example. Hispanic
grocery stores can be found in the Southwest and south Florida as well as in
areas with strong migrant populations, such as Chicago and cities in Indiana
and North Carolina. Stores specializing in natural and/or organic foods are
found along the coasts and in major cities in Midwest (Earthfare, Whole
Foods). These often overlap with global foods markets (Trader Joe's).

With this wealth of various shopping experiences, regional stores often
try to develop their own character or be innovative in their services. An
example is Wegman's in Rochester, New York, which offers seating for
meals selected from the store's wide variety of world cuisines. These options
are often accessible only to the middle and upper classes, however, because
the stores are typically in more upscale neighborhoods or on the outskirts of
towns and suburbs, thereby requiring private transportation.

One alternative way to purchase food that personalizes the experience
somewhat is through co-ops. These are formed by groups of individuals who
purchase in bulk in order to take advantage of lower prices. The products
are then divided among the members. Many co-ops started in the 1960s in
order to gain access to vegetarian foods and bulk grains, and most today
tend to emphasize organic and vegetarian foods. Co-ops tend to survive primarily in college towns and in areas where other outlets for purchasing
alternative foods are not available. They also frequently form a social
community as well with members sharing other interests and values. Some
co-ops also sponsor classes and activities, particularly related to food, such
as beer brewing.

Farming and Gardening

Although most Americans procure their food from commercial outlets,
many still either grow or gather from the wild some portion of their diet.

This self-reliance is due more to region and family tradition than it is to socioeconomic class. Frequently, the urban poor rely heavily on high-priced store-bought goods, whereas the rural poor, particularly in the upland South, the Deep South, and the Pacific Northwest have more of a tradition of self-sufficiency.

Ever since Thomas Jefferson proclaimed that every true citizen worked the soil of the land, the family farm has been central to mythic America. Family farms are, by definition, family owned and operated, usually working on an open-market system and with an annual income of less than $250,000. The number of these farms has decreased from 6.5 million in 1900 to 2 million in 1997, and although they make up 90 percent of all U.S. farms, they produce less than 41 percent of the food used in the United States. Fewer than 1 percent of farms are organic, and only 8,000 are officially certified as such.[11] These farms often supply local grocers, but more frequently must rely on farmers' markets to sell their produce. A growing trend is community-supported agriculture, or CSA, a concept based on the writings of the European philosopher/theologian Dr. Rudolph Steiner. In CSA, a group of individuals agree to support a local farm, usually committing to pay a monthly fee (or "share") in return for a portion of whatever is produced. The supporters agree to share in the windfalls of the farm as well as the losses due to unexpected weather or other disasters. The first CSA group was established in New Hampshire in 1986 (the Temple-Wilton Community Farm), and the concept thrived in New England and on the West Coast, particularly in northern California and Oregon. Although CSA was initially popular among individuals leaning toward progressive, countercultural values and lifestyles (the stereotypical back-to-land communes), and CSA groups are still found primarily in those regions, the idea has become more mainstream and is being adapted throughout the country. The rural Southeast, upland South, Mid-Atlantic, and Midwest, in particular, are developing these farms.

Another trend is networks connecting small farmers with local distributors, grocers, and restaurants, attempting to guarantee a market for the farmers as well as a dependable supply for the outlets. The Midwest seems to be leading the way in this concept, which acknowledges the role of market forces and tries to work within the system, rather than attempting more radical changes in philosophy. An example of this type of networking is Food for Thought: A Local Food Initiative, directed by the Rural Life Center at Kenyon College in central Ohio. The initiative is developing a sustainable system that connects local farms and local buyers.[12] Developed by sociologist Dr. Howard Sachs, the project is providing a national and international model. Similarly, the Leopold Center for Sustainable Agriculture, connected to the University of Iowa in Ames, "explores and cultivates alternatives that secure healthier people and landscapes in Iowa."[13] Similar programs are starting all over the country.

Yet another trend is community gardens and school gardens. Similar to the Victory gardens of World War II, community gardens are being promoted not only as a way for individuals to supply themselves with fresh produce but also as a way to create safer communities, preserve natural areas, beautify neighborhoods, and create positive relationships among neighbors. Oftentimes, master gardeners are on hand to offer advice and education. Such community gardens are frequently found in urban areas and promote diversity within a democratic, inclusive public space. The earliest influential models were on the coasts—Peralta Community Garden in Berkeley, California, and Clinton Street Garden in New York City. These were bottom-up organizations cooperatively owned and run; however, numerous communities are now establishing community gardens through their parks departments. The Midwest and Southeast, particularly in university towns, are seeing a number of these.

The school garden movement, in which gardens are tended to by schoolchildren and the produce is then used for school meals, was started by chef and food activist Alice Waters. Owner of the restaurants Chez Panisse and Café Fanny in Berkeley, California, Waters revolutionized American eating and approaches to food. She promoted the use of local, fresh, seasonal produce from small farms with minimal but refined cooking techniques. Her innovations were the basis for what is known as California cuisine.

Waters also developed the "edible schoolyard" at Martin Luther King, Jr., Middle School in Berkeley, a program that, through gardening, teaches children compassion, responsibility, and a sense of connection to nature and other people. The program has been copied and adapted in urban areas throughout the Northeast, Mid-Atlantic, and Midwest.

All of these gardening trends show differences by region. Each area supports different crops and different methods of growing them. For example, apple and pear orchards can be cultivated in colder states—in New England, the eastern Midwest, the Appalachian Mountains, and the Pacific Northwest—whereas peaches tends to grow better in temperate zones—Georgia and South Carolina in particular, although Michigan also produces peaches. Similarly, citrus fruits are only found in the warmest regions, and many homes in Florida and Southern California enjoy fruit from an orange or lemon tree in their yard. The climate has an obvious impact, so that greenhouses are more necessary in northern zones than southern ones.

Farmers' Markets

For those who appreciate fresh produce, there is the possibility of farm stands and farmers' markets. Farm stands (also called "produce stands") are informal operations offering fresh produce at the farm or field itself. Ranging from a simple table set out with food and a tin can for self-serve purchase on the honor system to permanent structures offering produce and other goods (e.g., crafts, jams, and preserves) from local farmers or just backyard gardeners, these stands are most common in small towns and communities of family farms, particularly in the South and Midwest.

Farm stands offer a direct connection between producer and consumer in which (in theory) what you see is what you get, and people get to meet the people who grew their food. Tailgate markets tend to be a step up from the farm stands, usually occurring on a weekly basis. Common throughout the South, these are gatherings of individuals who sell their produce, farm goods, and other homemade items from the back of their truck (the tailgate).

Farmers' markets are similar but tend to be more formal institutions, often with permanent structures housing the market and open throughout the week. Such markets have a long history in the United States. The oldest public market is the French Market in New Orleans, which started in 1791 as a trading post. It now is a daily flea market, but offers food only on Saturdays. The oldest continuously operating farmers' market is in Philadelphia—the Reading Terminal Market. Started in 1892, it reflects its regional identity, offering, among other things, cheesesteaks, seafood, and Pennsylvania Dutch and Amish specialties (scrapple, apple dumplings, egg sandwiches, soft pretzels). Portland, Oregon, is also famous for its market, which reflects the area's history of back-to-the-land small farmers.

Farmers' markets are currently undergoing a revitalization, and many newer ones are being established, particularly in smaller cities in the Midwest, upland South, and Pacific Northwest. These new markets tend to serve as community centers featuring organic and locally produced (often artisanal) foods—breads, cheeses, preserves and jams, and heirloom produce—as well as entertainment and family activities. They also reflect the ethnic and cultural history of each region. The farmers' market in Asheville, North Carolina, for example, has been in operation since 1977, offering local produce, along with honey, preserves, molasses, pies, cider, and other homemade items. Starting in the 1990s, however, many Mexican tenant farmers and their families were brought to the mountains to run the farms while the owners have had to find manufacturing jobs or work more farmland. As a result, the Asheville market has a large Hispanic population and offers boxes of salsa ingredients ranging from hot to mild.

Meanwhile, the bulk of American food is raised either by industrial farms or imported. Industrial farms make more than $250,000 per year but are also defined as those farms using scientific farming techniques (i.e., heavy reliance on technology and chemicals; adaptation of mass-production processes). These farms tend to grow the crops guaranteed for purchase by the agricultural industry, and more and more are being run as and by corporations that often have no geographic connection to the region housing the farm. The produce is often shipped to processing plants and distributors in other regions, so there is little regional quality to the resulting food. Region, in this case, is often a marketing tool or brand name, rather than an actual cultural or social connection. Supermarkets and groceries across the country then offer a uniform selection of produce with uniform prices.

From The Land—Hunting, Fishing, Gathering, Gardening

Hunting as a means of procuring food is a central part of America's past and is tied to the image of the self-reliant frontiersman, but it is still a vital tradition for many rural families throughout the inland East, the Midwest, and the upland South. The U.S. Fish & Wildlife Service oversees hunting and fishing, issuing licenses and determining restrictions in order to manage wildlife populations and their habitats. According to their 2006 national survey, 12.5 million people participated in recreational hunting and spent a total of $22.9 billion.[14] The game differs by region and often draws hunters from other regions. Moose and deer are in the Northeast, and elk are in the western plains states. Alaska offers large game, including bear. Deer are hunted throughout the Midwest, and venison is often a staple of farming families who not only supplement their diet that way but also hunt to keep wild deer out of their crops. Small game such as rabbits, squirrels, raccoons, and groundhogs tend to be hunted primarily in the upland South but also provide meat to hunters in the Midwest. Migratory birds and waterfowl are found throughout the eastern part of the United States.

Fishing is both a recreational and a commercial means of procuring food. Although no longer the thriving industry of the past, commercial fishing is still an occupation along the Great Lakes in the Midwest (walleye, perch, bass), the New England coast (cod, lobster, clam, mussels), the Mid-Atlantic (crab, clams, oysters), the Southeast and Gulf Coast (shrimp), California (bonito, halibut, red snapper, mackerel, and others), and the Pacific Northwest (salmon, clams, crabs, spiny lobster). Alaskan seafood, particularly salmon, represents almost 38 percent of seafood in the United States, and the industries connected to it (fishing, fisheries, canning) are the largest employment sector in the state.

Recreational fishing is found everywhere water is abundant enough. Deep-sea fishing draws in numerous tourists and residents along all coastal waters but is particularly popular off the southeastern, Florida, and Gulf Stream coasts. Cold mountain streams offer excellent trout fishing, and fly-fishing for trout in the western plains region is a huge hobby and recreation industry. Mountain trout is a delicacy throughout the Appalachian region. The Northeast has numerous clear-running lakes, and the Midwest has broad rivers and ponds with plentiful fishing. The South has warmer, usually muddier streams and rivers that are famous for catfish. Bullfrogs and turtles thrive in these waters and are still considered good eating in some of the rural areas. "Frogging" or "going gigging" at night with flashlights for frog legs used to be common both in the South and the southern Midwest. The inland waters of Louisiana and the southern Delta states abound with crawfish. These are not the one- to two-inch "toe pinchers" of the upper South streams; these grow to six to eight inches and look like small lobsters. Residents of the Pinewoods region of New Jersey pride themselves on living off the land and eating creatures deemed undesirable for many Americans—eels, in particular.

Wild birds and waterfowl also vary by region. New England and the Midwest still abound in numerous hunting birds—including turkey, quail, pheasant, and ducks and geese. The western prairie states depend on game bird hunting licenses and additional hospitality services for hunters as a major source of income. Ring-necked pheasant, short tail grouse, bobwhite quail, greater and lesser prairie chicken, and wild turkey are found throughout that region.

Although thought of as a pioneer or back-to-nature method, many people still gather edible plants from the wild. The types of plants obviously differ by region and climate. Greens, such as poke sallet, dandelion leaves, cattails, and lamb's-quarters are eaten in Appalachia and other parts of the South, while cactus leaves (*napoles*) are consumed in the Southwest. Wild mushrooms can be found throughout the eastern woodlands as well as the Pacific Northwest. The upper Midwest (Minnesota in particular) is known for its wild morels, and hunting spots are kept secret for generations. Similarly, ginseng roots are hunted and dug (and often illegally poached) in Appalachia (particularly in West Virginia, Kentucky, and North Carolina), and the roots are sold to pharmaceutical companies.

Wild berries are a favorite item to pick to make pies and preserves. Blueberries can be picked from Maine to the southern Appalachia, and blackberries are found from the Pacific Northwest to the South. Raspberries can be found in the same areas but seem to be more prevalent in the Midwest, along with mulberries, serviceberries, and a Native American fruit, the ground cherry. Pawpaws and persimmons grow wild in the Midwest and the southern mountains, and although they are not eaten much now, they are often celebrated in Indiana and Ohio as a heritage food.

Nuts supplied a significant part of Native American diets. They still grow wild in many regions but are now more of a supplement or snack for most Americans. Black walnuts, butternuts, and hazelnuts thrived in the eastern mountains, as did the American chestnut that was killed off by blight in the early 1900s. Chinese chestnuts are now grown as a replacement but tend to be cultivated rather than wild. A few of the original chestnuts survived the blight—one in Washington, D.C., still supplies a generous harvest every fall. Ohio is famous for its nonedible buckeye chestnuts. The Pacific Northwest grows acorns, hazelnuts, and chinquapins (also called bushy chestnuts and found in Appalachia). Pecans are gathered in the South, and piñòn (pine nuts) in the Southwest. Trees can also be tapped for their sap, which is then boiled down into sweet syrups and sugars. Although New England is best known for maple syrup, the Midwest (Ohio, Indiana, Michigan) has an established tradition of sugar tapping. Birch, elm, and oak trees are also tapped for their sap.

METHODS OF STORING AND PRESERVATION

Refrigerators are standard kitchen fixtures across the nation; however, some regional differences in food preservation remain. Many older rural people still call refrigerators "iceboxes," referring to the past in which

A traditional way of keeping foods cool in Appalachia was to store them in a root cellar, such as this one in West Virginia. Courtesy of the author.

blocks of ice kept the food cool. It is also common in areas of the East Coast, Midwest, and Pacific Northwest, where people raise their own meat or hunt, to have an additional "deep freeze." Frozen produce from the garden or orchard is also stored there, while canning (heat sealing in glass jars) is still a family tradition in the Midwest and South. Many Appalachian homes still have several structures for preserving food: root cellar, a room, often built into the side of a hill, where root crops, squash, and apples are stored through the winter; spring house, a small building over a spring where milk, butter, and eggs are kept cold (and the water kept clean); and smokehouse, where meat is smoked over a low fire. The meat was then either stored there or hung from rafters in an attic. Smokehouses for fish used to be common along the banks of the Great Lakes. The Amish in Ohio and Indiana are famous for pie chests, wooden cupboards for storing pies, and other handmade storage boxes for potatoes, onions, and preserves.

COOKING PRACTICES: KITCHEN EQUIPMENT AND TOOLS

Cooking practices in the United States today tend to be similar across the nation. Home cooks rely heavily on microwave ovens and equipment such as blenders, mixers, and toasters. Standard home kitchens are equipped with at least an oven and stove (also called a range) and a refrigerator with a freezer. These machines are promoted as timesavers as well as necessary for food safety. Climate differences may affect the use of this equipment in different regions; for instance, warmer zones may use more outdoor cooking implements, and colder ones may make more use of the ovens and slow cookers. Generally, though, they tend to be seen as all-American and are found everywhere.

Regional differences show up in some historical cooking practices, and specific equipment may be tied to those traditions. For example, the Southwest traditionally uses a beehive-shaped clay oven of Spanish origin or baking bread. New England is famous for boiled dinners and pots large enough to hold meat, potatoes, and vegetables for a family. Large pots are also used to boil lobsters. Similar pots are used along the Mid-Atlantic and Pacific Northwest to boil crabs, and in the Gulf Coast for crawfish. The South and upland South still rely on well-seasoned cast-iron frying pans. These can be used on top of the stove to fry meat or eggs or in the oven to bake cornbread. Also common are corn stick pans—cast-iron molds in the shape of corncobs.

Grilling foods over charcoal or wood-fire backyard barbecues is associated with the suburbs throughout the country, but particularly with the California year-round outdoor lifestyle. Although the technique is most

Native Americans in the Pacific Northwest traditionally
grilled salmon around coals. Here a woman from the Jamestown S'Klallam Tribal Center in western Washington pre-
pares the coals for a salmon bake. Courtesy of Mary Kay
Gaydos Gabriel.

traditionally used for steaks, hamburgers, and hot dogs, California cooks
introduced the idea of grilling vegetables and fish. The Pacific Northwest's
tradition of cooking salmon on cedar boards has also spread around the
country, as has coastal New England's tradition of grilling lobsters.

Although grilling is now an all-American cooking technique, there are
interesting variations in the names used for it. The term "barbecue" is used

In a traditional Pacific Northwest Native American salmon bake, the salmon is split and spread out so that the heat from the coals smokes it. Courtesy of Mary Kay Gaydos Gabriel.

in much of the Midwest and West Coast, while "grill" or even "cookout" are more common in the South and on the East Coast. Barbecue in the South, meanwhile, refers specifically to slow cooking with indirect heat, usually in a pit or large metal container, and usually of an animal in its entirety (pork is most common, but also chicken and beef). Even within the South, however, there are numerous debates over the exact method to use. The meat is sometimes basted as it cooks, and sauce can be added by individual eaters. Sauces are the basis of much debate and often reflect regional and racial traditions—tomato-based sauces being African American and vinegar-based being Anglo American. The eastern Southeast tends toward "dry barbecue," meaning that the sauce is not added into the meat before serving, as opposed to "wet," which is more common in the western part of the South. Similar techniques of slow cooking are found in other parts of the country with different names (and different contents): the Midwest has hog roasts, the Southwest has Mexican traditions of pit cooking of beef and goat (*barbecoa*, which refers to a cow's head cooked in this way, is often confused with barbecue), and New England has its distinctive clambakes. These reflect Native American traditions of cooking seafood in pits dug into sand along the seacoast. Fires are lit in the pits; after these have burned down to charcoal, lobster, clams, mussels, fish, sausage, and vegetables (corn on the cob, potatoes, sweet potatoes, onions) are placed on top and lined with sea-weed. The seaweed steams and gives a salty, sea flavor to the food.

Roasting and baking of food in indoor ovens are standard American prac-tices, but, for obvious reasons, are more popular in colder regions and in colder seasons. Baked casseroles mixing meats or fish with starches and veg-etables are frequently associated with the Midwest and are a staple of every-day and festive meals. Often made with canned creamed soups and frozen or canned ingredients, they are often misunderstood as resulting from a lack of taste and culinary sophistication rather than reflecting a regional aesthetic and ethos that emphasizes hearty, plain, and familiar fare. The upper Mid-west, in fact, uses the "hot dish" as an icon of the region.

Roasting or baking large cuts of meat grew out of British and pioneer cul-ture, but it tends to be considered a national cooking style, as seen in the roasted Thanksgiving turkey. The Sunday roast is still common in more tra-ditional families in New England and the Midwest, but turkeys are now pre-pared with regional differences: smoked turkey (cooked in an oversized barbecue grill) originated in California, and deep frying comes out of cook-ing styles of the Deep South.

Apple butter is made the traditional way at the Grand Rapids Apple Butter Fest in Ohio. Cider is boiled down and then cooked with chopped apples in a copper kettle. The mixture must be stirred to keep it from burning. Cour-tesy of Nathan Crook.

Even though most Americans conform to national patterns, some cooking techniques and styles are unique to regions. Large copper kettles are used over outdoor fires in Pennsylvania Dutch areas of the Mid-Atlantic and in German heritage areas of the Midwest to make apple butter. The same kettles can be used to make kettle corn, popcorn sweetened with melted sugar. Also in those areas, many families still have special sauerkraut boards for cutting and shredding cabbage, which is then packed into pottery crocks for fermentation. Boston is known for its ceramic bean pots and the Southwest for its pepper roasters. Maryland has its crab boils, in which crabs are steamed over a combination of water, beer, and vinegar, giving them a salty-spicy crust. Baltimore residents sprinkle Old Bay seasoning (celery salt and other spices) onto the crabs as they are steamed. Large pots are also needed for crawfish boils in Louisiana and crab boils in the Pacific Northwest.

NOTES

1. All Culinary Schools, www.allculinaryschools.com/about/.

2. The first televised cooking show is usually credited to the *Galloping Gourmet* in Britain.

3. Food Network, "Advertise with Us," www.foodnetwork.com/home/advertise-with-us/index.html.

4. Frances Moore Lappé, *Diet For a Small Planet* (New York: Ballentine, 1971).

5. Anne R. Kaplan, Marjorie A. Hoover, and Willard B. Moore, *The Minnesota Ethnic Food Book* (St. Paul: Minnesota Historical Society Press, 1986).

6. Irma Rombauer, *The Joy of Cooking: A Compilation of Reliable Recipes with a Casual Culinary Chat*. The first edition was self-published in 1931. It has been updated and revised numerous times, most significantly in 1963, when it was written by Rombauer's daugher, Marion Rombauer Becker (published by Bobbs-Merrill Company). A 75th anniversary edition was published in 2006 by Simon and Schuster and included Irma's grandson, Ethan Becker, as one of the authors. Betty Crocker cookbooks have gone through a similar history and have branched into a line of cookbooks and cooking products. Lori Fox, ed., *Betty Crocker's Cookbook: Everything You Need to Know to Cook Today* (New York: Hungry Minds, 2000).

7. This book was republished with an introduction by Louis A. Pitschemann as *Pickled Herring and Pumpkin Pie: A Nineteenth-Centry Cookbook for German Immigrants to America* (Madison, WI: Max Kade Institue, 2003).

8. Mollie Katzen, *Moosewood Cookbook* (Berkeley, CA: Ten Speed Press, 1977).

9. Alice Waters, *Chez Panisse Café Cookbook* (New York: HarperCollins, 1982).

10. Tracey Deutsch, "Untangling Alliances: Social Tensions Surrounding Independent Grocery Stores and the Rise of Mass Retailing," in *Food Nations: Selling Taste in Consumer Societies*, eds., Warren Belasco and Philip Scranton, 156–174 (New York: Routledge, 2002).

11. Catherine Greene, "Data Track the Expansion of International and U.S. Organic Gardening," USDA Economic Research Service, *Amber Waves: The Economics of Food, Farming, Natural Resources, and Rural American* (September 2007). Available online at wwwe.ers.usda.gov/AmberWaves/September07/DataFeature.

12. Food for Thought, http://rurallife.kenyon.edu/FFT/index.html.

13. Leopold Center for Sustainable Agriculture, www.leopold.iastate.edu.

14. U.S. Fish and Wildlife Service—Hunting, www.fws.gov/hunting/hunstat.html.

4

Typical Meals

Three meals a day is typical throughout the United States. Breakfast is the morning meal, literally to "break the fast" from the night's sleep. It is usually eaten before work or school. For many adults, a midmorning coffee break can occur between breakfast and lunch, which is frequently a relatively light and informal meal around noon. The evening meal, called either supper or dinner, usually occurs early evening, immediately after work, and is idealized as a time for family members to spend quality time together. A late dinner is common for romantic occasions or entertaining. Snacking throughout the day is common, although controversial as to its health implications.

The usual evening meal structure is a main dish (usually focused on meat, but it can be a hearty soup or casserole) accompanied by a starch (potato, pasta, rice), vegetables (oftentimes a cooked one and a salad), and bread. Food is served all at once, rather than in courses, and the meal can be followed by sweet dessert.

Although this meal structure shares a common national heritage, the names, times, contents, and contexts for these can differ across regions. These differences reflect the varying histories and cultures of each region. The following discussion focuses on these differences but cannot include every local tradition known. In spite of mass marketing and commercial, industrial foods, there are still numerous local variations in dishes and eating habits.[1]

MEAL TIMES

Taking time out for healthy and relaxed meals three times a day is frequently not a priority in contemporary American society, and food is oftentimes eaten on the run, as simply fuel to get through the day. Some regions and communities, though, have kept the more traditional approaches to meals. The Midwest and South, as well as rural pockets elsewhere, tend to be more socially conservative. At times, maintaining the meal structure is treated as symbolism of a romanticized past (actually a fairly recent past— the 1950s as captured in the *Ozzie and Harriet* or *Leave it to Beaver* television series). Increasingly, some of the more progressive urban regions are emphasizing set mealtimes as a way to maintain physical health and to create family rituals.

Nationally, the typical times for weekday meals are 7:00–8:00 A.M. for breakfast, 12:00–1:00 P.M. for lunch, and 5:30–7:00 P.M. for the evening meal. This schedule grew out of the rural, agrarian lifestyle foundational to American foodways. Farmers would rise with daylight to do early chores, and then eat a hearty breakfast filled with proteins and carbohydrates. They would break at noon for a long and equally hearty lunch featuring meat, bread, vegetables, and dairy. The evening meal would commonly be a light supper, often leftovers from the noon meal or a simple porridge or bread and butter. With the shift to industrialization and urbanization in the later 1800s, the meal structure split into rural and urban patterns, although the urban retained some of the contents, particularly the heavy breakfast, of the rural. In cities and towns, however, the meal times began reflecting work in factories and offices, so breakfast tended to be lighter and quicker to prepare. Lunch was still a family meal and a social time for upper classes and white-collar professionals, but it turned into a meal of a homemade sandwich or inexpensive but filling commercial food for working classes. Supper began to emerge as the family meal partly because it was the first occasion for the entire family to gather after working separately all day, but also because social workers began encouraging working classes and immigrants to become Americanized and stabilized by eating at home. Later, Prohibition also encouraged men to go home for meals rather than eating at bars or pubs. The noon lunchtime as family time remained common until the 1950s, when the new suburban lifestyles meant people were farther away from their work and could not easily travel home for a midday meal. Schools began offering lunches in cafeterias, or children brought lunches from home. National requirements for school lunches have since standardized these meals, but lunch still shows regional differences. Sandwiches became popular for lunch and were often paired with canned soup.

The 1950s ideal was that supper or dinner was ideally served at 5:30 P.M. or 6:00 P.M., so working men could come home to a meal prepared by an attentive housewife who had spent the day developing a healthy and pleasing menu. The evening meal was expected to fit the national menu of meat and starch, usually a potato, with vegetables, accompanied by bread and butter and followed by a dessert and coffee. In urban areas, an alcoholic drink—a cocktail—might be enjoyed before the meal to relax after the hard day's work, but this differed according to region, religion, and class.

After-school and bedtime snacks are standard, and new understandings of healthy diets (eating small meals throughout the day) have encouraged "noshing" or "grazing" on nutritious snacks. At the same time, the habit of snacking while watching television is heavily discouraged because it may lead to obesity.

WEEKEND MEALS

The national pattern for weekend meals tends to shift simultaneously to meals that are more informal and more celebratory. The morning meals are frequently more leisurely than on weekdays with dishes that require longer cooking or consumption time, such as waffles, pancakes, or omelets. Going out for breakfast on weekends as a social event is quite common and may feature a "farmer's breakfast" of eggs, bacon (or sausage), hash browns or home fries (potatoes), and toast or pancakes in the Midwest; eggs, grits, and biscuits in the South; and bagels in the Northeast and West Coast. Late breakfasts often turn into brunch, a combination of breakfast and lunch items served from midmorning to early afternoon.

Saturdays tend to be a day of errands, catching up, children's extracurricular activities, sporting events, socializing, and general relaxing. Meeting friends for lunch or dinner is common. Saturday evening, in particular, tends to be a time for going out to eat or having friends in for a meal.

Sunday tends to be more of a family day or for personal rejuvenation and relaxation, reflecting the historically Protestant foundation of American society, although patterns change according to religious affiliation (Jewish tradition celebrates Sabbath from Friday evening to Saturday sundown, and Seventh-Day Adventists hold church services on Saturday morning.)

Sunday brunch buffets are common in restaurants, and Sunday afternoon is traditionally a time for a formal family dinner, a pattern still found in rural areas and more conservative parts of the country, particularly the South and Midwest. Sunday evening then is ideally a light supper of leftovers or easily prepared comfort foods (soup and sandwich).

DRINKS

Although the national drink accompanying meals is milk or water, soft drinks are often included, particularly in the South and Midwest. Breakfast drinks tend to be juice and coffee. Fresh citrus juices are typical of Florida and Southern California. Buttermilk is still popular in the rural South and Midwest. Midmorning snack would be accompanied by coffee or hot tea. Lunch would be accompanied by cold drinks—soft drinks, iced tea (sweet tea throughout the South), milk, fruit juice, or Kool-Aid for children. Wine might be included at an upscale Continental restaurant or a business lunch with professional colleagues, particularly in the Northeast or on the West Coast. Beer might appear at lunch in areas settled by Central and Eastern Europeans, but, unless it is one of the higher-priced local brews, it tends to have working-class associations. Afternoon drinks can range from milk or soft drinks after school to iced tea in the South or hot tea in other parts of the country. Fruit drinks—juices, variations on slushes—would also be appropriate. Evening drinks may include alcohol. Bedtime snacks are typically hot chocolate or a nightcap of brandy, hot toddy.

BREAKFAST

Historically, breakfast was a major meal with a wide range of dishes; however, it is now generally much lighter, except in rural areas, particularly in the Midwest, for special occasions (weekends, holidays, birthdays), or for breakfast meals eaten out. Also, Seventh-Day Adventists eat their biggest meal in the morning. Breakfast seems to be a meal in which people both retain tradition and adopt new, more convenient foods, but generally breakfast foods tend to be sweet and heavy on carbohydrates. Many of the same foods have different names across regions. The basic foods used in breakfast across the nation are fruit, eggs with meat, cereal (hot or cold), and some type of bread. Each of these might appear in regional variations—an ingredient is varied or the ingredients are combined in different ways.[2]

Eggs are a common feature of breakfast nationally. Eggs benedict, an English muffin topped with poached eggs, ham or bacon, and covered with hollandaise sauce, is associated with formal breakfasts and the East Coast. Legend has it that it was invented in a New York restaurant (possibly the Waldorf Hotel in 1894 or Delmonico's around the turn of the century). Probably of French origin, it is also popular in New Orleans. Regional variations change the meat—the Pacific Morthwest uses salmon; eggs Chesapeake uses crab cakes, Dutch benedict in Pennsylvania uses scrapple, eggs Sardou from Antoine's Restaurant in New Orleans replaces the muffin and ham with artichoke and anchovy fillets, and then sprinkles chopped ham and a truffle slice over the hollandaise sauce. Creamed spinach can also replace the artichoke.

Soft-boiled eggs are common in those regions with a strong British influence—New England, the Mid-Atlantic and Southeast. They are often shelled and served on buttered toast or served in the shell in an eggcup and eaten with a spoon. Wedges of buttered toast are also dipped into the runny yolk. (Hard-boiled eggs tend to be more for lunch or picnics.) Scrambled eggs are found everywhere, but they often have regional ingredients mixed in, especially if the breakfast is a more festive or social one (salsa and chorizo in the Southwest; crab or shrimp in the Southeast).

Omelets are often served for special breakfasts and have regional variations. A Denver or Western omelet has diced ham, onions, and green bell peppers; a farmhouse omelet in the Midwest can have a variety of meats (bacon, ham, beef, hamburger), diced onions, green peppers, and mushrooms. Some varieties include sliced cooked potatoes, and the entire mixture is cooked in a skillet that is then baked (similar to a Spanish tortilla). Southwestern omelets include salsa and slices of chorizo.

Hangtown Fry (a San Francisco breakfast dish from the Gold Rush era)

4 oysters	2 slices bacon
3 eggs	Cracker crumbs
1 tablespoon milk or heavy cream	Vegetable oil or bacon grease
	Salt and pepper

1. Prepare the oysters. Shuck and pat dry.
2. Either sauté the oysters for 1 minute over moderate heat or dip them in mixture of 1 beaten egg and 1 tablespoon of milk, then dredge in cracker crumbs and pan fry for 1–2 minutes.
3. In another pan, fry the bacon.
4. Beat the eggs. Add salt and pepper. Add milk or cream.
5. Place bacon on either side of pan. Pour half of egg mixture over the bacon.
6. Place oysters on bacon and pour egg mixture over top.
7. Cook until eggs are set. Fold the omelet over and serve.

Fried eggs can be sunny side up, over easy, or over hard. Over hard (cooked on both sides so that the yolk hardens) tends to be more common in the upland South, where eggs are fried in lard or bacon grease with the edge of the whites are crispy. The Southwest is famous for huevos rancheros, fried eggs served with refried beans and tortillas, possibly carne asada and *carnitas*, and usually with chili Colorado and chile verde to spice it up.

Although bacon tends to be a national favorite, other breakfast meats frequently vary by region. The Southeast and upland South favor salty country ham, bacon, and sometimes even fried chicken or chicken hash. They also thinly slice and fry liver mush and pork sausage, oftentimes making a sausage gravy with big chunks of sausage to pour over biscuits or grits. In the Deep South, breakfast might include fried catfish. Along the coastal Southeast and Mid-Atlantic, oysters are deep fried or mixed in with scrambled eggs, and parts of the South with a strong Scottish heritage serve kippers. New England breakfasts could include corned beef hash or codfish balls, and the Mid-Atlantic offers creamed chipped beef or porterhouse steak. Pork breakfast sausage is common throughout the Midwest, and is spiced differently according to ethnicity and region. Biscuits and sausage gravy are popular in the eastern Midwest, in particular where southerners have migrated. Pennsylvania has scrapple, and Cincinnati has *goetta*, a German sausage made with pinhead oats. The agricultural and ranching heritage of the Midwest and West show up in their inclusion of beefsteaks and lamb chops. Hawaii boasts Spam with its breakfast.

Breakfast usually includes some sort of starch or carbohydrate to provide energy for the day. Toast is common everywhere, but the types of bread can vary—for example, white bread in the Midwest and South. Muffins and pie are popular in New England, and bagels are still associated with New York and the urban West Coast, although they are now available everywhere.

Pancakes, raised battercakes cooked on a griddle, are known by different names according to region. Flapjacks tend to be the older name, and it is associated with areas where lumbering was an occupation—inland New England and the Pacific Northwest. Vermont flapjacks usually use buckwheat flour. Johnnycakes are made with cornmeal and are a specialty in the Mid-Atlantic. Dutch baby pancakes comes from Pennsylvania and are usually eaten with powdered sugar. Topping for pancakes is usually sweet—molasses or sorghum in the upland south and maple syrup in New England and the Midwest.

Various forms of deep-fried dough are popular for both breakfast and snacks and tend to have regional variations. Doughnuts are now a national snack, but were brought to the United States (New York) by the Dutch and are still a favorite in New England. Dunkin' Donuts is a New England standby, and Krispy Kreme is popular throughout the South. The Canadian company Tim Horton's sells doughnuts and muffins in the Great Lakes regions close to the Canadian border. Crullers were also brought by the Dutch and still have an Old World East Coast associations. New Orleans offers beignets, from the French tradition, usually sprinkled on top with powdered sugar. Churros are the Mexican American variation found throughout the Southwest.

Other breads, usually sweet, are popular for breakfast. Cinnamon rolls are particularly traditional in Pennsylvania, and coffee cakes are traditional to the upper Midwest, particularly the areas with Scandinavian heritage. Muffins, small single-serving cakes, are most popular and traditional in New England, where they are sold commercially in coffee shops and bakeries, including the Pewter Pot franchise in southern New England. Maine is famous for its blueberry muffins, but apple and cranberry are also traditional. Although corn bread is generally not eaten in New England, corn muffins are also popular there. Muffins can now be found nationally, but often display regional ingredients—pecans in the south, hazelnuts in the Pacific Northwest, and healthy whole grains in cities.

Fried potatoes are common in homes in the upland South and the Midwest, whereas hash browns are offered at most restaurants nationally. Rice is a breakfast choice in Hawaii, and tortillas accompany breakfast in the Southwest.

Breakfast cereal (processed grains usually heavily sweetened and covered in cold milk) are an international favorite now; however, western Michigan still claims strong ties to it because the industry started there. Battle Creek calls itself "Cereal City" and is home to the companies that invented cold cereal in the 1800s—Kellogg and Post (now owned by Kraft). Some of these varieties still have old-fashioned connotation, such as shredded wheat (introduced by Kellogg in 1904) and grape nuts (introduced by C.W. Post in 1897).

Granola, invented in 1863 in New York and adapted by Kellogg in the late 1890s in Michigan as a part of the health movement, was revived by the 1960s counterculture. Although now national and mainstream, granola still has connotations of hippies, California's freewheeling lifestyle, and interior New England's back-to-the-land culture. The word is even used dismissively to refer to environmentalists and social liberals.

Hot cereals are still sometimes eaten, particularly oatmeal and cream of wheat. Cornmeal mush is common in Pennsylvania. These hot cereals are usually sweetened with sugar or honey.

A cooked grain that is eaten unsweetened is grits, an icon of the southern foodways. They (grits are usually plural in the South) are usually eaten with butter and salt and a variety of gravies. Red-eye gravy made with coffee and country ham pan scrapings is distinctive to the Appalachian region. The proper way to eat grits is to serve them on a plate with fried egg and sausage or bacon, which are cut up and mixed in with each spoonful of grits. A regional joke is that northerners can be identified because they always ask for syrup or sugar for their grits. Fried hominy might be served in place of grits in the southern mountains.

Baked Cheese Grits

4 cups water
1 teaspoon salt (or garlic salt or
   parsley salt)
1 cup quick grits
3 tablespoons flour

3 tablespoons butter (or
   margarine)
3 cups grated cheese (preferably,
   cheddar)
2 eggs, beaten

1. Make grits according to the package directions. Bring water and salt
   to a boil in a saucepan. Add grits slowly, stirring constantly. Return
   water to boil, lower heat, and cook for 5 minutes. (Cover so that grits
   do not "pop" out of the pan.) Stir occasionally while cooking.
   Remove pan from heat
2. Add butter and flour to grits. Stir until butter melts. Add cheese and
   stir until the cheese is melted. Add a little hot grits to eggs and stir.
   Then add this to remaining grits and stir until well blended. Pour into
   greased 1½ quart baking dish. Bake at 350°F for 30 to 40 minutes or
   until mixture is firm. Serve hot.

Leftovers can be sliced ½ inch thick, dredged in flour, and fried to make
fried grits.

Fruit is a common feature of American breakfasts, but the specific types
can differ regionally (and with the type of restaurant). Half a grapefruit or
orange slices are national favorites, but even more so in Florida and Southern California where they are grown. Hawaii is famous for its pineapple.
Tropical fruits, such as mango, kiwi, and papaya, are now being produced
along the southern and southwestern coasts, and these are frequently served
for breakfast as well. Most restaurants throughout the United States serve a
breakfast fruit platter with banana, pineapple, strawberries, and berries. The
Southwest offers special Mexican lime-chile salt for dipping pineapples,
mangoes, oranges, and other tropical fruits. Stewed prunes are still common
in parts of the South, whereas cooked apples are served in the more temperate zones—fried apples in the Appalachian region, applesauce or apple butter in the Midwest, and apple pie in New England.

Fruit juice is also a standard part of breakfast. Orange is a national favorite, and Florida is famous for its fresh-squeezed juice. Tropical and exotic
juices, such as mango, guava, or papaya, are more common along the Gulf
Coast and southern West Coast, and Floridians sometimes add coconut for

a Caribbean flavor. Also popular in Florida are *batidos*—tropical fruit shakes of crushed iced, fruit, sweetener, and milk or water, similar to fruit smoothies.

A more recent innovation for breakfast that has become a mainstream healthy alternative is yogurt. As with granola, it came out of the 1960s counterculture, but then turned into a calcium supplement and diet food, particularly for women. Even though commercial natural yogurts (made of organic milk without additives) are produced in Northeast dairy country, where there is still a back-to-the-land association, the food is now mainstream.

Some regional breakfast specialties include menudo for Sunday breakfast in the Southwest; the Hangtown fry in San Francisco, coke and peanuts (peanuts soaked in the coke) as a breakfast snack in the deep South, and the breakfast burrito found throughout Tex-Mex and Cal-Mex communities. Consisting of fried potatoes, bacon, and eggs, rolled up in a flour tortilla and served with salsa, these burritos are available at convenience stores and gas stations. New Mexico has its own variations—chorizo, potato, cheese, and green chili in some towns; red chili and beef in others.

MIDMORNING SNACK (COFFEE BREAK)

A midmorning break is common throughout the United States for all ages and occupations, and it is often referred to as a "coffee break." It can be anything from a quick cup of coffee to a more elaborate coffee and pastries, but it usually involves socializing as well. Any of the breakfast breads are appropriate, as are fresh fruit or yogurt. Stoughton, Wisconsin, holds a Coffee Break Festival every year to celebrate its claim of originating the coffee break by Norwegian immigrant wives there in the late 1800s, Coffee breaks did not become national until the Pan-American Coffee Bureau started promoting the concept in 1952. The proliferation of coffee shops since the 1990s also helped establish it as a national tradition, so that going out for coffee is a common way to socialize. Stay-at-home parents often meet for morning coffee klatches in each other's homes. Cookies, crackers, and juice or raw vegetable and fruit slices are the usual midmorning snack for younger children at home and school.

LUNCH

Lunch on weekdays tends to be squeezed into people's work hours or schooling. It often consists of foods that can be transported from home to office or eaten informally. Although it is often eaten outside the home and with friends or coworkers, it tends to be less formal than the evening meal. Soups, salads, and sandwiches dominate the meal and vary across regions.

Sandwiches

A distinctly American food that relies on bread is the sandwich—that is, any sort of filling between two slices of bread or on one piece as an open-face sandwich. American sandwiches differ from British and European sandwiches in that fillings tend to be thicker and heartier. Sandwiches vary by region according to what ingredients tend to be available, what types of breads are traditional, and what flavorings and sauces are favored. Peanut butter and jelly is the quintessential American children's sandwich, but in New England marshmallow fluff (invented in Massachusetts in 1917) is a favorite alternative to jelly and makes a fluffernutter sandwich. Southerners enjoy banana and peanut butter on white bread, sometimes fried in butter, as made famous by Elvis Presley in Memphis Tennessee. Tomato sandwiches—slices of fresh garden tomatoes between bread—are also popular wherever tomatoes are grown. A Southern twist is homemade mayonnaise slathered on white bread with lightly salted and peppered tomato slices. Also southern is toasted pimento cheese sandwiches (grated cheese mixed with chopped pimentos, onions, and mayonnaise). Bacon, lettuce, and tomato sandwiches are now a staple of American cooking, but they tend to be found especially in the Midwest and northern East Coast. The club sandwich (a double-decker sandwich of toasted bread layered with bacon, turkey, chicken, or ham, tomato, lettuce, and mayonnaise) is claimed by Boston and New York and is still a popular lunch item at diners and restaurants. Louisville, Kentucky, produced the "hot brown," an open-faced sandwich of toasted white bread covered with thick slices of turkey or chicken. Ham, bacon, and tomato slices are layered over that, and the sandwich is covered with a cheddar cheese sauce, sprinkled with Parmesan cheese, and then broiled. It was invented in 1923 at the Brown Hotel for guests after dinner dances. The Denver sandwich or Western sandwich consists of an omelet of chopped ham, green pepper, and onion (Western omelet) on toasted white bread. Usually eaten for breakfast, it is sold in diners in the West as a cowboy sandwich. The French dip sandwich, popular in Los Angeles, was invented there in a sandwich shop in 1918 when the owner accidentally dropped a French roll with a beef filling into the juice from the beef roast. Iowa is famous for its pork tenderloin sandwich, a flattened, breaded, deep-fried round of pork tenderloin on a hamburger bun. Almost every region has a distinctive local sandwich: shredded chicken sandwiches (canned chicken stewed in canned cream soup and served on a bun) in Ohio; chow mein sandwiches (chow mein on a bun) in southeast Massachusetts and Rhode Island; snoot sandwich (fried pig's snout on white bread) in east St. Louis, Missouri.

Thick sandwiches using rolls and stacked high with fillings have a variety of names. The hoagie—thin slices of Italian ham, prosciutto, salami, provolone cheese, tomatoes, lettuce, and onions with a dressing of oregano vinegar on an Italian roll—is the official sandwich of Philadelphia. Legend has it that immigrants living in a section of the city called Hog Island created it. They took the sandwiches to work for their lunch and the idea caught on, so that now hoagies are made with any type of meat or cheese and are also called submarine sandwiches, subs, grinders, heroes, and a number of other names. Portland, Maine, is the home of the Italian sandwich, which was created in the early 1900s for Italian workers on the docks. It is a long, soft, Italian roll filled with meat, cheese, and fresh vegetables (no lettuce), sour pickles, and a dressing of salt, pepper, and oil; and sour pickles. Other varieties include Chicago Italian beef sandwiches (sliced beef in a spicy gravy); Binghamton, New York, spiedies (grilled cubes of marinated beef or lamb); Philadelphia cheesesteak (fried strips of steak with fried onions and melted Cheese Whiz on a crusty Italian roll); the New Orleans muffulettas (a Sicilian bread filled with meats, cheese, and a distinctive olive salad), po'boys (also called poor boys, which feature a variety of fillings, including oysters and gravy, in French bread), and oyster loaf (a hollowed French loaf filled with broiled oysters); and the Chicago and northeastern Italian sausage sandwich (grilled pork sausage flavored with garlic and fennel seed and topped with fried green peppers and onions in an Italian roll). Italian sausages, along with Polish sausage sandwiches, hot dogs, and bratwurst or kielbasa, are commonly found at fairs throughout the Midwest.

Seafood and fish are frequently used as sandwich fillings as well—canned tuna fish mixed with mayonnaise and pickle relish is an all-American staple. New England is famous for its lobster rolls (lobster meat in a mayonnaise dressing stuffed into a New England–style hot dog roll) and serves deep-fried clams and scallops in the same way. The Chesapeake Bay area serves soft-shell crab sandwiches (deep-fried whole crab on white bread), and crab cake sandwiches are a favorite along the coast from Maryland and Delaware to South Carolina. Lake perch or walleye are filleted and deep fried and served on a bun for fish sandwiches throughout the Great Lakes region of the Midwest, similar to catfish sandwiches in the South. Salmon is more likely to be the fish of choice in the Pacific Northwest, but it is usually grilled rather than deep fried. San Francisco is famous for an oyster loaf similar to ones sold in New Orleans.

Two hot sandwich varieties that are quintessentially American are hot dogs and hamburgers. Both exist in multiple variations on meat filling, bun type, condiments, and toppings, and both are commercially mass produced and distributed yet are staples of home cooking. Hot dogs and hamburgers can be used for special occasions and are evocative of American identity, yet both can also be purely functional and quotidian, often being served for children's meals.

Hot dogs, in some ways simply a variation of sausage, are mainstays at baseball parks, communal and family cookouts, street food stands, and children's lunches. Numerous variations abound for hot dogs.[3] Even the name has variations—hot dog is generic, but they are also called franks, frankfurters, or wieners. Hot dogs are notorious for being made of any combination of ground meats—pork is common, but the all-beef varieties are kosher and are found more in the Northeast and on the West coast. Chicken and turkey are healthy alternatives. Even tofu and soy dogs are available. The casing can be "natural" (intestine) or synthetic. The standard hot dog bun is a rounded oblong that opens on the side, but New England's hot dog rolls open from the top. Toppings can range from the most standard ones of ketchup, mustard, and relish (with variations on these as well) to chili (usually all meat, as in Coney dogs found in the Detroit area) to salsa (common in the Southwest) to vegetables (tomato slices, cucumber, dill pickle spear, and celery salt for a "garden on a plate" in Chicago) to pickled vegetables and relishes (sauerkraut throughout the Northeast and Midwest, chowchow in the South, spicy relish in the Southwest and on the West Coast) to fruit (mango chutney or pineapple in Los Angeles.; pineapple in Hawaii). Cheese dogs, invented in Mobile, Alabama, are common throughout the Deep South.

Although many hot dog variations have been invented by commercial establishments as their signature food and then become associated with a city or region, other variations emerge out of a region's history and resources. In the Southwest, for example, hot dogs might be wrapped in a flour tortilla and served with salsa, refried beans, and rice. A Hispanic addition that has caught on regionally is wrapping the dog in bacon before it is grilled, and then serving it with salsa and taco toppings (chopped tomatoes, onions, shredded cheese) as well as standard American toppings (for example, the Sonoran hot dog has bacon, salsa [tomatillo or red chili], and pinto beans, all on bread and topped with mayonnaise, ketchup, and mustard). Chicago-style hot dogs include the vegetable toppings with a special bright-green sweet pickle relish. Hot dogs in the Southeast (Carolina dogs) tend to have coleslaw, similar to barbecue sandwiches. Las Vegas, in keeping with its reputation for ostentatious extravagance, offers a foot-long hot dog. Some southern establishments also deep fry their dogs. Alaskans offer dogs made of reindeer.

New York is often considered the home of the hot dog—Nathan's on Coney Island claims to be the first hot dog stand and is still active today. Hot dog carts are a fixture on the streets of New York. Chicago challenges New York's claims of hot dogs' origins and boasts a number of historical and famous hot dog eateries. Connecticut claims to have more hot dog establishments than other states, and hot dog pushcarts selling dogs wrapped in bacon with pineapple salsa are an icon of Los Angeles. In general, the food seems to lend itself to colorful and idiosyncratic variations, so that hot dog establishments offer variations throughout the United States.

Hamburgers, the other quintessential American food, appear in a similar variety of forms, ingredients, buns, toppings, condiments, and serving styles. Like hot dogs, they are a staple of backyard grilling and community gatherings. They differ from hot dogs, though, in that they are generally not sold on street stands (because of health regulations), are a ubiquitous fast-food standby, and can be very upscale and gourmet. Variations are often purposely invented by restaurants and home cooks, but they can also reflect regional traditions. For example, butter burgers in Wisconsin—the dairy state—are fried in butter. Local cheeses are added to make cheeseburgers in Vermont and the upper Midwest; and avocado is a popular topping in California along with fresh greens, sprouts, and gourmet fruit relishes.

Hamburgers and hot dogs are frequently accompanied by other iconic American foods—french fries or potato chips, pickles, coleslaw (particularly in the South), and baked beans (particularly in the Northeast). In some versions, the fries are added to the sandwich itself (hamburgers in Pittsburgh have the fries directly on top of the burger but inside the bun). Of course, variations on the fries are possible—sweet potato fries were popularized in California as a healthy alternative to white potatoes, for example. Utah is famous for its fry sauce, similar to Thousand Island dressing, and some Midwesterners like ranch dressing on theirs instead of the national favorite, ketchup. Potato chips are often the nationally distributed commercial brands, but like many popular foods are now being created with distinctive cooking styles and flavorings with regional associations. Cape Cod Potato Chips, for example, were one of the earliest homestyle commercial chips and come in salt and vinegar, a New England-British condiment for fish and chips (french fries). Battered and deep-fried onion rings are often an alternative accompaniment, and the Midwest and parts of the South seems to lead the way in offering these.

Southwestern cuisine has become another popular option throughout the country. Tacos and burritos have been Americanized to the point that they are often included in school lunches. Although the national version of the taco usually uses ground meat on a hard tortilla shell (an Anglo invention), the more traditional form of marinated cubes of beef in a fresh tortilla with salsa and cilantro can be found in eateries throughout the Southwest as well as those catering to the more recent Mexican migrant populations in the Southeast and Midwest. Fish and shrimp tacos with shredded cabbage are popular throughout southern California. Burritos similarly have been adapted from their Tex-Mex origins of a tortilla wrapped around beans, meat, and rice to include favored meats, vegetables, and cheeses. A variation on both the burrito and the sandwich is the wrap, a sandwich filling rolled up in a flat bread.

Utah is famous for its distinctive fry sauce used on
french fries, hamburgers, and anything else that
suits the taste. Courtesy of Nathan Crook.

Another sandwich alternative comes from Middle Eastern pita bread and
Greek gyros. Diners in the Mid-Atlantic and the eastern Midwest are frequently run by Greek Americans who have introduced their traditional
sandwich of roasted lamb enclosed in half a round of flat bread. A Middle
Eastern version of this flat bread, pita, has been adapted into pita pockets
that can be filled with anything from the traditional middle eastern falafel
to fusion foods, such as Thai flavorings or Mexican spices.

Sushi is now also a popular lunch item, although not completely mainstream. Coming from Japanese immigrants, sushi was popularized in California and has been adapted to regional tastes—cream cheese for a Philadelphia
roll, barbecue for a southern flavor, all fresh vegetables for a California roll,
and native salmon in the Pacific Northwest. Hawaii offers its own brand,
Spam *musabi*, a small slice of Spam wrapped with a piece of seaweed paper
onto a wedge of rice.

Although beef, pork, and chicken are the favored meats in the United States, lamb is common among Mediterranean immigrants. Courtesy of the author.

Pizza is another ubiquitous lunch food. Originating in this country in Italian neighborhoods in New York City, it was adapted to American tastes with a thicker crust, melted cheese (usually mozzarella), and thick tomato sauces and called Italian pie or tomato pie. Italian sausages may be added; pepperoni slices are the most common. After World War II, American serviceman returning from Europe had developed a taste for southern Italian food and accepted this American version. It spread throughout the Northeast first, where it developed several regional variants. Today, New York style is a thin crust with tomato sauce, mozzarella cheese, and toppings. Connoisseurs claim that New York City tap water gives the dough a specific flavor. Sicilian style is also found in New York; it has thicker dough and is usually cut into squares.

New Haven, Connecticut, boasts of its distinctive white clam pizza (a haphazardly shaped crust with littleneck clams on olive oil, oregano, garlic, and grated parmesan or Romano cheese). Mozzarella cheese tends to be standard elsewhere, but in New Haven, "mootz," as it is called, should only be sprinkled on after the pizza has baked. Chicago, with its large ethnic Italian population developed its own version, a deep-dish pizza. St. Louis, Missouri, makes an unusually thin, unleavened crust topped with a three-cheese mixture called "provel" (made of provolone, Swiss, and white cheddar), unique to the city. The pizza is also cut into squares rather than wedges. Detroit pizzerias offer a thick, chewy crust similar to New York style. Mexican-style pizzas developed in the Southwest with stereotypical Hispanic ingredients, but tortillas covered with refried beans and salsa and cheese, similar to a pizza (also called a tostado) are also available. Hawaiian pizza with ham and pineapple on a tomato and cheese base was not invented in Hawaii.

Pizza quickly became commercialized, and many of the commercial innovations came from companies in the Midwest. Pizzeria Uno, in Chicago, is home of the deep-dish pizza invented in 1943. The largest pizza franchise in the world, Pizza Hut, started in Kansas in 1958. Domino's, the second largest franchise, originated in Ypsilanti, Michigan, in the 1960s and developed home delivery, promising under thirty-minute waits for the hot pizza. In the 1980s, California pizza was developed in the San Francisco area, based partly around Alice Water's restaurant, Chez Panisse. Her idea of fresh vegetable, exotic flavorings, and unusual pairings was translated into gourmet pizzas. In 1985, Ed LaDou started a restaurant, California Pizza Kitchen, that introduced these pizzas to a broader public.

Barbecue is another frequent lunch item in the South.[4] Served as a sandwich or a "plate," it is meat that is slow cooked in a pit or smoker away from direct heat rather than grilled. It is usually marinated or basted while it cooks and is served with barbecue sauce either mixed in or poured on top. Its historical roots in African American traditions in the South are still evident in the association with black cooks and eating establishments today, but it has definitely transcended race, class, ethnicity, and region. Barbecue joints can be found across the nation, and variations of barbecue are served everywhere. Controversy abounds, however, over the correct cooking style, equipment, type of meat, and sauce ingredients. Pork is the dominant meat in the Piedmont and Deep South, and "pulled pork" refers to the meat literally pulled apart into smaller strands, while "slabs" are barbecued pork ribs. Texas, which also claims barbecue as its own, prefers beef, particularly brisket, and often includes sausage (made by German American butchers). Chicken is popular nationwide. Kansas City, Missouri, is famous for its barbecue, which mixes a variety of meats in one serving, including sausage and turkey. Mutton barbecue is found in isolated pockets in Kentucky and the Southwest; lamb is featured in Denver.

Memphis is world famous for its barbecue and hosts an annual world championship contest. Pork is the favored meat, and it is usually cooked "dry"—that is, rubbed before cooking with a mixture of salt, garlic, onions, cumin (and usually other secret ingredients in secret recipes). Sauce is usually tomato based and served on the side. Memphis also offers "wet" barbecue, meaning the sauce is poured over the meat. In other regions, "wet" can mean that the meat is basted with the sauce while it cooks.

North Carolina barbecue often uses a vinegar-based sauce, although black cooks tend toward the tomato-based ones. There also tends to be a difference between the eastern and the western parts of the state—ketchup or tomato sauce is added to the sauce in the west. Also, barbecue was not a part of the mountain tradition, probably because slavery was not affordable or profitable there, and there is not the history of black cooks as in the "flatlands." Regardless of where in the state, though, North Carolina barbecue always comes with hush puppies and coleslaw (on top of the pulled pork if it is served as a sandwich). Georgia barbecue frequently includes a side of Brunswick stew. South Carolina, meanwhile, offers a mustard barbecue sauce, and Louisiana uses a fiery hot pepper sauce.

Soups are frequently served as a main dish or partnered with a sandwich. They can range in texture from a clear broth to a thick stew. They can also

Typical barbecue plates in the South—meat with sides and corn bread. Courtesy of the author.

contain any variety of meats and vegetables. Although canned soups are nationally distributed and popular among all classes, some of these celebrate regional favorites. These commercial soups as well as homemade traditional ones usually use the natural resources of the area and reflect settlement heritage.

Fish and seafood soups, for example, are often tied to where the ingredients are freshly available. New England is famous for its clam chowder, and New York has tomato-based Manhattan clam chowder. Louisiana serves gumbo, a stew of chicken, seafood, and whatever meats are available, thickened with filé (dried, powdered sassafras leaves), whereas other areas of the South often call any okra-based soup gumbo. The Pacific Northwest offers chowders and bisques of local clams, oysters, mussels, Dungeness crab, and fish, particularly salmon. She-crab soup with sherry is distinctive of the southeastern coast, and a fish stew, *cioppini*, is traditional in San Francisco.

Poultry is a mainstream favorite for soups, and chicken and turkey broth and meat form the basis for many soups with regional vegetables and flavorings added. Chicken is frequently paired with noodles, but there can be variations on these—homemade flat noodles are common in Eastern and Central European heritage areas (Mid-Atlantic and Midwest), and dumplings made of flour, water, and egg are popular in the southern Appalachians as well as in Hungarian and German soups as spaetzle. Matzo ball soup is a staple in Jewish homes and delicatessens. The Italian influence shows up in the use of small pieces of pasta (pastina, orzo) in chicken broth with small meatballs, as in Italian wedding soup, which is popular throughout the Northeast and Midwest. Chicken is used as the base for a number of ethnic soups in the United States, particularly those of Asian origin (Seattle's Shanghai soup dumplings, for example). Mexican American flavors are popularized in tortilla soup, a spicy chicken soup with rice, chilies, strips of tortillas, topped with cilantro, sliced avocado or guacamole, and sour cream. In fact, any soup can be given a southwestern association by adding peppers, beans, and corn. Black beans and pinto beans tend to be especially associated with the Southwest, even though Caribbean cuisines often use black beans as well.

Not surprisingly, beef is frequently a main ingredient in soup, often paired with pasta and basic vegetables (carrots, celery, onion, green beans). Beef and barley or beef and noodle tend to have an all-American, pioneer aroma, and strips of round steak are mixed with tomatoes, potatoes, carrots, celery, onions, and a flour roux for Kansas City steak soup. Beef with dumplings is a mainstay of the Midwest (dumpling soup), as is hamburger soup, browned ground beef with tomatoes and vegetables. Beef stew is also a hearty, all-American dish.

Beef is also the traditional ingredient in most chilies. Texas-style chili has strips or chunks of beef slow cooked with chili peppers and herbs and is still a common way to use cheaper cuts of meat. Texas claims it as the official state dish, referring to it as a "bowl of red," and it was probably based originally on Native American stews. Texan chili has no beans, although pinto beans might be served in a separate dish, and some purists do not even include tomatoes or onions. Texas chili was introduced to the nation at the 1893 World's Columbian Exposition in Chicago, and packaged chili mixes were first produced commercially in Texas soon after. San Antonio is still famous for chili, drawing on its history of "chili queens," Mexican women who sold homemade chili (and tamales and enchiladas) on the streets.

Chili, like many other popular American dishes, has been adapted to each region's tastes.[5] Other parts of the Southwest, for example, use a block of chili paste and frequently include beans and roasted chili peppers. In New Mexico, chili is red or green peppers stewed with onions, garlic, and spices, and chili stews are meat with posole, corn, garbanzo beans, and green or red peppers. Much of the Midwest has adopted chili as a family and community tradition but has added kidney beans and cut out much of the spiciness. Cincinnati chili is a distinctive tradition that was started by Macedonian immigrants to the city who opened restaurants in the 1920s. The chili itself is ground meat simmered with spices (cinnamon, cardamom, allspice, and cloves) and served over spaghetti. Kidney beans, chopped raw onions, shredded cheddar cheese, and oyster crackers can be added for a three-way, four-way, or five-way according to the additions. A similar sauce is used in the eastern Midwest and the Mid-Atlantic on hot dogs to make a chili dog or on pasta for chili mac. Chili cookoff competitions are popular fund-raisers and community gatherings throughout the Midwest and Texas.

California chili, also known as "white chili," uses chicken, navy beans, and white pepper, so that the dish is literally white instead of the usual reddish-brown color.

Soups and stews using game meats are common in rural parts of the Midwest, Pacific Northwest, and South. Squirrel is a traditional ingredient of both Brunswick stew on the Southeast coast and of Kentucky burgoo, which also uses mutton.

Turtle soup is a vernacular food in southern Indiana and the Pinelands region of New Jersey, and it is a popular "diner" food in the Delaware valley. Upscale Philadelphia restaurants serve snapper soup, and Creole cuisine in New Orleans gives its distinctive twist to it. Along the same lines, Philadelphia is famous for its pepper pot soup and Texas for menudo, both made from tripe.

Borscht, soups made from beets or other root vegetables, are common in the Pacific Northwest, as are nettle and wild mushroom soups thickened with potatoes. The Upper Midwest has distinctive fruit soups from Scandinavian settlers, while soup beans (usually navy beans cooked into a thick soup) and corn bread are a basic meal in the southern Appalachians. Although bean soups are a basic old-fashioned food throughout the United States, Washington, D.C., is associated with a particular recipe of bean soup served in the Senate's cafeteria.[6] Georgia peanut soup, made of minced vegetables, potatoes, and peanut butter, is a traditional colonial soup that probably has African roots.

Salad as a main course for lunch first became popular in California and then spread to the rest of the nation. Similar to soups, they can use local ingredients. Salad bars are common nationally, but the ingredients often vary regionally. Midwestern and southern salad bars tend to rely heavily on iceberg lettuce and mayonnaise-based pasta and bean mixtures. Salads on the coasts and more progressive urban areas tend toward a variety of greens and fresh vegetables, including sprouts, beans (garbanzos, soy, black beans), tofu, cottage cheese, yogurt, and sunflower seeds, along with the more standard chopped carrots, celery, tomato, and green peppers.

Several regional salads have become popular nationally. California introduced the Caesar salad (originating in Tijuana, Mexico, in the early 1920s), the Cobb salad (invented in 1936 by Bob Cobb at the Brown Derby restaurant in Los Angeles), the Crab Louis salad (in San Francisco in 1910, although Seattle also claims it), the Palace Court salad (San Francisco again—crabmeat salad in an artichoke shell), and green goddess dressing (distinctive because of the inclusion of anchovies, first served at the Palace Hotel in San Francisco in the 1920s). Seafood salads usually refer to chunks of crab, lobster, or shrimp in a mayonnaise. In the Northeast, these are often served in a roll, and in the Southeast, they are served on a bed of lettuce. Steak salads (iceberg lettuce topped with strips of steak) and chef salads (iceberg lettuce with small squares of American cheese and deli meat) seem to be popular throughout the Midwest and western plains. Taco salads are associated with the Hispanic Southwest, although they are probably not traditional there.

AFTERNOON SNACK/TEA

An afternoon snack is an unofficial ritual for many Americans and can be anything that tides them over until dinnertime. The South adapted the British tradition of afternoon tea with iced tea or lemonade (hot tea is also a possibility) and light foods, such as tea sandwiches (open-face sandwiches, or larger sandwiches cut into squares), cookies, cakes, crackers, and fruit. Office workers frequently take a quick break around midafternoon with a soda, candy bar, fruit, or yogurt, and children eagerly anticipate their after-school snack. This is traditionally cookies and milk, ideally with home-baked cookies fresh from the oven.

Cookies are distinctive to American foodways. The word itself derives from a Dutch term and culinary tradition, but cookies are now widespread throughout America, eaten for snacks and dessert, and often used as an incentive for good behavior for children. Their central place in the family kitchen is suggested by the standard cookie jar sold nationally. Cookies are usually baked from a dough of flour, sugar, and fat (butter, shortening, or margarine) and are usually eaten by hand in several bites. They can be made with a wide variety of ingredients and flavorings, and they come in different forms—drop cookies, pan cookies or bar cookies, rolled and cut into shapes with cookie cutters. Some varieties have become all-American (chocolate chip, peanut butter, raisin cookies, and brownies), but there are some varieties that have regional associations. Moravian sugar cookies come from eastern North Carolina. German peppernuts (also called Russian teacakes or Mexican wedding cakes) are found throughout the Midwest and Northwest. Gingersnaps made from molasses have an old-fashioned flavor and are popular in both the South and Amish country. Toll House cookies, made with chunks of chocolate, originated from a Massachusetts inn from the 1930s. Cookies often include locally favored nuts—pecans in the South, black walnuts in the Appalachians, hazelnuts in the Northwest, and macadamia in Hawaii.

Some commercial snacks have regional associations as well. MoonPies are icons of the South. A large cookie with a marshmallow filling, then dipped in chocolate, they are now available in several flavors (vanilla, chocolate, banana) and are ideally paired with an RC Cola. Similar commercial snacks have regional associations—Tastykakes in Philadelphia and Twinkies in the Midwest. Fried dough in New England is literally that—a large thin round of fried dough, usually sprinkled with cinnamon and sugar. Midwesterners call the same thing "elephant ears," and usually offer them at fairs and festivals. The Pennsylvania Dutch have a similar snack, funnel cakes, and the Southwest offers sopapillas, which are frequently covered with honey.

Ice cream might be a snack, particularly in areas with a dairy tradition—New England (Bostonians are known for high consumption of ice cream), Ohio, Indiana, and Wisconsin. Hawaiians prefer "shave ice" finely shaved ice on ice cream and covered with flavored syrups and even condensed milk. "Snow cones," which are similar but without the ice cream, were invented in Texas and are popular in summer throughout the South. In Texas, they are frequently called "shaved ice," and use tropical fruit and Mexican flavors (cinnamon, chili, tamarind, cucumber, guava). Snow cones in the Midwest tend to use crushed ice rather than shaved. Baltimore, meanwhile, has snowballs, shaved ice with syrup flavoring and topped with a marshmallow.

Not all afternoon snacks are sweet, and many regional snacks supplement the standard potato chips or leftover pizza. Wisconsin offers fried cheese curds (cheddar or white)—no toppings. The curds have to be fresh so that they are squeaky. New Mexico boasts of Frito pie (Frito bag with melted cheese and salsa poured into it) and Indian tacos (taco ingredients on fry bread), which have become favorites at Native American events everywhere. Fried pork rind (skin) is associated with the South ("hillbillies" and African Americans) and Southwest (*chicharrones* in Hispanic foodways). Popcorn is popular nationally, although it still has lingering images of Native Americans and settlers in the East. Kettle corn, popcorn sweetened with melted sugar, is especially popular in the Midwest. Large soft pretzels are Philadelphia treats, as are boiled peanuts in the Southeast. Stands along the California and Northwest coast sell native Olympia and Hog Island oysters, and roadside lobster shacks in New England sell lobster rolls. Some snacks have regional associations because they were invented there, for example, Buffalo chicken wings.

Fried pork rinds are traditional snack throughout the South. In the Hispanic Southwest, they are called *chicarronés*. They became popular nationally in the early 2000s as part of a no-carbohydrate diet, often replacing potato chips. Courtesy of the author.

Many of these savory snacks are also offered as appetizers to a formal or celebratory meal or as hors d'oeuvres or finger foods at a social event. Again, local resources and history are often expressed. San Francisco has oysters Kirkpatrick, oysters broiled with butter, then topped with cooked bacon, ketchup, Worcestershire sauce, and Parmesan cheese and broiled again. Deviled eggs are a mainstay throughout the South, and cooks pride themselves on their personal recipes and presentations. Shrimp is a standard appetizer but is local to the Southeast and gulf coasts. Seviche, a marinated mixture of raw fish, has Mexican origins and is popular throughout Southern California. The western plains pride themselves on their Rocky Mountain oysters (bulls' testicles) and dare outsiders to relish them.

SUPPER OR DINNER

The evening meal has become the expected family gathering time throughout the nation, but depending on schedules, it can be a light meal, similar to lunch, or a heavier, complete meal with a main dish (usually a meat), sides of vegetables, a starch, and dessert. It tends to be the meal Americans try to make sure has a full complement of proteins, carbohydrates, and vitamins and is likely to have more components than other meals, usually involving a main dish, cooked vegetable and/or salad, and bread followed by a sweet dessert. An appetizer might precede the meal if the occasion is formal or festive.

Although traditional patterns have fallen by the wayside in many homes and eating establishments, there are still some reflections of region in this meal. The word "supper" is often used in the South for the evening meal, though dinner is favored elsewhere. Southerners use the word "dinner" for formal and social meals regardless of the time of day. Also, the national pattern of meat as the centerpiece of the meal varies regionally, both in terms of the actual meat and the foods it is paired with. "Meat and potatoes" is the stereotype of American meals, especially of the Midwestern Heartland, but this varies widely. The main dish can also be stews or casseroles or fish, seafood, and meat substitutes.

The stereotypic American dinner plate, however, features a large piece of meat (animal flesh), preferably in the form of a steak, which is assumed to be beef unless specified otherwise. Steak is particularly preferred in New England, the Midwest, and the western plains. Chicago is famous for its steak houses, as is Texas and cowboy culture in general. The meal tends to be about the steak, usually paired with a baked potato or french fries (or deep-fried, battered onion rings) and accompanied with a salad (coleslaw or lettuce) and bread. The western plains claim to have originated chicken-fried steak, in which thin-cut steaks are dipped into batter and fried. Similar to fried chicken, these are popular throughout the South as well.

Other meats can also function as the centerpiece of the meal. Pork chops are served with mashed potatoes and gravy, although in the South, they are usually accompanied with sweet potatoes and fried apples, and in the Midwest and Mid-Atlantic, they are likely to be accompanied with sauerkraut and homemade noodles. Country ham is standard in the South, and lamb chops are favored in New England and the Basque areas of the western plains. The Navajo in the Southwest also have a tradition of eating mutton. Steaks from game meats are popular regionally—moose in the Northeast, venison in the Midwest, and elk in the western plains and Pacific Northwest. Organ meats are not as popular now as they used to be, but calf's liver with onions is still available in many homestyle diners, and breaded, fried chicken livers are sold nationally through certain fast food establishments.

Fried chicken is favored in the South, as well as in the Midwest, while baked or roasted chicken is popular nationally. Abalone steaks are popular in northern California. Salmon steak is a Pacific Northwest tradition that has become widespread, as hasve tuna and swordfish steaks from the southern Atlantic waters. Both ocean and freshwater fish are often filleted and fried, and served with fried potatoes and coleslaw for fish and chips. This is a typical Friday evening meal in many traditional Catholic homes, particularly in the Northeast, where cod and haddock would be the preferred fish, and in the Midwest, where walleye and perch from the Great Lakes are favored. Trout (fried or grilled or smoked) are a treat in the western plains, sturgeon with chopped hazelnuts in Oregon, san dabs along the Northwest Coast, and catfish in the South. Other seafood are traditional to each region and are often the centerpiece for the meal—lobsters and clams in New England; crabs, oysters, and clams in the Mid-Atlantic (boiled crabs with Chesapeake Bay seasoning, crab cakes); shrimp along the southeast Gulf Coast (shrimp and grits, shrimp roulade with crawfish and other ingredients for jambalaya, étouffée) and southern California coast (shrimp tacos); oysters, Dungeness crabs, and clams further north; and King crabs in Alaska.

Salmon in Hazelnut Breading (from the Pacific Northwest)

4 salmon fillets $^1/_4$ teaspoon garlic powder
$^1/_2$ cup chopped hazelnuts   Salt and pepper to taste
$^1/_4$ cup breadcrumbs

1. Mix the hazelnuts, breadcrumbs, and spices.
2. Season salmon with salt and pepper.

3. Place salmon in an oiled baking dish.
4. Sprinkle hazelnut mixture over salmon.
5. Bake in preheated 400°F oven until golden brown (about 12 minutes).

Lobsters and crabs are often centerpiece foods and may be served whole on a platter surrounded by "sides," which can include other seafood items as well as potatoes and corn. This kind of presentation is distinctive to coastal areas, where the seafood is freshly caught, although modern refrigeration and transportation allow seafood to be a gourmet meal anywhere.

A variation on the main dish centerpiece is the roast or boiled dinner, in which a large cut of meat or whole animal is served. Pot roast (beef roasted with potatoes, carrots, and sometimes onions and celery) or a pork roast is a traditional Sunday dinner throughout the Midwest, similar to roasted or baked chicken popular in the Midwest, but also in New England. These dishes are similar to the roast turkey dinner held nationally at Thanksgiving and can also include stuffing (of white bread crumbs) or dressing (Southern, made of corn bread). Regional variations on the roast include ham roast in the South in which the ham is covered with a sweet marinade of brown sugar, molasses, honey, or pineapple juice; rutabagas and turnips are added in the upper Midwest. Appalachian hillbillies are stereotyped as serving opossum cooked in this way with sweet potatoes, and "smothered chicken" in Maryland is a roast chicken with white gravy covering it. A whole salmon is frequently the centerpiece in the Pacific Northwest. The boiled dinner, common in New England, is just that—a dish in which the meat (usually beef) is boiled with potatoes, carrots, and onions. Corned beef is also prepared this way, and if it is served in the Midwest on St. Patrick's Day or in an Irish setting, it is referred to as a Jigg's dinner. Other regional boiled meals include Chesapeake Bay crab boils, New England lobster boils, Louisiana crawfish boils, and Wisconsin fish boils.

Numerous regional dishes offer ways to either deal with cheaper, less desirable cuts of meat and fish or to stretch them to feed more people. Ground beef is often made into hamburgers or meatloaf, and family as well as regional variations on meatloaf flourish, particularly in the Midwest and South. Ground meats are also used for meatballs for Italian dishes as well as for Americanized Hispanic entrées throughout the Southwest (tacos, burritos). A special beef dish in Texas is fajitas, a marinated and grilled tough cut of beef that has been Anglicized to mean any marinated and grilled meat or vegetables that are then wrapped in a tortilla. An Eastern and Central European dish common in the Midwest and Mid-Atlantic is beef tips and noodles, similar to a beef stroganoff with sour cream. Sausages are a way to stretch and preserve meats, and they are frequently a main dish across the Midwest and Pacific Northwest. Grilled bratwurst or kielbasa served with mashed potatoes and sauerkraut is a mainstay in households of German, Hungarian, and Polish heritage. French-influenced *boudin* is popular in southern Louisiana.

Similarly, fish can be mixed with other ingredients and made into cakes or loafs. Crab cakes are specialties along the southeastern seaboard, as in Maryland crab cakes. Crab cakes made with mashed potatoes rather than breadcrumbs are a specialty of San Francisco. Canned salmon is frequently used to make salmon patties in the South and Midwest. Seafood tacos or enchiladas are a way of extending fish in Southern California.

Meat or fish is also frequently mixed with a starch, vegetables, and sauce to create casseroles, or hot dishes, as they are known in the upper Midwest. Campbell's Soup Company encouraged casseroles as a national dish with its invention of condensed cream of mushroom soup in 1934, and these are now a fixture of family meals and community potlucks in the South and the Midwest. Some casseroles have regional associations, even though they probably did not originate in those regions; enchilada casseroles are associated with the Southwest and lobster casseroles with New England. The starch used in the casserole can also carry regional associations—wild rice with the upper Midwest and grits or sweet potato with the South. Casseroles can also leave out the meat, frequently substituting cheese and more vegetables. Macaroni and cheese is a staple of African American meals as well as many southern and midwestern meals. Homemade "mac-and-cheese" is frequently similar to egg and milk custard, particularly in the South, or it can be similar to a quiche, as is more typical in the Midwest. Lasagna and spaghetti with meatballs are centerpiece dishes traditional to Italian American families. Although both have become national favorites, it is still more common in the Northeast and eastern Midwest for them to be homemade from family recipes and used for celebratory and holiday meals.

Pies, turnovers, and dumplings are another way to stretch meat and fish. Meat pies are traditional to the French-heritage areas of interior New England and Louisiana, and fish and seafood pies reflect the Russian heritage in the Pacific Northwest. Savory pastries filled with meat or fish and vegetables have a long history in the United States, particularly in the upper Midwest and Great Lakes. Cornish miners brought pasties, large turnovers filled with beef, potato, carrot, and onion with them to the Upper Peninsula of Michigan in the early 1800s. Finnish immigrants then adopted them, added rutabaga, and helped popularize them as a regional dish. Russian meat pies are sold in Nebraska as "*runzas*," Montana offers Butte pasties (Cornish meat pies), and variations on bite-size dough pockets filled with meat, potatoes, onion, cabbage, or cheese (among other possibilities) are found among numerous ethnic groups—ravioli among Italian Americans, pierogi among Poles, *pirozhki* among Russians. *Bierocks* in the western states (Kansas and Nebraska, in particular) are filled buns, sometimes considered identical to *runzas*.

Vegetarians and vegans often replace meat with beans, tofu, tempeh, textured vegetable protein made from soy flour (TVP), seitan (wheat gluten), or any number of commercial "veggie burgers." These variations are more common along the coasts and in areas associated with socially progressive or back-to-the-land lifestyles (such as college towns). Historically economically disadvantaged ethnic groups and regions often feature beans as the centerpiece or the meal, as in the cuisines of the Southwest, the southern Appalachians, and the pioneers on the western plains. Native Americans in the Southwest cook pot beans, pintos simmered with a seasoning of salt pork, onion, garlic, and salt, and Mexican Americans there cook *frijoles negroes* (black or turtle beans) the same way. Chili peppers and salsas are usually added to individual servings. Appalachian foodways is defined by soup beans and corn bread, similar to pioneer diets in the Midwest and western plains. Bean casseroles or Crock-Pot beans (multiple dried bean varieties slow simmered with tomatoes, onions, and a sweet sauce) are popular in the Midwest, and New England still has community traditions of baked beans and bean pot suppers.

Evening meals are not considered complete without a starch. A baked potato slathered with butter, sour cream, and chives is the stereotypical accompaniment, particularly at steak houses throughout the country. It is typical of home cooking throughout the Northeast, Midwest, and Northwest. Fried potatoes are iconic of the upland South, home fries of home cooking in the Midwest, and hash browns of New England. French fries can probably be considered a national food. Boiled potatoes are preferred in New England and the upper Midwest, although boiled new or red-skinned potatoes are common in many restaurants and homes. Potatoes can also be mashed, and Irish American traditions fold in cooked cabbage, leeks, or parsley. Garlic mashed potatoes seem to have come out of California innovations. Potato salad accompanies lunches or light suppers. A sweet-and-sour dressing is popular in the Mid-Atlantic and Midwest (German potato salad), and a cold mayonnaise dressing is more common in the South.

Sweet potatoes frequently replace white ones (also called Irish potatoes in the Appalachians) throughout the South. In Appalachian and soul-food cuisine, they are often baked in the skin and served whole, though the rest of the South prefers them pureed or in a casserole topped with bread crumbs and brown sugar (and pineapple). Sweet potato casserole is popular throughout the Midwest as well, and it frequently has a marshmallow topping.

Rice is a standard starch in the coastal Southeast (Charleston), the Gulf Coast (Texas is one of biggest producers of rice), and the West Coast. New

Orleans cuisine contains famous rice dishes—jambalaya and étouffée served over rice, red beans and rice, or "dirty rice." The Southwest displays its Hispanic influence in Mexican rice cooked with tomato sauce. New Mexico serves green rice, long-grain white rice cooked with beef or chicken stock and covered with a puree of cilantro, jalapeño peppers, green onions, garlic, and salt. Both Hispanic and Asian influence is seen in California where sushi is popular and chop suey was invented. Hawaii includes rice as a standard side, including in its plate lunch. The upper Midwest has its distinctive wild rice, which is used as a starch as well as a stuffing for game and poultry.

Grits can replace rice or potatoes in the South, and hominy serves the purpose in some Appalachian homes. Pasta or noodles are also a basic starch, with pasta referring more to Italian meals as well as the nationally distributed commercial varieties. Noodles, on the other hand, tend to reflect a more old-fashioned or German culture, and they are commonly homemade throughout the Midwest.

Dinner salads and hot, cooked vegetables also accompany a complete dinner. These tend to reflect regional resources as well as attitudes toward health and taste. California focuses on freshness, variety, and innovation. Southern meals tend to include greens (collards, kale, turnip greens, chard, or kale) and green beans cooked with bacon grease, and the stereotypical midwestern meal smothers basic American vegetables, such as green beans, corn, and carrots (maybe broccoli and cauliflower), in butter or melted cheese sauce. Appalachian and New England meals might include turnip, while the upper Midwest enjoys rutabaga and kohlrabi.

Bread usually accompanies the meal. Dinner rolls made of white flour are a national standard. Corn bread is likely in the South, and a tortilla in the Hispanic Southwest. Sliced white bread is still prevalent throughout Midwest and South, though pumpernickel and rye are associated with Eastern and Central European settlement areas. Artisan whole-grain breads are expected on the West Coast and most urban centers.

A sweet dessert at the end of the evening meal is an American tradition. Reflecting their origin in the British tradition of "puddings," they are often some combination of sweetened dough and fruit, in the form of cakes, pies, puddings, cobblers, and a host of regional and ethnic variations.

Puddings in American tradition are always sweet. They are usually some combination of a grain or cereal with milk or egg and some variation of sugar. Indian pudding, associated with historic New England, contains cornmeal and molasses. Tapioca pudding is another traditional pudding now found throughout the United States, although southern cooks may be some of the few using actual tapioca pearls. Inexpensive packaged mixes for vanilla, chocolate, or butterscotch puddings now transcend regional boundaries and seem to be especially popular in the Midwest, where salad bars often include puddings.

A dessert with a similar consistency to puddings is custard, a sweetened baked dish of eggs and milk. Sweet custards with or without a crust can have additional ingredients—sugar or honey, raisins, fruit—and are usually eaten for dessert. They tend to have an old-fashioned association and are common in New England as custard pie and in the South as custard pudding. They are also common in Hispanic foodways and are found throughout the Southwest as flan. New Mexico has *natillas* ("floating islands" of meringue on top of custard). Rice puddings, popular in the South and in Jewish American traditions, are technically a rice custard with raisins and nutmeg sprinkled on top. Bread puddings can also be similar to custards. Historically a way to use stale bread, they are made similar to rice puddings (oftentimes with raisins, cinnamon, and nutmeg), and are popular in New England and the South. New Mexico bread pudding, *capirotada*, is spiced with cinnamon and cloves and made with cheese, sugar, and pine nuts (no eggs or milk). Some of the Amish and German parts of the Midwest have a sweet tomato pudding that is actually a bread pudding made with tomato juice.

Cake is another common dessert item in the United States, usually reserved for special dinners or celebratory occasions, such as birthdays, weddings, and parties in general. The original English cakes laden with fruits and spices and made by early settlers carries over today somewhat in fruit cakes and spice cakes. Generally, however, American cakes are made with cake flour, which gives the cake a lighter texture, and is then iced with a soft, creamy icing (variations on powdered sugar, butter, cream cheese, or sour cream). One regional variation is Boston cream pie, actually a cake layered with whipped cream and covered with chocolate icing.

Pie is another all-American dessert, tending to have more filling than its British counterparts (called tarts). Fruit fillings are common and often reflect the region. Although apple pie is considered the American pie, it has special associations with New England, as does blueberry. The South has of peach and blackberry, and the upland South has wild huckleberry, blueberry, blackberry, and apple pie. The eastern Midwest, particularly Indiana and Ohio, claim apple pie and associate it with local hero Johnny Appleseed. Cherry pie is particularly favored in the Mid-Atlantic (where George Washington cut down a cherry tree) and the Midwest (Michigan cherries are widely distributed). Rhubarb, also known as "pie plant," grows well in the colder zones and is traditional to much of the Midwest, especially paired with strawberries. Serviceberry pies are a tradition in areas with strong pioneer heritages, so called because they were the first berries to ripen in the spring, so were used for pies for the rash of funerals and memorial services that always followed the first thaw. Cooks in the Pacific Northwest and western plains use their native blackberry, huckleberry, and marionberry, as well as the cherries and apples commercially produced in Washington and Oregon.

A number of regional pies have specific names. Florida key lime pie uses the small limes distinctive to that state. The Pennsylvania Dutch and the Amish in the eastern Midwest make shoofly pie of molasses, brown sugar, and cake or cookie crumbs. Another Midwestern pie, probably harkening back to pioneer days, is vinegar pie (egg custard with vinegar replacing lemons). Ohio and Indiana seem to specialize in candy-filling pies—Snickers, Mars bars, and so on—along with sweet meringues and pudding pies. New England has a cider pie (egg custard with cider), and the South offers pecan pie (popular nationally), chess pie (pecan pie without the pecans), Mississippi mud pie (chocolate brownie crust with chocolate pudding filling and topped with crushed Oreo cookies, and Jefferson Davis pie (custard maybe with dried fruits and nuts and topped with meringue). Oregon specializes in hazelnut desserts, including pie.

Another dessert uses fruit fillings without the crust. Southern cobblers have a biscuit topping, and crisps have a crumbly topping made of oatmeal, brown sugar, and butter. Similar biscuit-topped dishes are called brown Betties or buckleys in New England, and the western plains have a deep-dish version called a pandowdy. German strudels are sometimes confused with these dishes, the difference being that the dough in strudels is on the bottom and studded with fruit.

Fruit salads are a common dessert today throughout the nation, particularly in areas where tropical fruits abound. The French tradition of fruit and cheese has influenced gourmet or more health-conscious eaters, and the Asian tradition of ending the meal with fruit is part of the food heritage of Hawaii, California, and the Pacific Northwest.

Ambrosia, fruit salad with shredded coconut, is a southern and midwestern specialty (often made with miniature marshmallows in the Midwest). The same regions enjoy gelatin molds, both as salads (filled with vegetables and meats or fish) and desserts (often filled with canned fruits.)

Ice cream can be a dessert in itself or used as an accompaniment or topping on other desserts. "Cake and ice cream" are a standard pairing, and in the South, ice cream is considered a necessity with cobblers and crisps. Whipped cream made from fresh cream is a topping (often gourmet now) for ice cream (for sundaes) and other desserts. Commercial variations come in aerosol cans (Reddi-wip) or tubs (Cool Whip). *Cajeta* (a Mexican caramel sauce made from goat's milk) is used in many desserts in the Southwest. Fried ice cream is associated with the Southwest, and Eskimo ice cream (not actually ice cream, but whipped fish oil) is a specialty of Alaska.

A number of ethnic desserts have become traditional to certain regions. Italian cannoli are standard in the Northeast, and Middle Eastern baklava is prevalent in the eastern Midwest (Detroit to Cincinnati). Greek-run diners in the Mid-Atlantic and Midwest often offer their own version of the honey-soaked pastry.

CANDY

Americans tend to have sweet tooths, and this shows up in the many regional candies. These are not necessarily related to the local natural resources; certain candy companies become well known and associated with a region, for example, Hershey's chocolate in Pennsylvania, See's candy in California, Mackinaw Island fudge in Michigan, and the list can go on. Certain types of candies are regional as well: saltwater taffy in New England, old-fashioned molasses candy and horehound drops in Amish areas, buckeyes (peanut butter confection dipped in chocolate) in Ohio, and salmon candy (dried or smoked salmon strips soaked in honey) in the Pacific Northwest.

Buckeyes, a peanut butter, powdered sugar, and chocolate confection, are made to look like the inedible buckeye nut, a symbol of Ohio and of the Ohio State University football team. Courtesy of Nathan Crook.

Buckeyes Candy

$1/2$ stick (4 tablespoons) butter,
softened to room temperature
$2^1/2$ cups powdered sugar
1 teaspoon vanilla

1 cup smooth peanut butter
(some prefer crunchy peanut
butter)
$1/2$ teaspoon salt
1 cup milk chocolate or dark
chocolate

1. In a mixing bowl, combine the softened butter, peanut butter, powdered sugar, vanilla, and salt. Mix until very smooth and well combined.
2. Form mixture into balls the size of a quarter (use hands or a teaspoon). Place balls on cookie sheet covered with foil and chill in refrigerator for 30 minutes.
3. While the balls chill, melt the chocolate.
4. Use a toothpick to skewer each ball. Dip it partially into the melted chocolate, leaving a dime-sized circle on top of the ball (so that it looks like a buckeye nut).
5. Place the dipped balls back on the cookie sheet and chill until firm.

Chocolate is one of the most popular flavorings for desserts and sweets in the United States. It is added to milk or drunk hot; used as cake icing; used as the main ingredient in fudge, brownies, and many candy bars, cookies, and cakes; and used as a dip or sauce for nuts, fruit, and other foods. European traditions of candy making were brought to the United States in the second half of the 1800s, and numerous businesses developed, many where they had access to dairy production. The oldest producer is Hershey Chocolate Company in Pennsylvania, begun in 1894. Today the town of Hershey is a favorite tourist site for chocolate lovers and offers tours of the factory.

American chocolate tends to be mild and sweet—milk chocolate—but in the 1970s Americans started developing an interest in the European darker chocolates. These expensive "fancy" chocolates are available everywhere now. Many confectioners add local ingredients to their chocolate, attaching regional associations—pecans in the South, hazelnuts in the Northwest, and chilies in the Southwest. Hot chocolate as a drink can have a regional flavor in the Southwest where cinnamon and chilies are often added (following Mexican origins).

Fudge is a soft candy made of sugar, butter, and milk boiled until the sugar caramelizes. Popularized in late 1880s at the Seven Sisters women's colleges in the East, it is still a specialty of New England. Different flavorings can be added—though chocolate is standard. Mexican Americans in the Southwest make a brown sugar fudge called *penocha*, and New Orleans makes a round version with pecans called pralines. Divinity is a variation in the South using corn syrup, egg whites, and water (pecans are a frequent addition).

BEDTIME SNACK/LATE NIGHT SNACKS

Because the evening meal in the United States is relatively early in the evening, it is common to have a snack later, particularly before bedtime. Milk and cookies tend to be a traditional snack for children, and warm milk or hot chocolate is often advised for adults and children who have trouble going to sleep. Molasses is stirred into the warm milk in the Appalachians. Americans frequently snack while watching television (variations on chips, popcorn, and ice cream tend to be favorites) and while socializing. Standard snacks include tortilla chips with salsa and guacamole in the Southwest and on the West Coast (and are increasingly popular everywhere), and chips and dip (meaning potato or corn chips). Pretzels tend to be more common in the East, particularly in the Mid-Atlantic, where a number of family-run companies have produced them for generations. A number of eating establishments have acquired names for themselves by offering special foods late at night. A Rochester eatery, Nick Tahou Hots, offers the Garbage Plate, a cheeseburger, hamburger, or hot dog on top of a choice of home or French fries, pasta salad, baked beans, or macaroni and cheese, all covered with fried eggs, onions, chili meat sauce and mustard. This might be served with another central New York (Syracuse) specialty, salt potatoes, which are young "new" potatoes boiled in heavily salted water. The dish reflects the area's natural resources of salt springs and the ethnic heritage of Irish immigrants who started the tradition.

NOTES

1. There are numerous resources describing these foods and offering recipes. The publications by Jane and Michael Stern ferret out many local delicacies, as do Linda Stradley, Jeff Smith, and many other cookbook authors. Stradley's Web site (http://whatscookingamerica.net) is particularly useful and convenient. Also, many folklorists at state or regional folk arts councils, museums, and heritage sites have produced excellent Web sites and materials describing local food traditions. Each state also has an official Web site, which often includes references to agriculture, local resources, and state-designated iconic foods.

2. Because the United States is a land of immigrants, American meals actually use many cuisines and foodways traditions from around the world. Numerous websites are available for almost every food item consumed in the United States and demonstrate the rich variety of food choices made by Americans.

3. A good overview of these variations is provided by the PBS Home Video, *A Hot Dog Program* (1999).

4. The Atlanta History Museum has developed an extensive barbecue exhibit.

5. Jane and Michael Stern, *Chili Nation* (New York: Random House, 1998).

6. For information and recipes, see the official Web site www.senate.gov/reference/reference_item/bean_soup.htm.

5

Eating Out

Eating out in the United States is a convenience, a means of socializing, and a source of entertainment. The varieties of eating establishments offer different price ranges, eating styles, and cuisines, so that most Americans can afford to eat out somewhere.[1] As work schedules have increased over the past few decades, more and more families have both parents working full-time to make ends meet, and children have many scheduled activities outside of school, going out to eat or bringing home takeout often seems to be the best way to have a meal and some family time.

Aside from convenience, eating out is a frequent way to socialize—for families, coworkers, romantic couples, friends, and individuals on their own. Restaurants come in all varieties of price ranges and types of food, and in some ways, offer one of the few public venues for gathering that were historically offered by churches and town squares. Fast-food restaurants even offer birthday parties for children and coffee hours for senior citizens, which provides a sense of community. In addition, for many Americans, food has become a source of entertainment, so going to restaurants and trying out new menus is a major leisure activity.

A substantial amount of eating out occurs while Americans travel. With many families dispersed across the country (usually to pursue work or education), families often travel long distances to visit other family members or attend family reunions. Eating outside the home also occurs because work schedules often demand that workers take only a brief half-hour lunch break, so they must stay close to their place of work (business lunches are generally longer). Furthermore, school hours generally run through lunchtime, and children are expected to eat in the school cafeteria or bring a lunch from home.

These trends toward eating out are national; however, they vary across regions. Some eating establishments are found only in specific regions, but other regional restaurants and food traditions have become nationally known. Regional dishes appear at every type of food venue and even show up in national chain restaurants.

Urban and rural populations often have different approaches to eating out. Cities offer a much wider variety of establishments, and farming regions tend to be more cost-conscious and "down home." In between, however, are small towns, suburbs, and wide varieties of offerings.

STREET FOODS—HOT DOGS, ICE CREAM, AND MORE

Street foods in the United States are usually found only in urban areas. These are generally foods that can be held in the hand and consumed informally in public. The foods may be purchased from simple pushcarts selling a single item, such as hot dogs or ice cream, or from a truck vendor selling a number of pre-prepared, quickly cooked items, usually the all-American hot dog or hamburger with potato chips and drinks. East Coast cities are particularly well known for their street foods. The regional variations are enormous, however, and frequently reflect the local natural resources as well as ethnic history. Philadelphia, for example, is known for roast chestnuts and soft pretzels as well as its ethnic food trucks and vegetable vendors, New York is known for its hot dogs, and San Antonio for its tamales. In the Southwest, vendors offer fruit on a stick, often with a chili salt dip. Los Angeles is famous for its fruit slushies and Southern California for its fish tacos. Ice cream stands are frequently seasonal and offer basic all-American foods as well. Washington, DC has *papuseria* trucks selling *pupusas*, a Salvadoran stuffed tortilla, as well as other Latin American items. New England takes great pride in its ice cream parlors, as does the upper Midwest (Wisconsin in particular) and the eastern Midwest (Ohio, Indiana). Hawaii is famous for its "shave ice," literally shaved ice with flavoring poured over it.

Even if the foods are national ones, condiments and sides may differ. Ketchup, mustard, chopped onion, and pickle relish are the standard toppings, but others are frequently available according to region. Salsa, for example, is usually offered in southwestern establishments and soy sauce in Hawaiian ones.

Many of these street foods are also available at public sporting events, civic celebrations, and community events, again with local variations. Cleveland stadium, for example, boasts its own brand of mustard.

LOCAL EATERIES

The range of locally owned and run small eateries catering to local customers with local down-home food is enormous. Food writers Jane and Michael Stern, who have traveled the States eating at these places, call this food "road food."[2] Frequently, local residents gather at these venues after social events—church, high school football games, and life celebrations. The owners often know the customers by name, the customers know each other, and eating there is part of people's routine. These places often have an atmosphere of nostalgia to outsiders—this is the way that Americans like to imagine the past. Decor is often in keeping with that—down-homey and with photographs and artifacts affirming the establishment's ties to the local community and its past.

Although road food tends to be inexpensive and often more functional than aesthetic, it is inexpensive, filling, and familiar to the locals who frequent the restaurant. This means road food often uses local resources as ingredients and traditional, often family, recipes well liked by the community. Ethnic influences are often evident, but the foods are not typically sold as "ethnic" but just as the food of that local community. National foods are usually included as well—hot dogs, hamburgers, french fries, and homemade desserts, including pies, cakes, muffins, and brownies.

Some of these eateries are found only in specific regions: for example, lobster shacks in New England, barbecue joints throughout the South and in cities where southerners have migrated to (Detroit, for example), taquerias in the Southwest, crab shacks in the Mid-Atlantic.

Breakfast is often a big meal at local eateries and standard national breakfast offerings of eggs, bacon, omelets or pancakes with coffee and juice are often mixed with local specialties—scrapple in Pennsylvania, grits throughout the South, and salsa and refried beans in the Southwest.

Diners

Diners are an American tradition of eateries that stay open long hours, have a no-nonsense setting, and offer plain, straightforward fare of sandwiches, pie, coffee, and other hearty but simple hot meals at inexpensive prices. They cater more to the working people of any class. They often serve as a meeting place before or after work.

The name "diner" probably came from dining cars on trains, and some discarded railroad passenger cars have even been turned into diners. The history officially begins in Rhode Island in the 1870s, when a street vendor who offered food from his wagon stayed open late in front of offices. In the 1880s, Samuel Jones started building food wagons specifically to go to public

This restaurant in Pittsburgh, Pennsylvania, plays on nostalgia for diners and home-style cooking. Courtesy of the author.

places. These were mobile wagons, but in 1905, permanent lunch wagons started being built, mostly in New York and New Jersey. These first diners had stainless steel exteriors with efficient and clean interiors, laminated tables, and tile. Food was fast and filling—"meat and potatoes."[3]

Delicatessens and Sandwich Shops

Delicatessens (the name means "to eat delicacies") commonly serve German Jewish foods (e.g., meats, breads, sauerkraut, pickles, potato salads, herring, sausages) both for takeout and eating in. Delicatessens were first established in the 1880s by Jewish immigrants to New York, and they serve kosher and pareve foods, such as chicken soup, corned beef, lox, chopped liver, and garlic pickles. Bagels and cheesecake were introduced in 1920s. This ethnicity and these foods are still associated with delis, but the use of the word has expanded to include supermarket sections where fresh meats and cheeses can be purchased to specification. Traditional delicatessens are still associated with New York (Katz's, the Carnegie Deli, and the Second Avenue Deli) and the East Coast but are also found in major urban areas with large Jewish populations—Cantor's deli in Los Angeles and Eli's Stage Deli in Chicago. Some of these, such as Zingerman's in Ann Arbor,

Michigan, are now famous primarily for their fresh-baked artisan breads and have grown into high-priced establishments offering gourmet items.

Sandwich shops are similar to delicatessens, but lack the ethnic association and usually focus solely on serving some sort of food on bread. Every region has its own specialties—po' boys in New Orleans; cheesesteaks and hoagies in Philadelphia; hot browns in Louisville, Kentucky; pork tenderloin or "loose meat" in Iowa; barbecue on a bun in the south; and chicken-fried steak in Texas.

PIZZA PARLORS

Although pizza parlors started as ethnic Italian eateries in New York City in the 1940s, they spread after World War II so that pizza has become one of the all-American foods with both local and national chains. Many national chains started locally and still have that connection for their region—Domino's, for example, nationally famous for starting home delivery, is still considered a hometown pizza in Detroit, Michigan. Most towns and cities also boast a locally owned "pizza joint" that caters to families and groups of friends socializing. Some offer beer, particularly in college towns. They often use a signature sauce recipe, make their own dough, and use toppings favored in that locality. Pizza places in the Midwest, for example, emphasize a variety of sausages; those in the South usually offer barbecue; California pizza features numerous fresh vegetables and exotic sauces and ingredients; and New Haven, Connecticut, is famous for its white clam pie.

Hamburger and Hot Dog Joints

Like pizza, hamburgers and hot dogs are all-American foods. They are often sold in small mom-and-pop eateries and have either distinctive ingredients or forms. Local resources and toppings are frequently used—Coney dogs throughout Ohio, Michigan, and Indiana have a ground-beef sauce; Chicago joints serve sliced tomatoes, pickle spears, and celery salt on their hot dogs. Burgers might be made out of different ingredients—buffalo in the western mountain states, steak burgers in Texas and the Midwest, and vegetarian burgers in college towns and the West Coast.

Lunch Places and Plate Lunches

These are family- or work-oriented establishments have limited hours but offer a more substantial hot meal of home-cooking types of foods at inexpensive prices. A variant throughout the South is a "meat and three" where customers can get the blue-plate special, a set menu of a main meat course with a selection of two or more sides, all accompanied by corn bread and sweet tea. Standard main dishes are fried chicken, pork chops, Salisbury steak, or fried catfish, and sides commonly include collards, yams, green beans, fried potatoes, corn, stewed tomatoes, and fried okra. Many smaller establishments are run by African Americans and offer soul food. These can be found in urban centers that have a sizable black population, such as Detroit, Chicago, and Washington, D.C. Plate lunch eateries in Hawaii often offer mixtures of American and Asian foods—Spam with sides of macaroni salad and potato salad; rice with fried chicken or pork teriyaki.

Fast Casual—Fast Food, Drive-Throughs, and Chain Restaurants

"Fast casual" is the industry term for chain restaurants offering inexpensive meals from a limited menu of corporat-controlled recipes and service style. The first chain restaurants were the Harvey Houses established along the Santa Fe railroad after the Civil War. With their uniform service and menu, reasonable prices, and commitment to cleanliness, they provided respectable places where travelers could get a quick, home-cooked meal. This idea, however, was quickly adapted by others and developed into a huge industry.

Fast food has become almost synonymous the world over with American food and is often considered the worst of American dining. For many people, fast food represents the American obsession with efficiency, speed, quantity over quality, and a misplaced attitude toward food as simply fuel and a commodity. A sociologist, George Ritzer, even coined a term based on the most successful fast-food business—"McDonaldization"—that refers to the globalization of the practices developed by McDonald's—uniformity and predictability of product and service, efficiency, and an "emphasis on the quantitative aspects of products sold and services offered."[4] American fast food is also characterized by corporate control over the menu, the customers, and the workers, which leads to the increased use of technology to replace human workers. In 2009, there were 25,663 McDonald's throughout the world. Other fast-food establishments have successfully copied the McDonald's approach—Burger King, Wendy's, Pizza Hut, Kentucky Fried Chicken, Taco Bell, A&W Root Beer, Long John Silver, and Subway, to name a few.[5]

These restaurants represent a national American foodway; however, there are regional variations in the popularity of certain restaurants, condiments, and menu items. Some restaurants try to fit into the local regional food culture, and there are smaller fast-food establishments specific to different regions. Also, consumers often use fast food in ways that, in spite of its mass-mediated character, end up building a sense of community and family, for example, by using them for children's birthday parties, senior coffee hours, informal gatherings with coworkers, and even family times that give the parents a break from food preparation.

There were logical reasons why fast food developed into the major share of the food service industry in the United States. Aside from America's preoccupation with efficiency and speed, the cleanliness, uniformity of dishes and quality of food, quick service, standards for courteous service, and low prices fit into people's busy schedules and the car culture of most citizens. Fast-food establishments also offer an informal public place to meet and socialize, something that is sorely lacking in much of the country. Only in communities that highly value local food and businesses and have the resources to support them is fast food not established. Some towns in New England and California, for example, have tried to ban fast-food restaurants on the basis of maintaining the local heritage or keeping neighborhoods noncommercialized.

Some claim that the first fast-food establishment was A&W Root Beer in Lodi, California, in 1912. The fast-food concept evolved around hamburgers, however, and from that perspective, some historians date the beginning of the industry to 1916 when Walter Anderson developed his Wichita, Kansas, hamburger stand into the White Castle System of Eating Houses. These were common throughout Midwest in 1920s and are still popular there, offering an inexpensive, bite-size burger. The original White Castle is still in operation in Columbus, Ohio.

McDonald's is the leading fast-food chain, but two cities are associated with its beginnings. The originator, Ray Kroc, got the idea from Dick and Mac McDonald, who ran a restaurant in San Bernardino, California. They ran eight multimixers that served 15-cent hamburgers to large crowds. Kroc opened up the first McDonald's in 1955 in Des Plaines, Illinois. That original "golden arches" restaurant is now a museum. Although the Big Mac is its trademark hamburger, McDonald's now tries out new menu items that have regional associations and leaves specific menu choices to local managers— McRib in the South and Midwest, lobster roll in New England, salsa in the Southwest, noodles and rice in Hawaii, chicken fried steak on a biscuit in the upland South, tacos and burritos in southern California, and crab cakes in the Baltimore area.

Burger King and Wendy's are the two other leading fast-food restaurants, and they similarly offer variations according to region. Wendy's was founded by Dave Thomas in 1969 in Columbus, Ohio. He named it after his youngest daughter and came up with the drive-through concept. Wendy's offers slightly more upscale food than its two main competitors, and markets itself as fast food that can be personalized—made to order "old-fashioned hamburgers" with a condiment table for customers. Although Wendy's is now national and is not necessarily associated with Ohio, its old-fashioned concept connects it to the Midwest.

A number of other chains are either regional or have regional associations. Hamburger establishments include White Castle (Ohio and the Midwest), Whataburger (the South), Arctic Circle (Utah), In-N-Out Burger (the Southwest: California, Arizona, Nevada), Hardee's and Carl's Jr. (West Coast), Burgerville (Portland, Oregon), Dick's Drive-in (Seattle), Tommy's (Southern California), Krystal and Bojangles (the Southeast), and Jack-in-the-Box (the South and West Coast).

Hot dogs have their own fast-food franchises, although for some reason, these tend to be local to a city rather than regional or national. Hot dogs seem to be a national food that defies standardization, and local establishments cater to local tastes. Variations occur with the ingredients of the dog, the size, the casing, the cooking method, the type of bun, the condiments, and even the name. Two New England restaurant chains that offer hot dogs on New England–style rolls rather than the usual hot dog buns are fast-casual restaurants, Friendly's and Howard Johnson's. Hot dog places in the Detroit area offer Coney dogs with a ground beef–based chili sauce.

For fried chicken, two chains stand out: Kentucky Fried Chicken and Popeye's. Kentucky Fried Chicken, based in Louisville, Kentucky, is international, but the name automatically associates the chain with the South. The founder, "Colonel" Harlan Sanders, began by selling his recipe to franchises and played up his southern gentleman image by dressing in a vest and string tie and sporting whiskers. Popeye's Chicken and Biscuits offers Cajun-style fast food, "inspired by the foods of southwest Louisiana and New Orleans." It not only sells spicy fried chicken with Cajun spices, but its menu includes dishes that are specific to Cajun cuisine, such as dirty rice (sold as Cajun rice), red beans and rice, jambalaya and étouffée. Popeye's originated in New Orleans in 1972 and was called "Chicken on the Run." The Cajun theme has helped make it successful as well as giving it a distinctive regional association. In the 1990s, it started offering "Louisiana Legends," which celebrated the New Orleans one-pot cooking that produced such dishes as gumbo and étouffée. It also blended Creole and Cajun cuisines (the African-French-Spanish and the French-Anglo ethnic traditions of Louisiana).

Pizza is often considered a fast food, although the time it requires to bake a fresh pizza means it is generally not a drive-through takeout item. Many towns have a national pizza chain (such as Pizza Hut) as well as a locally run and owned pizza parlor.

Doughnuts are often a takeout food as well, and some chains have regional associations: Dunkin' Donuts in New England and the Midwest;

Krispy Kreme in the South; and the Canadian chain, Tim Horton's, along the American-Canadian border.

As American tastes expand and food businesses seek new marketing niches, new chains develop. Ethnic foods tend to be featured currently, with southwestern or Tex-Mex cuisine (Chipotle, Qdoba) and Chinese leading the way. The most successful national chain serving Chinese food, Panda Express, reflects the multicultural character of contemporary American corporations as well as traditional regional culinary cultures. It was started in California, home to numerous Asian immigrants as well as to innovative cuisine, and owned by a Chinese American couple. Middle Eastern food is also being adapted to fast food, with businesses such as Pita Pit that also meet the demand for fresher and healthier foods and more international tastes. Hispanic chicken franchises are popular in the metropolitan Washington, D.C., area. These businesses tend to be popular in different regions—usually those with historical associations with that ethnicity. Some national chains also vary their menus and recipes by region. A representative of the Manchu Wok points out that spicy dishes tended to sell best in the South, while Northerners preferred their food more bland.[6]

FINE DINING AND GOURMET RESTAURANTS

Gourmet restaurants are those establishments following more articulated aesthetics of high-quality finely prepared foods. Generally, the chef and the kitchen staff have formal training, and customers are expected to have enough experience to appreciate the details of fine dining—and the higher prices associated with it. These places focus on food as an artistic production and try to create an atmosphere of eating as an aesthetic experience.

New York City restaurants are rated according to the Michelin star system was started in France in the 1920s by the owner of Michelin tires to assist traveling motorists. A team of inspectors would assign stars: three being "exceptional cuisine, worth a special journey," two for "excellent cooking, worth a detour," and 1 for "a very good restaurant in its category." Numerous other rating systems are now used—Zagat's is nationwide, as are the rosette awards given by the American Automobile Association (AAA). Many Web sites and newspapers also offer reviews of restaurants, and personal blogs frequently include accounts of dining experiences.

Historically, these upscale restaurants emphasized their continental character, offering French cooking not as an ethnic cuisine but as the epitome of haute cuisine. They tended to be expensive and formal, frequented by wealthy connoisseurs or for special occasions by the middle classes. Today, fine dining restaurants still tend to draw a wealthier clientele, but with the growing interest in food in the American public and the development of the chef as rock star phenomenon, they are not limited to the upper classes. They still tend to be found in urban, cosmopolitan centers, however, and every city boasts at least one or two restaurants striving for three stars. Some of the more famous have regional associations. The Union Oyster House in Boston, for example, was established in 1826 and claims to be the nation's oldest restaurant. Today it features local seafood and local recipes, such as Boston baked beans, chowder, and other "Ye Olde New England Favorites."

Some cities lay claim to particular foods, and their restaurants reflect that identity. Chicago, for example, is famous for its steak houses, reflecting the city's role as the meatpacking capital of the world in the late 1800s. It can be argued that these restaurants helped to establish steak as the quintessential dish in American fine dining. New Orleans is renowned for its fine restaurants. One that stands out is Antoine's, founded in 1840 and specializing in French Creole food. It claims to be the oldest single-family owned restaurant in the United States. Chez Panisse, of Berkeley, California, is famous as the home of California cuisine. It was established in 1971 by Alice Waters, one of the most vocal advocates of eating organic and local foods.

ETHNIC RESTAURANTS

Ethnic restaurants are those that serve a cuisine distinctively not "American." This is tricky, however, especially because defining what is American is equally complex. Immigrants, recent citizens, and persons of strong ethnic backgrounds often own, manage, and cook in American restaurants as well as ethnic ones. In addition, many restaurants include one or two dishes or ingredients from an ethnic cuisine, and over time, some foods originally though of as ethnic—such as pizza—become so fully embraced by American culture that they are no longer treated as ethnic. Frequently, as foods become familiar, they become commonplace and lose their attractiveness as curiosities for those eaters who enjoy being adventurous. Restaurants may then try to tweak these dishes in some way that makes them seem distinctive or exotic again.[7]

Ethnicity is possessing a particular heritage and having a sense of that heritage being a part of one's identity. That identity is expressed through traditions, particularly foodways, in specific contexts that display membership in an ethnic group as well as attitudes toward that identity. Food is often used to define ethnic identity and its boundaries. For example, certain foods thought to be disliked by the American public are often not included on menus given to nonethnic customers or are watered down for American tastes. If they are offered, it is almost a test to see whether the consumers are really "one of them." For example, Korean restaurants offer a number of dishes thought to be disliked by or offensive to Americans—particularly, kimchi stew and a buckwheat noodle dish with soy paste. Both are very popular among Koreans but oftentimes are not included in the English section of the menu. Ethnic food also brings people together and is used to build a sense of fellowship and community. Many ethnic restaurants have back rooms available for parties or meetings for community members. Menus, serving styles, and even consumption styles may differ from those offered in the public dining area and be closer to the home country's.

Eating in ethnic restaurants, though, is not necessarily tied to a person's ethnicity or personal history. Americans, in general, are now open to a variety of cuisines, and trying new foods is often a form of entertainment and means to socialize well as a way to demonstrate social status as a cosmopolitan person (cultural capital) for many. Regional variations in numbers and types of ethnic restaurants, then, reflect regional food ethos and histories. The findings from a foundational survey in the 1980s hold true for today, in which geographer, Wilbur Zelinsky, found that the popularity of ethnic restaurants differs by region. Not surprisingly, the Northeast and West Coast had the most ethnic restaurants, and within those regions, they tended to cluster in cities. Surprisingly, there was "no strong relationship between the relative strength of an ethnic cuisine and the distribution of most ethnic groups."[8] Tourism seemed to make a difference as well as the presence of a cosmopolitan middle and upper class. Those conclusions, however, might not include the inexpensive eateries established wherever immigrant populations can support them. These are frequently not found in restaurant listings, as they often are in a home or a small, hole-in-the-wall establishment known only to locals. The food is often inexpensive and closer to the tastes of the ethnic group.

Ethnic restaurants can be venues for displaying ethnicity and creating public spaces for members of that heritage, but they are also businesses that need to make profits to survive. Therefore, they frequently adapt their menus, recipes, decor, and serving styles to whatever locale they are in, resulting in regional variations in the distribution of ethnic restaurants as well as in the food served in those restaurants.[9] In Zelinsky's survey, Chinese, Italian, and Mexican restaurants made up more than 70 percent of all ethnic restaurants, Chinese accounted for 29 percent, Italian for 22 percent, and Mexican for 20 percent. Although the variety of ethnic foods has widened considerably, Chinese, Italian, and Mexican still dominate. In 2000, the National Restaurant Association found that 90 percent of diners in a national survey had tried restaurants serving those foods and 50 percent of them eat at them regularly.[10] Also, as all three cuisines have become more familiar to Americans, restaurants featuring regional specialties within those cuisines have become popular, especially in urban areas.[11]

Chinese food can be found everywhere in the nation. Starting in California and the Pacific Northwest, Chinese immigrants, primarily from southern China, followed the railroads and other lines of commerce to small towns and cities throughout the country, establishing small Cantonese-style eateries that easily adapted to local tastes and resources. In the Mississippi Delta region, for example, collard greens are used, and along the Gulf Coast, crawfish replace shrimp. Neighborhoods of Chinese immigrants, or Chinatowns, are established in cities in California (San Francisco), the Pacific Northwest (Seattle), and the East Coast (Boston, New York City, and Washington, D.C.), and these cities host numerous restaurants, many of which maintain authentic dishes and cooking styles. Almost every small city and larger town in the United States has a Chinese restaurant. These are often lunchrooms serving only the most stereotypical and Americanized Cantonese-style food—rice or noodles with stir-fried meat and vegetables in cornstarch sauces. In the 1970s, China opened its doors to the West, and immigrants from other regions of the country began establishing restaurants that offered a variety of regional Chinese cuisines. Although this variety has filtered into the general American eating possibilities, Chinese cuisine tends to be found primarily in major urban centers. Now considered a familiar food, Cantonese-style restaurants have expanded their menus to offer sushi and basic American items. This juxtaposition of Americanized ethnic foods along with more authentic cuisines and innovative fusion dishes is representative of more contemporary trends in American dining habits. New York City, for example, continues to host numerous Cantonese restaurants, even though a wide variety of regional and fusion Chinese restaurants are also available.[12] All-you-can-eat Chinese buffets are popular throughout the Midwest, and many include sushi, salad bars, and some American foods (macaroni and cheese and chicken fingers for kids). Inexpensive Chinese takeouts are commonly found throughout the country in suburban strip malls, small towns, and big cities.

Italian restaurants accounted for 22 percent of all ethnic establishments in the 1980 survey. They tended to dominate the market in the Northeast, from southern New England through New York City to western Pennsylvania. This is not surprising given the strong immigrant neighborhoods that developed in Boston, New York, and Philadelphia at the end of the 1800s. Large immigrant populations, however, are no guarantee that ethnic restaurants will be established. A taste for Italian food seems to have been taken to central and southern Florida by northeastern city folk heading south, while the western plains states, particularly Utah, have numerous Italian immigrants but few Italian restaurants.[13] A study examining the foodways of

Italians settled in Utah in the 1970s demonstrated that the contrast in food aesthetics between Italians and the surrounding Anglo American culture was too stark to enable the Italians to be accepted. They were holding onto rural Italian traditions such as eating goat meat, home butchering, an emphasis on fresh vegetables rather than canned, "strange" vegetables (eggplant, broccoli), and placing vegetable gardens in the front yard rather than the back. Although Americanized generic Italian food (spaghetti, pizza) is now common throughout the country, Italian restaurants are also frequently the upscale, gourmet-quality establishments in an area, reflecting a common pattern in which ethnic foods in the United States tend to grow in popularity from the ground up, so to speak. They often start as working-class cuisines, become common partly because they are inexpensive, then become cuisines available for more adventurous eating and innovation.

The number and variety of Mexican restaurants have similarly expanded enormously since the 1980s when they represented 20 percent of the ethnic restaurant industry but were primarily found in the Southwest (Texas to Southern California up through the southern Great Plains states).[14] Large migrant populations brought Tejano culture and Tex-Mex cuisine to the rural Midwest starting in the 1940s. Many of these migrants settled in nearby cities, establishing barrios (neighborhoods) where they ran taquerias and groceries. Their food, however, was often looked at with suspicion by non-Hispanic Americans, and even now, many rural areas with large Hispanic populations publicly offer only the Americanized and sanitized version of Mexican food found at national chains, such as Taco Bell.[15] Different regions do now have varieties of Mexican food, with southern California offering Cal-Mex versions, Texas offering Tex-Mex, New York City upscale restaurants featuring authentic Mexican regional cuisines, and the Southwest presenting a unique blend of Native American and Hispanic traditions that many think represents the soul food of Mexican American cooking.

In the restaurant survey, only 5 percent of ethnic restaurants were French, although this number is deceiving because many pricier restaurants that are not identified as ethnic serve French-style cuisine. These tend to be perceived as sophisticated and upscale and are found particularly in northeastern cities, San Francisco, Los Angeles, and New Orleans, as well as scattered around the country in other major cities.

Since the 1980s, there has been a boom both in the number and variety of ethnic restaurants throughout the country, including Asian restaurants. Japanese food was introduced first in the 1960s through Japanese steak houses where chefs would perform astonishing knife and carving tricks. These were expensive, but family oriented, and established teriyaki sauces and tempura batter as "safe" ethnic foods. The Japanese tradition of eating raw fish (i.e., sushi and sashimi dishes) initially met with great suspicion and was commercially available only in ethnic enclaves and cosmopolitan centers on the East and West coasts. Californians, however, popularized sushi, even creating a California roll of avocado and cooked crabmeat in rice rolled in a sheet of seaweed. A Philadelphia roll of cream cheese and vegetables was also invented, and now sushi, both in its Americanized and Japanese forms, is commonly available in Asian restaurants throughout the country, as well as in many mainstream supermarkets. Sushi stands similar to those in Japan in which the sushi is freshly made are starting to appear in more upscale urban centers where eaters might be more adventurous and experienced. (The North Market in Columbus, Ohio, is an example.) Korean restaurants, meanwhile, are found primarily in urban areas along the coasts, most notably, New York City, northern Virginia, and Los Angeles. Although large numbers of Koreans immigrated after the 1965 Immigration Act opened the way (numerous "war brides" immigrated in the 1950s), Korean food was not perceived as appealing to Americans, so restaurants were established only within neighborhoods with large Korean populations.

Vietnamese restaurants emerged with the influx of immigrants after the end of the Vietnam War in 1975. Similar to Korean, these restaurants tended to cluster in New York City, northern Virginia, and cities along the West Coast, but Minneapolis–St. Paul, Chicago, Houston, Atlanta, and St. Louis also have a number of Vietnamese eateries. Because of the French colonial history in Vietnam, some of these restaurants offer upscale French and French Vietnamese fusion cuisines.

Thai restaurants started out in California in the 1980s and are now very popular throughout the country, although they are still found primarily in urban, industrial areas. Unlike other Southeast Asian cuisines, selected Thai flavorings (e.g., fresh basil, lemongrass, chopped peanuts) and dishes (e.g., pad thai, iced coffee) have even entered mainstream American eating habits.

Middle Eastern food in general has become popular—hummus and pita bread are sold in most groceries—and restaurants range from quick carryouts to family-run groceries with attached cafes to very upscale, fine dining. The largest numbers of Middle Eastern restaurants are in the Detroit, Michigan, and Toledo, Ohio, area, where, beginning in the 1940s, the auto industry initially helped to attract the largest Arab population in the country. A variety of Middle Eastern countries are represented there. Lebanese tend to dominate in Toledo.

Greek restaurants are common in the eastern Midwest, where they have also contributed to two regional specialties—Coney dogs (hot dogs with a hamburger-tomato sauce) and skyline chili (a cinnamon-flavored meat sauce on spaghetti).

This combination grocery store/restaurant in Toledo, Ohio, features Middle Eastern food. Courtesy of the author.

Portuguese food is found primarily in the Boston area, where Portuguese fishermen settled along the North Shore in the early 1900s. It is generally not presented as gourmet cuisine, although Portuguese sausage has recently become popular outside of the ethnic communities.

Polish and Hungarian restaurants are generally found in urban areas in the Northeast and Midwest. A Hungarian restaurant in Toledo, Ohio, Tony Paco's, is nationally famous because a character in the 1970 hit movie *MASH* frequently talked about how much he missed it. Russian food in commercial establishments is found primarily in the Pacific Northwest and western plains. The Nebraska-based chain, Runza Drive Inn, even serves *bierocks*, a meat-filled pastry originally from Russia.

German restaurants are common in the eastern Midwest and Pennsylvania, although they frequently do not call attention to their ethnicity—reflecting the regional assumption that their food is all-American, but also reflecting past discrimination against Germans during World War I and World War II. Many Amish restaurants in those areas serve German foods.

Northern European restaurants appear primarily in the upper Midwest. Swedish food has been introduced on a national level through the IKEA department store chain.

Restaurants serving food from the Indian subcontinent are plentiful in the United States. A 2009 Web site on Indian culture in the United States lists more than 10,000 restaurants and grocery stores, most clustered around urban centers along the coasts, the Gulf Coast, and the eastern Midwest.[16] (The western plains states have the fewest.) Unlike some other ethnic cuisines, this abundance is due partly to the large number of Indian immigrants who are successful professionals and can afford to eat out. Also, Indian food tends to be especially popular around college campuses, where the food is still associated with 1960s counterculture interests in Eastern religion and alternative lifestyles. Indian cuisine offers numerous vegetarian and vegan dishes, making it especially popular among the growing population of non-meat-eaters in the United States. It makes sense, then, that they tend to be in cities, notably Seattle and San Francisco. Most Indian restaurants offer selections from the various regional cuisines of India.

Pakistani restaurants are often mistaken for Indian, although the Muslim affiliation of Pakistan forbids pork, while the primarily Hindu religion of India forbids beef. Restaurants specializing in Pakistani food are found where there are large Pakistani populations—New York City (Queens and Brooklyn hold the largest number in the United States), New Jersey, Chicago, Houston, Los Angeles, Detroit, and Washington, D.C.

Afghan food is less known in the United States, but is sometimes included at Pakistani restaurants. The first Afghan restaurant opened in St. Paul, Minnesota, in the late 1970s, and such restaurants are now found primarily in California (Los Angeles and San Francisco), New York, and the northern Virginia/Washington, D.C. area. They frequently feature kabobs, a staple dish of Afghani cuisine and thought to have originated there. Many Afghans who have immigrated recently (due to military conflicts) work in the food service and fast-food industries.

African food, although historically very influential on the foodways of the American South, was rarely recognized as a culinary culture with multiple cuisines until Ethiopian restaurants began opening in the late 1970s and early 1980s in cosmopolitan centers along the East Coast. These often hired as cooks immigrants from Central America who could transfer their experience making tortillas to *injera*, the large, flat bread unique to Ethiopia, which is made from teff rather than wheat or corn. The food consists of curries and sauces served on the bread and eaten communally. Other African cuisines are found only occasionally and only in larger cities with large immigrant populations.

COFFEEHOUSES AND TEAHOUSES

Coffee has been the American beverage since the Boston Tea Party, after which American patriotism was expressed by drinking coffee rather than tea. At the beginning of the 20th century, however, coffee shops offering primarily coffee and pastries were mainly found in Italian communities in cities on the East and West coasts. In the late 1950s, coffeehouses emerged as venues for folk music and meeting places for the growing countercultural movement. Smoke-filled, darkly lit, basement coffeehouses were a staple of the Beat poets and their followers during the 1960s, hippies, and "the cool." New York City's Greenwich Village was particularly famous as a hangout for the counterculture, as were coffeehouses in the Pacific Northwest. Churches and other organizations also established coffeehouses as outreach. The concept gradually became more mainstream, and Starbucks, started in Seattle in 1971, established a model offering specialty coffees and specialty coffee drinks, which rapidly spread across the country and even internationally. Many duplicates quickly sprang up, and it is common now for most towns and cities to have a coffeehouse that serves as a sort of informal community center as well as café.

Tea has long been associated in the United States with either British or Asian culture. Although cold sweet tea is an icon of the South, establishments specializing in tea tend to have definite cultural meanings. Tea was considered a feminine type of drink, and from the 1880s onward, tearooms in upscale hotels offered places where ladies could respectably gather. Today, tearooms can be found primarily in the South where formality still reigns.

BARS AND WINERIES

Alcohol has a problematic place in American culture, and attitudes toward it differ according to region as well by class and religion. Although beer and hard cider were staples of the everyday diet for most colonists, and wine was considered a tonic, fears about the effects of too much alcohol began sweeping the country during the religious revivals of the mid-1800s, ultimately leading to the Prohibition, which lasted from 1920 to 1933. Today, many conservative Protestant churches consider alcohol sinful and allow no alcoholic beverages at all. The South, with its strong Protestant heritage, has many dry counties and towns where alcohol cannot be bought or consumed. Even though bourbon is produced in Kentucky, and wineries have sprung up throughout the South in the last decade, there still tends to be a hesitation about alcohol among the middle class, and certain drinks are associated with upper classes or lower classes.

Except in more cosmopolitan urban centers, bars tend to be considered less than respectable and are often in down-and-out parts of town. Similar prohibitions against alcohol are found among Mormons (who predominate

The name of this restaurant in Louisville, Kentucky, identifies its regional connection, suggesting that the beer is produced locally. Courtesy of the author.

in Utah) and some Muslims (who have large populations in Detroit, Michigan; their restaurants are usually alcohol free even though they frequently
run beer carryouts). Seventh-Day Adventists also avoid alcohol (and coffee,
pork, shellfish, and tobacco). Other regions of the country do not attach
morality to alcohol in the same way, and college towns throughout the
country are notorious for their bars.

Names of establishments selling alcohol tend to differ by region—the
term "tavern" appear in the Mid-Atlantic and New England; saloon in the
Wild west; and pub in Irish neighborhoods across the nation—and some
regions are associated with different types of alcohol.

For many years, commercial beer production was centered in the Milwaukee, Wisconsin, area, where German beer makers established breweries in
the 1800s that are still synonymous with American beer—Pabst, Schlitz,
Miller, Blatz. St. Louis, Missouri, is home to Anheuser-Busch, which started
in the 1850s and produces two of the top-selling beers in the United
States—Budweiser and Bud Light.

SCHOOL LUNCHES

Free school lunches were first started in 1853 by the Children's Aid Society in New York City. The Works Projects Administration (WPA) under

President Franklin D. Roosevelt established hot lunches for school children in 1937, and the 1946 National School Lunch Act provided federal funding for public school lunches, to be run through the U.S. Department of Agriculture. Various rulings since then have established nutritional guidelines, some of which have recently come under severe criticism by observers who think that certain food industries have too much influence.[17] Free school breakfasts were first offered in the late 1960s in low-income districts. Because public school meals programs are federally run, there are not supposed to be regional variations; however, the cooks can make selections from the overall guidelines and can adjust to suit local tastes and familiar recipes.

NOTES

1. Eating out also plays into social status, and certain restaurants are associated with different socioeconomic levels. According the French theorist Pierre Bourdieu, people choose things like restaurants as a way to demonstrate taste that distinguishes them from lower classes (*Distinction: A Social Critique of the Judgment of Taste*. Cambridge, MA: Harvard University Press, 1984.).

2. Jane and Michael Stern describe these eateries as places that offer "informal food made by the cooks, pit masters, bakers and hash slingers who are America's culinary folk artists." They also are not attempting to offer a "dining experience" but one of community and familiarity and comfort. The Sterns continue their description, stating that these places "express the soul of their region, where you can sit down with locals and enjoy real food in a place where real people feel comfortable." *Roadfood* (Rev. ed, New York: Broadway Books, 2005), xi.

3. American Diner Museum, www.americandinermuseum.org/site/history.ph.

4. George Ritzer, *The McDonaldization of Society* (Thousand Oaks, CA: Pine Forge Press, 2004), 13.

5. NationMaster, "McDonald's restaurants by country," http://www.nationmaster.com/graph/foo_mcd_res-food-mcdonalds-restaurants. For more information on McDonald's, see www.mcdonalds.com. Other fast-food businesses also have their own Web sites. The fast food industry has received much criticism for how it has taken over smaller, locally run restaurants. Some writers are also concerned that the industry homogenizes the eating experience, so that local tastes and values are erased. The theory of globalization, in contrast, suggests that even globalized products are adapted to those local tastes and values—both by the industry as a marketing measure and by consumers who fit the globalized foods into their own needs and eating habits. For studies on globalization, see James L. Watson, ed., *Golden Arches East: McDonald's in East Asia* (Stanford, CA: Stanford University Press, 1997). For more information on the fast-food industry, see Andrew F. Smith, *Encyclopedia of Junk Food and Fast Food* (Westport, CT: Greenwood Press, 2006).

6. Described in a newspaper article by Matt Krantz, "Panda Express Spreads Chinese Food Across USA," *USA Today*, September 13, 2006.

7. Such intentional exploration of new foods is "culinary tourism" or "eating out of curiosity." The need to constantly exoticize the food so that it is not too familiar and mundane is one reason the American food and restaurant industry introduces new items and/or new variations. See Lucy Long, ed. *Culinary Tourism: Eating and Otherness* (Lexington: University Press of Kentucky, 2004), 20–37.

8. Wilbur Zelinsky, "You Are Where You Eat," in *The Taste of American Place: A Reader on Regional and Ethnic Foods*, eds. Barbara G. Shortridge and James R. Shortridge (Lanham, MD: Rowman and Littlefield, 1998), 248.

9. The fact that restaurants are businesses raises a number of questions about the nature of the food they serve. Some question the authenticity of such food, believing that because it is commodified, it automatically loses some of its emotional meanings for its producers and consumers. Food historian Donna Gabbacia suggests, though, that the business aspect of restaurants has enabled the friendly interchange of new cuisines in the United States. Consumers and producers feel free to try new foods, adapt old ones, and mix styles of foodways in these business contexts precisely because they are commodities—not symbols of identity. Donna R. Gabaccia, *We Are What We Eat: Ethnic Food and the Making of Americans.* (Cambridge, MA: Harvard University Press, 1998).

10. Life in the USA, "Ethnic Dining Trends in the United States." http://www.lifeintheusa.com/food/ethnic.htm

11. Krishnendu Ray, "Ethnic Succession and the New American Restaurant Cuisine," in David Beriss and David Sutton, eds., *The Restaurants Book: Ethnographies of Where We Eat* (Oxford: Berg Publishers, 2007).

12. That popularity may be partly because it is a favorite among Orthodox Jews, who see it as cosmopolitan and American, yet kosher (following the rules of kashruth). Gaye Tuchman and Harry Gene Levine. "New York Jews and Chinese Food: The Social Construction of an Ethnic Pattern," in *The Taste of American Place*, eds. Barbara G. Shortridge and James R. Shortridge, 163–186 (New York: Rowman and Littlefield, 1998). One writer refers to such food as "kosher treif." Miryam Rotkovitz, "Kashering the Melting Pot: Oreos, Sushi Restaurants, 'Kosher Treif,' and the Observant American Jew," in *Culinary Tourism*, ed. Lucy Long (Lexington: University of Kentucky Press, 2004), 158.

13. Richard Raspa, "Exotic Foods among Italian-Americans in Mormon Utah: Food as Nostalgic Enactment of Identity," in *Ethnic and Regional Foodways in the United States: The Performance of Group Identity*, eds. Linda Keller brown and Kay Mussell, 185–194 (Knoxville: University of Tennessee Press, 1984).

14. Zelinsky, "You Are Where You Eat," 248.

15. Some scholars think the watered-down versions of Mexican food have at least introduced Americans to the idea of consuming that food. Once they develop a taste for it, they then are willing to try more authentic versions. There is also a feeling, though, that the fast-food Mexican establishments appropriate or steal Mexican culinary traditions and identity simply for monetary purposes and are ultimately disrespectful to the culture of that food. Amy Bentley, "From Culinary Other to Mainstream America: Meanings and Uses of Southwestern Cuisine," in

Culinary Tourism, ed. Lucy Long, 209–225 (Lexington: University Press of Kentucky, 2004).

16. Thokalath Indian Resources, "Indian Restaurants in United States," www.thokalath.com/restaurant/index.php.

17. Marion Nestle was one of the first and most vocal critics. Her book *Food Politics: How the Food Industry Influences Nutrition and Health* (Los Angeles: University of California Press, 2002) has brought much attention to these issues.

6

Special Occasions

The United States has many special occasions surrounding food or involving food. These include national and religious holidays, regional and local celebrations of heritage or identity, events marking an individual's passage through life from birth to death, and festivities celebrating the seasons. These various occasions can be either public or private, frequently both, and often vary region to region.

The word "holidays" comes from the term "holy days" and were originally tied to religious celebrations. They are days officially set aside for observance. Many holidays, such as Christmas and Easter, have become nationwide cultural holidays that are observed in a variety of ways by people with a range of attitudes to the religious beliefs behind them. Many holidays also celebrate natural cycles, such as the changes of seasons—and activities associated with these cycles, such as harvest and planting. Thanksgiving, for example, officially recognizes a bountiful harvest, and many people treat Halloween as an autumn festival by emphasizing fall colors and fruits (pumpkins, apples). The solstices (December 21 and June 21) and equinoxes (September 20–22 and March 20–22) are officially celebrated by Wiccans and a number of ethnic groups. The lunar and solar cycles often form the calendrical timing of holidays even if they are not being celebrated themselves, for example, Easter and many of the Jewish and Muslim holidays (Hanukkah, Passover, Ramadan). Most Asian cultures celebrate their New Year according to the lunar calendar.

Celebrations of personal life-cycle events also provide special occasions for food. These include the milestones individuals pass through during the course of their lives, literally from birth to death. These celebrations can be both private and public, focused on a single person—such as birthdays, coming-of-age celebrations, weddings, retirements, funerals—or on a group, usually united by age, such as graduations. These celebrations often include certain expected foods popularly associated with them, but they can also be personalized to the tastes of the person or persons being celebrated.

Festivals are public, multilayered events containing a variety of activities and meanings. Some are tied to calendrical holidays, but others are moved around according to the needs of the groups holding them.

Many civic festivals celebrate a town or locality. Some are fund-raisers, and others showcase local businesses and institutions or attract consumers and tourists to the area. Food often plays a significant role in these events—sometimes as the focal point, as in apple festivals or pumpkin festivals set in a town or orchard. County and state fairs feature local food products and include cooking competitions and exhibits. Gatherings around food, such as fish fries, church suppers, chili cook-offs, and office potlucks, also bring people together and often showcase regional specialties. Every region seems to have a set of foods specifically for feeding large crowds.

This chapter describes some of the regional variations for all of these special occasions. They are organized initially by season, then by life cycle, and finally by gatherings as food events. Ethnic holidays are included if they have a regional variation or identity.

CALENDAR AND PUBLIC HOLIDAYS

Calendar and public holidays mix national, ethnic, and religious traditions and are often celebrated differently according to region. Variations may occur across regions, or in some cases, different regions have different holidays. For example, Chinese New Year's (based on the lunar calendar) is celebrated throughout the country, but the most visible public celebrations are in Chinatowns, most notably in New York and San Francisco. The following discussion mentions some of these holidays as they occur with regional variations. The holidays are discussed by season, beginning with New Year's celebrations and ending with Christmas and Kwanzaa.

Winter

New Year's Eve is often celebrated nationally with parties, party food (appetizers, pot lucks, special festive foods), and champagne. The traditional countdown of the seconds leading up to the new year are publicly celebrated in a number of places with food icons: Port Clinton, Ohio, a 600-pound walleye fish; Elmore, Ohio, an 18-foot sausage; Lebanon, Pennsylvania, a bologna (made by Weaver-Kutztown Bologna Company and donated to charity); Mount Olive, North Carolina, a three-foot pickle; Raleigh, North Carolina, acorn; New Orleans, gumbo pot; Easton, Maryland, giant crab; Plymouth, Wisconsin, cheese; and Pennsylvania, a 25-pound marshmallow Peep.[1] *Hogmanay*, Scottish New Year's, traditionally involves giving special foods to the "first-footers," the first person stepping into one's house, that include whiskey, bannocks of oatcake, shortbread, and blackbun cake (a type of fruitcake soaked in whiskey and aged for several weeks). Scottish societies, particularly in the South and on the East Coast, often host *Hogmanay*, and some Appalachian residents have memories of a similar observance.

New Year's Day tends to be celebrated with food traditions across the nation. Southerners eat hopping John, a rice, black-eyed peas, and pork (or ham hocks) dish, often accompanied by collard greens, while midwesterners and Mid-Atlantic residents favor pork (in a roast, chop, or sausage) and sauerkraut. The Pennsylvania Dutch serve *oliebollen* (doughnuts filled with raisins and apples), and Polish Americans in the Midwest and Mid-Atlantic celebrate with *biblos*, or hunter's stew, of various meats, vegetables, and cabbage, all washed down with vodka. The Far West celebrates with the Russian tradition of spicy ginger cakes.

Chinese New Year's celebrations are based on the lunar calendar and are often public festivities in urban centers with large Chinese populations. Along with parades and dragon puppets, the holiday features steamed and baked cakes and buns, rice dumplings with various fillings, and foods with lucky sounding names—tangerine (good fortune), fish (surplus), chicken (good fortune), chestnuts (profit), and tofu (riches). Japanese serve a type of rice cake, *mochi*, that is often sold in supermarkets during the season.

January 6 is known as Twelfth Night or Epiphany and is traditionally celebrated in French Louisiana with a three king's day cake. Trinkets are hidden inside the cake, and these tell the fortune of the person who finds one. The day was also celebrated historically in southern Appalachia as "old Christmas" with "breaking up Christmas" parties. These usually included quantities of food (corn bread, beans, roast chestnuts) and drink (moonshine, in particular). It is celebrated in the Hispanic Southwest with a king cake, an oval-shaped fruitcake with a ceramic or plastic baby hidden inside to represent baby Jesus. The finder of the baby is expected to take it to church on Ash Wednesday.

Burn's Night is celebrated on January 25 to recognize the birth of Scottish poet, Robert Burns (in 1759). It features the infamous haggis, a meatloaf-like pudding made of oatmeal, chopped liver (lamb or beef), and other ingredients (beef suet, beef heart, lamb shoulder, whiskey) that is steamed inside a cow's bladder or sheep's stomach. (An ovenproof bowl covered with tin foil is an acceptable modern alternative.) This is served with great ceremony, and is usually "piped in," carried on a tray followed by one or more bagpipers. A poem by Burns, "Address to a Haggis," is read, and the haggis is dramatically cut open. The meal frequently also includes cock-a-leekie (chicken stewed with leeks), tatties and neeps (mashed potatoes and turnips), tipsy laird (sponge cake, biscuits, jam, and spirits), or trifle. Haggis has been adapted to American tastes, and recipes are available that leave out some or all of the animal parts. Although ostensibly a celebration of Scottish heritage, it is borrowed by a number of other civic groups that have also adopted bagpipes. The Shriners in Toledo, Ohio, for example, hold a Burns' night with haggis and the trappings, even though most of their pipers are Polish.

Ground hog's Day on February 2 is a time of forecasting the end of winter. It is publicly celebrated in a town in Pennsylvania inhabited by the "official" groundhog, Punxsatawney Phil. Although no specific foods are officially associated with it, people often eat chili or other cold weather foods on that day, and, in recent years, the holiday has become more recognized nationally and used as an excuse for festive socializing and eating.

Though not a holiday, gatherings and festivals surround maple sugaring, particularly in Vermont, New Hampshire, and the eastern Midwest, where there are strong traditions of tapping trees for their sap. The long hours of boiling the sap down into syrup are often an excuse for people to come together.

Spring

Spring is seasonally a time of renewal and rebirth. Spring holidays and the foods associated with them reflect this natural cycle, oftentimes emphasizing newly harvested plants, eggs, and baked goods in symbolic forms. In the United States, the Christian observance of Easter is the basis for a series of holidays and celebrations, mostly centered on Lent, the forty days leading up to Easter, and Easter Day itself. Lent begins on Ash Wednesday, and the Tuesday prior is Shrove Tuesday, also called Pancake Day, Dollar Day, Fat Tuesday, or Mardi Gras.

The Lenten period is a time of somber fasting from meat and sweets as well as sacrificing of personal food favorites. Historically, homes were cleansed of fats and sugars before Lent, and traditions of foods and celebrations were built around using up those ingredients. In anticipation of the sacrifices to come, many of these celebrations feature excess and revelry as well as rich pastries. Some begin as early as January 6 (Twelfth Night), and the French Catholic heritage areas of the country celebrate this time of carnival with parades, revelry, rich foods, and "rites of reversal," in which participants act in ways not normally allowed (e.g., working classes take over the streets, dress is very revealing, and public drunkenness is common). New Orleans is famous for its Mardi Gras Carnival, although it was first celebrated in Mobile, Alabama, in 1703. Today, it is today a strong community and family tradition throughout the French heritage areas of the Gulf Coast. It is celebrated the weekend before Ash Wednesday with large amounts of regional foods and with the distinctive king cake, a large cake (oftentimes similar to a cinnamon roll), usually shaped in a ring, with icing or sugar colored purple, green, and gold, and a bean or coin hidden inside. Whoever finds the trinket is the king for the day.

Other regions of the country have pre-Lent food traditions without the revelry of Mardi Gras. Polish Americans in southern Michigan introduced traditional *paczki* (pronounced "punch-key" and similar to jam-filled doughnuts), and these are now available at mainstream supermarkets and bakeries throughout the Midwest. Chicago even holds a Paczki Day celebration. Eastern European poppy seed and nut pastries are also popular in the

Paczki are a Polish American pastry eaten on Fat Tuesday. The filling can be custard, lemon, apple, prune, cherry, or another fruit preserves. Courtesy of the author.

Midwest and Mid-Atlantic. The Pennsylvania Germans celebrate Fasnacht Day, with a similar type of doughnut, on Shrove Tuesday. They also offer sticky buns, rich soups and stews, homemade noodles, and cottage cheese or shoofly pie. Hungarian Americans celebrate Shrove Tuesday with pancakes, as do Russian Americans in the Pacific Northwest. The latter make buckwheat pancakes, blini, that are topped with butter, jam, sour cream, smoked salmon, or caviar. The Southwest, with its heavily Latino Catholic population, has a number of traditions, including the king cake, special tamales, and sweets.

Ash Wednesday is observed by Christians in various ways. Catholics, for example, hold special masses and by eating fish, marking the beginning of fasting. Hungarians brought their traditions of sour eggs and herring salad on that day to the Mid-Atlantic and Midwest.

Hungarian Americans mark Good Friday with stuffed eggs and baked fish. Similarly, the biggest meal of the year for them is Easter Eve, when they serve chicken soup with dumplings or noodles, roasted ham or lamb, cabbage rolls, pickled vegetables, cakes, pastries, and coffee.

Easter itself is usually celebrated with symbolic foods that both break the Lenten fast and mark renewal, rebirth, and fertility. Easter eggs (hard-boiled and dyed in the shell) are common throughout the United States. These eggs are often hidden for children to find or placed in Easter baskets with special Easter candies (marshmallow Peeps, chocolate eggs, jelly beans). A British tradition of rolling the eggs, however, is active in Washington, D.C., where the president hosts an annual egg rolling on the White House lawn. Eastern Europeans in the Midwest have a tradition of creating intricate wax designs on the eggs, often blowing out the egg so that the shell is left intact. Other Eastern Europeans bake the colored eggs into breads or cakes, and Cajuns in Louisiana serve hard-boiled eggs on a crust topped with cooked meats. German Americans still maintain a tradition of marzipan cakes and marzipan candies formed into complex shapes, including eggs.

Easter dinner is often a formal meal with special foods. Throughout the South, it usually includes baked ham with new peas and new potatoes, asparagus, deviled eggs, and cakes in the shape of lambs and rabbits (with a white coconut topping). In areas where Eastern Europeans have settled, butter is shaped into a lamb (*pasha*, or Paschal lamb) and served alongside the many pastries associated with Easter. Polish Americans eat sausages, hams, painted hard-boiled eggs, and a butter or sugar lamb. These foods symbolize the fertility and renewal associated with spring and are balanced by grated horseradish, symbolizing the bitterness of life. Slovaks feature a *paska*, a distinctive pyramid of cheese, cream, butter, eggs, sugar, and candied fruits, while Russian Americans in the Pacific Northwest have maintained traditions of Easter breads and *kulich* (a tall round cake). They also have the lamb butter *pasha* marked with the letters "XB," which stands for "Christ has risen."

Other spring holidays are tied to the Christian calendar, but not to Easter. The Portuguese community in coastal Massachusetts celebrates the Holy Ghost Festival one week after Easter. The celebration includes a procession with a queen, followed by community banquets featuring soup, potatoes, fish, sausages, and a sweet bread called *massa sovada*. Food is also distributed to the needy.

In the late 1800s, Irish-Americans introduced St. Patrick's Day, March 17, to major northeastern and midwestern cities (New York, Boston, and Chicago). They marked the day with parading in order to make a political statement about their presence. Although it is still most prevalent in heavily Irish urban areas, the holiday has grown into a national day of celebrating the Irish skills of making and consuming spirits. Beer is frequently dyed green, and unusually large quantities are consumed. Some cities allow the bars to open early in the morning on that day. Also, many restaurants serve a Jigg's dinner, a stereotypical Irish meal of corned beef, boiled cabbage, potatoes, and soda bread (which in the United States is usually make in a loaf pan with white flour, sugar, and raisins). Two days later, Italian Americans celebrate St. Joseph's Day with colorful altars piled high with food.

The Christian holy days are not the only excuses for celebrations in the spring. The Jewish holiday of Passover is observed with a number of ritual foods. Passover celebrates the exodus of the Israelites from Egypt, which was allowed because the angel of death passed over the homes of the children of Israel. The holiday includes a seder, a ritual feast in which the story of the exodus is read and special foods are eaten. These foods need to be kosher and not include any leaven, and most are symbolic of Jewish history. Charoset is chopped fruit representing the mortar used by the Israelite slaves to build Egypt. The fruits can vary—most common are dried or fresh apples, figs, prunes, dates, apricots, and raisins. Nuts are often chopped and added to the mixture. Matzo, an unleavened bread similar to a large cracker, is basic to the meal. It is also ground up as meal for matzo balls used in a chicken broth soup. Gefilte fish, roast chicken, and brisket are standard menu items as are vegetables prepared in salads or as sides. Potatoes are standard also. Elaborate kosher deserts frequently end the meal. The exact menus vary according to each family, but also reflect the availability of Kosher foods in different regions. Those areas with large Jewish populations have more variety. Matzo crackers, made without leavening agents, are now sold in mainstream groceries on both coasts and in most urban areas throughout the country. They also now appear in a variety of flavors.

The Kentucky Derby, an annual horse race in Kentucky, is celebrated there with burgoo and mint juleps. The race is televised and has become an informal national holiday, when people gather to watch the races and sip mint juleps.

Asian American communities celebrate spring 106 days after the winter solstice, frequently by honoring ancestors with food. Southeast Asians and Indians have a water festival that involves throwing colored water and dye on each other. The Thai New Year, for example, is celebrated in April. Called Songkran, it involves presentations of food to monks as well as the sprinkling of water in order to cleanse people of the old year and bring them good luck for the new one. In the United States, these festivals generally include special rice cakes, sweets, and noodle dishes.

May Day, the first of May, was traditionally celebrated in the South with maypoles, and throughout the South and Midwest with May Baskets, small baskets of newly picked flowers and grass that would be left on a friend's doorstep at dawn. Those traditions are being revived in some communities. Although no specific foods are traditionally associated with May Day, it is popular for those who celebrate the day to feast on Spring foods—asparagus, new peas, new potatoes, and wild plants. Edible flowers, such as violets, might be added to salads or used as garnishes.

Summer

For many Americans, summer unofficially begins on Memorial Day, the last Monday in May, and ends on Labor Day, the first Monday in September. Both of these days are national holidays, and the long weekends surrounding them are often spent setting up or putting away barbecue grills and marking the change in season with an outdoor meal. Although the specific foods vary with the season, regions tend to have favored picnic and grill foods. Hot dogs and hamburgers are the national favorites, but even then, there can be variations. New Englanders use a soft roll for their hot dogs that opens from the top rather than the side. They often fill the roll with a lobster salad for a lobster roll or fried clams for a clam roll. They also might cook lobster on the grill. Midwesterners (in areas with German or Eastern European herit-age) frequently grill a variety of sausages—particularly German bratwurst and Polish kielbasa—and barbecued ribs, along with hot dogs and hambur-gers, and southerners tend toward pork chops and chicken. Southwesterners grill fajitas (originally, a tough cut of skirt steak) or put salsa on their bur-gers and dogs, residents of the Pacific Northwest grill salmon and giant clams, and Californians typically grill vegetables with their meat or fish. Pic-nics often include sandwiches, chips, potato salad or cole slaw, cookies, and fruits, but these, too, vary by region. The South, for example, prefers pimiento cheese sandwiches and fried chicken, and New England,

California, and the Northwest frequently feature seafood fillings on their sandwiches.

Summer also tends to be a season of social gatherings, civic fund-raisers, and town celebrations, and each region tends to offer its own specialty for a communal meal. This often involves a large one-pot food that can vary widely in quantity and exact ingredients. The large containers seem to represent generosity and unity. Some of the events and foods are seasonal, but not always. (For more discussion of communal foods, see the end of this chapter.)

Juneteenth is a Texas holiday held on June 19 that commemorates the news of the Emancipation Proclamation (which came to Texas two years after President Abraham Lincoln made it official). It is usually celebrated with social gatherings and barbecues. Although historically Juneteenth was an unofficial celebration within African American communities in Texas, it is now official in at least seven states, has spread throughout the United States, and is frequently a celebration of black heritage, with foods representing southern, African American cuisine. Similarly, Emancipation Days are celebrated at different times in different places, and often include soul food. Washington, D.C., for example, holds an official Emancipation Day holiday on April 16.

The 4th of July, celebrating the 1776 declaration of independence from England, is the biggest national holiday. As the birthday of the nation, it is celebrated with foods decorated with red, white, and blue—cakes and cookies iced in those colors, ice cream, watermelon, and blueberries. It also tends to be a celebration because schools are out, government institutions are officially closed, and family reunions are common. Towns hold parades with patriotic themes, and parties and food are expected before the anticipated fireworks displays held in most communities. Food tends to emphasize national unity—hot dogs and hamburgers, potato salad, cole slaw, potato chips—but with the regional variations already described. Watermelons are ripening at this time, and eating and seed-spitting contests are popular. Although fresh slices are standard for picnics, in the South, they may be fancied up with sprigs of mint. Corn is usually not ripe by July 4—in fact, a saying in the Appalachians is that the corn stalks should by knee high by the 4th of July.

Summer also tends to see homecomings throughout the South, reunions of a church congregation involving potluck meals and memorial services for those who died the previous year. Also called "Decoration Day" in the southern Appalachian region because they involve cleaning and decorating graveyards, these reunions are celebrated with "dinner on the grounds" as potluck meals at churches are frequently called. Tables tend to be loaded with vast amounts of food—fried chicken, macaroni and cheese, green beans and baked beans (southern style), biscuits and corn bread, corn, homemade pickles, cakes, pies, watermelon, sweet tea, and any other foods attendees might bring.

August and early September tend to be when county and state fairs are held. These celebrate the agriculture of a region and feature local foods as well as "fair food," foods that can be carried and eaten by hand and that are known more for their enjoyment value rather than their nutritional value. State fairs in Minnesota and Wisconsin introduced deep-fried Twinkies and candy bars, and most fairs offer some sort of fried dough sprinkled with sugar—elephant ears in the eastern Midwest, funnel cakes in Pennsylvania, fry bread in the Southwest, fried coke (batter with coke syrup) in Texas, bear claws on the West coast, sopapillas in New Mexico, and beignets in New Orleans and Charleston, South Carolina. These fairs also include competitions and displays of baking (pies, breads, cakes) and canning (jams, jellies, preserves, and various fruits and vegetables).

Many towns also hold food-centered festivals during the summer. Sometimes the dates coincide with the time the food is ripening, for example, strawberry socials and peach festivals in the Southeast or ramp (wild garlic)

Towns frequently celebrate and market their identity through festivals. Food is often a part of these festivals and can be the focus of an event, as it is here with the Taste of Asheville, North Carolina. Courtesy of the author.

festivals in West Virginia, but the date may also be chosen for the convenience of tourists and local residents, for example, the Gilroy Garlic Festival in California draws thousands every July. Many of these festivals are connected to the region's agricultural or history. Some localities are connected to the food celebrated in unexpected ways. McClure, a small town in northwest Ohio, holds a radish festival because the town has a processing plant for radishes. Another town in Ohio, McComb is home to a cookie factory and holds an annual cookie festival. Some of these festivals grow into larger events so that the food being celebrated plays only a minor role and is just the excuse for an event.

Late summer is frequently the Muslim month of Ramadan, in which observant adults fast during the day for 30 days. The month is considered a holy time during which Muslims should reflect on their lives and seek spiritual renewal. Food can be consumed after sundown. The month ends with a three-day celebration, Eid al-Fitr (usually referred to in the United States as Eid), consisting of visiting family and friends and feasting.

Fall

The autumn months have special occasions marking the end of the growing season and the coming winter. School begins, and families settle into routines of school lunches and after-school snacks. Historically, this was a time for harvest feasts, both informal social ones in which neighbors gathered to help with harvesting and celebrate afterwards, and official town and church celebrations of the bounty. Some towns in the Midwest and upstate New York still offer "thrashers' dinners."

Today, seasonal autumn festivals are found throughout the nation, particularly in agricultural areas, and tend to celebrate foods thought to be connected to the area's history. The Midwest seems to abound with these festivals. Apple festivals in Ohio and Indiana frequently refer to Johnny Appleseed, who traveled in those parts from 1800 until his death in 1845. Several towns hold festivals celebrating him and the apples he planted. An apple butter festival in Grand Rapids, Ohio grew out of a local family tradition of making apple butter with the leftovers from from their own orchard. Other festivals celebrate pumpkins (Circleville, Ohio, has one of the largest), corn, persimmons (Indiana), and any other food item that catches people's fancy.

Ethnic harvest celebrations are also common during this time, often offering an occasion to celebrate heritage and the season. These tend to occur wherever a large enough population has settled. A number of Asian cultures, for example, celebrate on the first full moon of autumn. Korean Chusok is usually in late August and features pastries made of rice flour.

Persimmons and pear-apples add to the seasonal foods. Similarly, the Chinese Mooncake Festival features steamed rice flour cakes and buns filled with nuts and fruits. German Americans throughout the Mid-Atlantic, eastern Midwest, and west Texas celebrate Oktoberfest in late September or early October. Originally a celebration of the marriage of a Bavarian prince in 1810, it has become a major ethnic and seasonal festival, usually involving much beer, iconic German American foods (e.g., sausages, pretzels), and polka music. One of the largest Oktoberfests in the United States (and possibly the world) is held in Deshler, Ohio.

Apple-butter stirrings are found in German American areas of the Mid-Atlantic and Midwest. These usually involve several days of peeling, coring, and chopping apples, and then several days of cooking the butter in special, large pots (preferably copper) over an outdoor fire. The apple butter, a Pennsylvania Dutch tradition, is then used as a spread on bread. Recipes in the Midwest usually call for boiling down cider before adding chopped apples, whereas apple butter in the South is made directly from apples (similar to a thick applesauce) and tends to not be a celebratory event. Pennsylvanians tend to put spices (cinnamon, cloves, fennel, and nutmeg) in their apple butter, and midwesterners prefer theirs plain or possibly with red-hots (a cinnamon candy) stirred in for sugar and color.

Sorghum molasses making was a tradition in southern Appalachia that tends to be found today at historical reenactments and festivals. Sorghum festivals are scattered throughout Kentucky, West Virginia, southern Ohio, and other states. They usually feature old-time crafts, music, and food—corn bread, beans, beef jerky, fried pies, kettle corn (popcorn with a sugar glaze), and homemade ice cream. Hog slaughterings were also a traditional festive but domestic event, particularly in the southern Appalachians and the Midwest where families would raise one or two hogs for their own use.

The Jewish New Year, Rosh Hashanah, occurs this time of year, falling between Labor Day and Columbus day according to the Jewish calendar. It is celebrated with a festive meal and wine. Several foods are important symbols and are eaten as ritual wishes for a good new year. Honey is particularly important since it represents sweetness and goodness. Challah (bread) that is baked in round shapes to symbolize perfection is dipped in honey, as are slices of apple. A fruit not yet tasted that season is eaten the second night of Rosh Hashanah as a reminder to be thankful for the bounty of nature. Pomegranate is a favorite choice. A fish head or gefilte fish symbolizes leadership by righteousness as well as prosperity and abundance. The meal might include rice, meat baked in honey, tzimmes (carrots baked in honey), the head of a lamb, spinach, and honey cakes. The foods eaten vary according to the individuals' seriousness about their symbolism as well as their region. Stores in those areas with higher Jewish populations tend to offer the necessary ingredients more than in regions with low populations. The holiday Yom Kippur falls nine days after the first day of Rosh Hashana. It is a day of atonement and repentance and is commemorated by fasting and attending a special service at synagogue.

Halloween, October 31, is celebrated nationally with trick-or-treating and parties serving Halloween candy, but it also is frequently connected to local harvest celebrations and regional traditions of social eating. Popcorn balls, candied apples, and homemade cookies are all typical treats in homes and at parties, and bobbing for apples in a bucket of water is a traditional game. Meals that day may feature pumpkin soup, chili, and party foods that fit the scary theme of the holiday, such as spaghetti, grapes as eyeballs, and Jell-O squiggles. Some households celebrate the Irish origins of the holiday by serving traditional Irish foods, *colcannon* (mashed potatoes with stewed cabbage) and soda bread. Many communities now encourage families to use only mass-produced commercial candies for trick-or-treating because of urban legends suggesting that homemade candies might be tampered with or poisoned. Stories of razor blades in apples add a dimension of fear to the ritual, and hospitals frequently offer free x-raying of candy on Halloween night.[2]

Hispanic communities in Texas and the Southwest celebrate the Mexican Day of the Dead (*Dia de los Muertos*) on November 2. A variety of tamales are served, including ones with a sweetened cheese filling, and a special sweet bread, *pan de muertos* that comes in different shapes, including skeletons, skulls, and round shapes represent the soul. Colored sugar is sprinkled on top. Sugar skulls and lollipops shaped like skeletons and skulls are also common, and families erect elaborate memorials (called altars) containing photographs, flowers, and favorite foods for those who died the previous year.

Italian Americans, particularly in the East Coast, have a similar tradition for All Souls' Day with special cookies called *fave dei morti* (beans of the dead) and *osso dei morti* (bones of the dead) with chunks of almonds. Sold in Italian bakeries in Italian American neighborhoods, the dry texture of these cookies makes them resemble bones.

Election Day, the second Tuesday in November, is not widely celebrated today; however, many towns still hold fundraisers and dinners that day. Hartford, Connecticut, is famous for its Election Day cake. Actually more like a sweet yeast bread, it is full of raisins, nuts, chopped citron, and spices and is served with coffee. Published recipes go back to 1800.

Thanksgiving is the only national holiday that revolves around a meal. The Thanksgiving dinner officially commemorates the survival of the Pilgrims at Plymouth Plantation, and the traditional dinner represents the mythical meal shared by Native Americans and Pilgrims—roast turkey, stuffing, mashed potatoes, gravy, rolls, pumpkin pie, cranberries, and vegetables—green beans, corn, carrots. Many of these foods have Native American origins and associations.[3] Norman Rockwell canonized the New England version of the meal in his 1942 painting, "Freedom from Want," but every region has its own variations on this national meal. Even New England, which has the standard quintessential meal, adds mashed squash, mashed turnips, and apple, pumpkin, and custard pies. The South prefers a corn bread–based dressing and usually adds pecans. Pecan pie and mince-meat (today, a spiced mixture of raisins and dried citron replaces the meat) are also on the standard southern menu. Sweet potato casseroles (mashed sweet potatoes baked with brown sugar and chopped fruit) are also favored. Southern meals tend to contrast with the New England meals in that the southern table tends to be laden with as many dishes as possible, and frequently, foods have been "fancied up" in some way—with sauces or additions, such as pecans added to brussel sprouts or slivered almonds tossed in with the green beans. Southerners also like to add apple salads (apple Waldorf is popular), ambrosia (fresh and canned fruits mixed with miniature marshmallows), and aspics (gelatin molds filled with shredded vegetables). Southern traditions of deep frying have also been applied to Thanksgiving dinner, and both Texas and Louisiana claim to have invented deep-fried turkeys.

The Midwest tends to follow the New England menu but green bean casserole; numerous sweet gelatin salads, including a cranberry relish mold of Jell-O, cranberries, pineapple, Mandarin orange slices, and pecans; and mashed sweet potatoes with a marshmallow toppings are frequently added. The typical Midwest white-bread stuffing might include sausage or oysters, although the upper Midwest might include a stuffing of wild rice. Sauerkraut is a common side dish in the German heritage areas, as well as in Baltimore. Pies tend to be slathered with canned whipped cream and are frequently made of berries or candy (e.g., peanut butter bars, chocolate chips).

Cooks in the Southwest frequently serve turkey mole, salsa, tortillas, and chili peppers. Californians offer more healthful versions of the traditional foods and include more salads. Generally, the farther west one goes, the more innovative the cooking is and the less tied to the traditional New England meal. California, for example, introduced the concept of smoking the whole turkey in a grill rather than roasting it. Grilled whole salmon may substitute for the turkey in parts of the Pacific Northwest and Alaska. Also, many families with strong ethnic backgrounds purposefully include a favorite ethnic dish with the meal—spaghetti or lasagna for Italians; stuffed cabbage for Eastern Europeans; and rice, stir-fry, and egg rolls (or some other iconic stuffed pastry) for Asians.

Winter

The Jewish holiday of Hanukkah (also spelled Chanukkah), the festival of lights, is one of the first winter celebrations. Because of its proximity to Christmas, it has become more important to many Jewish Americans than it actually is in the Jewish calendar. It commemorates a time in the ancient past in which the oil in a temple lantern was miraculously able to last for eight days instead of one. Menorahs of eight candles symbolize the eight days, with candles being ritually lit every night. Foods rich in oil are eaten, including potato latkes (pancakes) with applesauce. Also, children play with a special top, called a dreidel, and are given special coins (gelt) as a gift. Both items are now popular forms for cookies and candies specific to the holiday. The eight nights of Hanukkah are usually celebrated with family and friends and often include festive meals. The menus for these meals can vary according the each family's taste, history, and region.

Many winter holidays have religious connections to Christmas, but they also acknowledge the coming winter solstice (December 20 or 21) and the increasing lack of daylight and warmth. These natural themes strongly affect the activities and foods used to celebrate the religious holidays, which is not surprising as they are the historical origins of many of them.

St. Nicholas Day, December 6, is a northern European Catholic tradition found in many German heritage areas of the Midwest. On the eve of this day, children set out a shoe, and during the night St. Nicholas fills it with small presents and candies (which does not preclude a visit from Santa Claus later in the month). Another version in New York State among Dutch and Flemish Americans celebrates the day (*Sinterklass*) with ginger cookies called *speculaas* (often shaped into windmills or gingerbread men and spiced with a mixture of cinnamon, cloves, nutmeg, coriander, allspice, aniseed, ginger, cardamom, and mace).

A Swedish holiday, St. Lucia Day, December 13, is celebrated among Scandinavian Americans, particularly in the upper Midwest. Early in the morning on this day, the eldest daughter dresses in a white gown with a wreath of candles on her head to portray the Queen of Light and brings saffron-flavored buns, called *lussekatt*, and coffee to the older members of the family who are still sleeping. The buns are made from a sweet, yeast dough with an abundance of butter, eggs, and milk and include saffron threads. Currants may be added as well. This dough is then shaped into individual buns or braided wreaths and crowns. Public Santa Lucia celebrations take place wherever Swedish American communities are established (primarily the upper Midwest), but the holiday is also celebrated privately in homes across the United States.

Holiday or Christmas parties at homes, schools, and workplaces are common throughout the country, regardless of people's religious affiliations. Public institutions in urban areas and on the East and West coasts make a point of recognizing all the winter holidays during this season, and some federal and state offices do not observe any holidays to maintain separation of church and state. Regardless of what these parties are called, cookies and sweets are often featured, and they frequently reflect regional traditions. Southerners tend to include sugar-dusted pound cake, eggnog, and fruitcake full of pecans. Peppernuts (translated from the German name, pfefferneuse), hard, round cookies with a peppery taste and dusted with powdered sugar, are a tradition throughout the Mid-Atlantic and the Midwest where people of Eastern European descent have settled. In Utah, Scandinavian Mormons make pepper cookies that are actually flavored with ginger. Baked goods are a specialty of various immigrant groups in the Upper Midwest and are often given as gifts. Norwegians make *fattigman* (a crisp cookie sprinkled with confectioner's sugar); Germans, *kuchen* (coffee cake); and Swedes, coffee crescents. New Englanders of French Canadian descent often serve meat pies and a festive drink called *caribou*, a mixture of white whisky and red wine. Eggnog is a common drink during this time and is sold nationally. Of English heritage, it is a cold drink made of cream, sugar, and eggs flavored with vanilla and nutmeg. It can be served as is or various alcohols can be added—brandy, rum, bourbon, and sherry—to personal and regional taste. The southern preference is for peach brandy, rum, and whiskey. Also popular for gatherings are mulled cider (hot cider with cinnamon, cloves, and other spices), mulled wine, and hot toddies (a Scottish drink of whiskey, hot water, lemon, sugar, and spices that New Englanders favor, with rum or brandy replacing the whiskey.

The tradition of decorating a fir tree for Christmas was brought from Germany to the United States in the later 1800s. Many German Americans, particularly in the Midwest and Mid-Atlantic, still decorate their Christmas trees with cookies, such as *pfefferneusse* and *lebkuchen*. Some still wait to put up the tree on Christmas Eve, loading it with cookies and small presents for the children. German traditions of marzipan (almond paste confection) in shape of fruits and animals, stollen (fruit cakes usually with an icing), gingerbread houses, and spice cakes and cookies are still common in German ethnic heritage areas, particularly Pennsylvania and Ohio. An unusual German tradition that seems to be practiced only in a few places in the upper Midwest is a large tree-shaped cake called *baumkuchen*,

Christmas caroling is a national tradition that probably has roots in wassailing in England; it is still found in the South and parts of the Midwest. Groups, oftentimes sponsored by a church or simply a group of friends, go out knocking on doors and singing carols to neighbors. A party usually ensues, with eggnog, mulled cider and wine, and Christmas cookies.

A distinctive regional tradition of Mexican Americans in the Southwest is the Posada, a ritual performance reenacting Mary and Joseph's search for shelter at Christmas. Food given to the participants includes specialties of the season, such as cheese (soft white cheese)-filled tamales, posole, hot chocolate, and coffee. Sante Fe, New Mexico, offers *bizcochitos*, unique cookies with toasted aniseed and cinnamon, flavored with orange juice or brandy, and often formed into the shape of a fleur-de-lis.

Christmas Eve dinners are traditions among a number of ethnic communities in different regions. Italian traditions of *la Vigilia* (the vigil), the "feast of the seven fishes" are found in Italian families throughout urban New England, the Mid-Atlantic, and the Far West. This meal has no meat but includes dishes made of various combinations of anchovies, smelt, salt cod, squid, octopus, clams, mussels, shrimp, eels, and sardines served along with pasta, bread, vegetables (kale patties), and wine. Hungarian Americans in the Midwest and Mid-Atlantic also have a meatless meal featuring fish and potatoes, and Russian Americans in the Pacific Northwest have a traditional dinner featuring 12 meatless dishes. German Americans have a similar tradition of eating carp on Christmas Eve.

Polish families in the Mid-Atlantic and Midwest often have a meatless meal for Christmas Eve called a *wigilia*. This is a solemn but festive family ritual in which family unity is celebrated through the passing around of the *oplatky*, a thin, wafer-like cracker stamped with pictures of the holy family. The traditional menu is mushroom barley soup, boiled potatoes (*kartofle*), pickled herring (*sledzie*), fried fish, baked carp, pierogi, beans and sauerkraut (*groch i kapusta*), a dried fruit compote, *babka, platek*, assorted pastries, nuts, and candies. Especially popular is a rolled cake filled with black poppy seeds, honey, raisins, and almonds. Norwegians in the upper Midwest celebrate with *lutefisk*, boiled dried salt cod served with a white sauce and boiled potatoes, a dish that is said to be a test of true Norwegian-ness. For good luck, many Scandinavians in the upper Midwest and Pacific Northwest serve a rice porridge flavored by sugar and cinnamon with one almond in it.

The Catholic tradition of not eating until after Midnight mass is still prevalent in some regions that have strong cultural identities connected to the religion, particularly the Northeast, Mid-Atlantic, and parts of the Midwest with strong ethnic enclaves. Cajuns in Louisiana, for example, eat *tourtire* (a pork pie) after mass.

Christmas dinner is often a large family gathering with a formal dinner. Although roast turkey is common nationally, ham tends to be favored in the South. Goose stuffed with chestnuts, onions, or potatoes harkens back to British tradition and is still found in New England as well as in some European immigrant traditions. Scandinavians in the upper Midwest have a Christmas goose, or the roast pork or ham with sauerkraut or red cabbage that is common with many Central and Eastern European ethnic

Americans. German Americans in the Mid-Atlantic and Midwest prefer goose roasted with apples and nuts. Hungarian and Czech Americans in the Midwest and western mountain states serve roast goose and sauerkraut with stuffed cabbage (cabbage leaves wrapped around a rice and ground meat mixture), barley mushroom soup, carp, and *kolaches* (yeast buns filled with poppy seeds or fruit, traditionally, prunes or apricots). Supermarkets throughout the Midwest and Mid-Atlantic sell *kolaches* and other poppy seed and nut pastries. Borscht soups made of beets and cabbage are frequently part of Christmas dinner in Russian-influenced areas of the Pacific Northwest. Cajun dinners in Louisiana might include meat pies, showing the French influence. Similarly, in New England, French heritage is reflected in *cretos* (pork pâté), meat pies, and Yule log cakes. The Southwest's Mexican heritage shows up in the tamales that are given as gifts or featured for Christmas gatherings. These often have special festive fillings of cheese and jalapeño peppers or honey-sweetened cheese.

Tourtiere (French Canadian Meat Pie)

This pie is eaten in western Massachusetts for New Year's Day.

Pie pastry	1/4 teaspoon nutmeg
1 pound ground pork	1/4 teaspoon mace
1 pound ground veal	1/4 teaspoon salt
6 slices bacon, chopped	1/4 teaspoon pepper
1/2 cup onion, chopped	1 1/4 cup water
1/2 cup celery, chopped	2 tablespoons cornstarch
1 clove garlic, minced	

1. Brown all the meats.
2. Drain off fat and add vegetables and spices.
3. Add 1 cup of water and bring to a boil. Reduce and simmer 10–15 minutes, stirring frequently.
4. Combine cornstarch with 1/4 cup water. Add to meat-vegetable mixture. Cook 2 minutes more until thick.
5. Place pastry in 9-inch pie dish. Fill with slightly cooled meat mixture. Top with remaining crust and seal edges.
6. Bake in preheated 400°F oven for 25–30 minutes.

Kwanzaa is an African American holiday starting December 26 and lasting a week. Invented in 1966 in California in order to celebrate African heritage, it features the first fruits of the harvest and seven principles thought to be integral to African identity. It often ends with a feast highlighting foods believed to represent African culture and the African American experience. It quickly spread to urban areas with large African American populations and is popular today in most cities.

Life Cycle Events

Special occasions for celebrating an individual's passage through life can be private or public. They often include celebratory foods, but the specific foods tend to relate more to ethnicity and religion than to region, although regional specialties might be included in the celebratory meal.

These life cycle events begin with birth and end with death. Birth, baptism, or christening are not associated with special foods, but birthdays are expected to be celebrated with a cake. Fried ice cream is frequently served at Mexican American restaurants for birthdays.

Coming of age events tend to be more regional. The Hispanic Southwest and pockets of Hispanic Americans throughout the United States hold elaborate parties for a girl's fifteenth birthday. Called a *Quinceañero*, these events often include lavish feasts of Mexican American as well as American foods. Similarly, some families of the "Old South" host debutante balls for the "coming out" of their daughters when they reach their teen years and are ready to be introduced to society. These also feature refined and festive foods. Jewish teenagers can choose to participate in a *bar mitzvah* (*bat mitzvah* for girls). These usually include a festive meal afterwards. Catholic confirmations, though not as elaborate, are often celebrated with cake and possibly a meal. High school graduations also serve a similar function as a rite of passage for children moving into adulthood. These are often celebrated with parties and party foods and large communal foods, such as chili, barbecue, clambakes, or salmon bakes.

Weddings, anniversaries, retirements, and other personal rites generally do not vary by region. Funerals, however, are frequently acknowledged in the South with a funeral supper and in the Midwest with a hot-dish potluck meal.

COMMUNITY CELEBRATIONS

Communal food events occur throughout the year and throughout the country and are often named for the foods they feature. They often have a regional flavor, reflecting different resources and settlement histories, and are characterized by large amounts of food, often large, one-pot meals. They function in a variety of ways—as affirmation of a community, as social gatherings, as celebrations of an ethnic heritage, as a marketing ploy of a town or local industry, and even as fund-raisers.

Many of the foods featured are also iconic of the region. For example, Kentucky offers burgoo, and the Piedmont and coastal South boast of Brunswick stew. Both are frequently made at outdoor community celebrations in large iron kettles. Brunswick counties in Virginia, North Carolina, and Georgia claim Brunswick stew. It has to have at least two types of meat (historically it would have been game, such as squirrel, but now is chicken, and pork), with corn, lima beans, tomatoes, and potatoes, seasoned with salt and pepper. Burgoo is a Kentucky specialty similar to Brunswick stew. It also historically included squirrel, but now uses chicken and beef, or mutton, stewed with cabbage, potatoes, green peppers, celery, carrots, corn, and okra. It is usually served during the Kentucky Derby.

Burgoo

This stew is normally made for large groups of people. The first amount makes 40 gallons; the second one feeds a smaller group.

1 pound (25 pounds) mixed cooked meats (beef, lamb, mutton, pork, chicken, squirrel, or other game. If meat is not cooked, first brown it before adding it to the burgoo.)

$1/2$ gallon (5 gallons) chicken stock

$1/2$ gallon (5 gallons) beef stock

1 cup (8 gallons) tomatoes, diced or stewed

1 large (3 gallons) onion, diced

1 stalk (4 bunches) celery, diced

1 small (4 large) green bell pepper, diced

1 large (1 bushel/60 pounds) potato, diced

2 large (3 gallons) carrots, diced

$1/4$ head (8 gallons) cabbage

$1/4$ cup (4 cups) peas

$1/2$ cup (7 cups) okra

$1/4$ cup (4 cups) lima beans

$1/2$ cup (7 cups) yellow corn

2 teaspoons (4 tablespoons) garlic, minced

2 teaspoons (4 tablespoons) paprika

1 ounce Worcestershire sauce (optional)

salt and pepper to taste

1. Combine all ingredients. Simmer for two hours until thick enough to stand a spoon in.

Serve with corn bread or buttermilk biscuits.

A Cajun crawfish boil in southern Louisiana is a frequent way for the community to gather and celebrate together. Courtesy of Nicholas R. Spitzer.

Every region seems to have its specialty communal food. Chili (all meat) is particularly popular in Texas as well as in the eastern Midwest (usually with meat and beans). Iowa has "loose meat" (boiled ground beef similar to a sloppy Joe) and northwest Ohio offers hot chicken sandwiches (canned, shredded chicken cooked in a gravy and served on a bun). Jambalaya and gumbo are common in Louisiana, and New England offers bean suppers. New England also boasts of clambakes (clams and lobsters steamed in a pit along with potatoes, corn, and other ingredients), whereas Wisconsin has fish boils (boiled white fish and white potatoes covered with melted butter and served with bread and cold slaw), Maryland has crab boils, Louisiana has crawfish boils, and the Northwest has quahog clam suppers and salmon bakes. Pit barbecue, in which a whole pig or cow is slow cooked in a metal drum or brick pit, is popular throughout the South, and different regions and makers compete with distinctive sauces. Vinegar-based sauces tend to be more in the southeastern states and are often associated with white southern cuisine, whereas tomato-based sauces tend to be found closer to the Mississippi River and are associated with African American cooking. Kansas City is also famous for its barbecue. A Hispanic variation in the Southwest is *barbecoa*, in which the head of an animal is slow cooked with spices. The eastern Midwest also slow cooks whole pigs, but refers to the events as hog roasts.

An annual gathering at a Pittsburgh amusement park celebrates Croatian heritage with traditional foods. Courtesy of the author.

Fish fries are commonly hosted during the Lenten season by Catholic churches but are also standard fund-raisers for civic organizations, particularly in areas with plentiful fishing waters. Typically, fish fillets are battered and deep-fried and served with fried potatoes, cold slaw, baked beans and desserts. Pie suppers are popular in the Midwest and New England, where many individuals pride themselves on their ability to produce a perfect crust.

NOTES

1. William Wan, "Forget the Big Apple—Drop a Peach," *The Washington Post*, December 31, 2008, A1, A6.

2. Russell W. Belk, "Carnival, Control, and Corporate Culture in Contemporary Halloween Celebrations," in *Halloween and Other Festivals of Death and Life*, ed. Jack Santino, 105–132 (Knoxville: The University of Tennessee Press, 1994).

3. The meanings of Thanksgiving and the typical menu are very problematic. One interpretation sees it as a "consumption" of Native American lands and peoples. Janet Siskind, "The Invention of Thanksgiving: A Ritual of American Nationality," in *Food in the USA: A Reader*, ed. Carole Counihan, 41–58 (New York: Routledge).

7

Diet and Health

American food today is often characterized as being unhealthy, with more attention paid to quantity or calorie counting than to taste and actual nutritional quality. Americans like lots of sugar, fat, and grease and tend to eat them all day long—and into the night, too. Many of the practices surrounding eating are also perceived as unhealthy. Family meals seem to be few and far between. People often eat on the go or in front of the television set, consuming too much and too often. Although these attitudes are currently changing, the diets of many Americans emphasize commercially processed foods that have little connection to the place they live or to the natural seasons. Instead of giving spiritual, social, and emotional nourishment, food is frequently a source of anxiety in its effects on bodily appearance, efficiency, and pocket books.

Americans vary enormously, however, in their eating habits, and these variations reflect class, religion, ethnicity, gender, education, and region. Not all Americans eat in the unhealthy way portrayed in the stereotypes. Furthermore, American eating habits cannot be blamed simply on greed, laziness, or ignorance—although those qualities definitely exist. Concepts of diet and health are tied into a culture's underlying attitudes and ways of seeing the world. The phrase "food ethos" refers to a culture's worldview surrounding food—what should or should not be eaten, what moral or social values are placed on food in general, where food fits into the larger economic system, and how people and food fit into the world. Food aesthetic refers to a culture's way of evaluating the quality and tastiness of food.

(For example, one culture might appreciate fishy tastes, but others may find such tastes disgusting.)

Although the various regions share a common national ethos and mass-mediated culinary culture surrounding diet and health, they also put their own slant on those practices, reflecting different histories and resources. New England, for example, is representative of the national ethos, especially as it is the mythic foundation of American culture. Although New England is now as varied as any other region and has a rich immigrant culture, its food-way is still characterized by frugality and austerity. These beliefs led to an aus-tere and frugal diet among the early settlers, and this view carries over to food in that region today. The strong British culinary heritage in that region also tended to de-emphasize food as an aesthetic and social experience.

The culinary ethos of New England contrasts vividly with that of the Mid-Atlantic states and coastal South, where business interests rather than religion seemed to dominate settlement history, and historical ties with France are reflected today in many of the dishes and culinary customs.[1] Sim-ilarly, Charleston, South Carolina, a bastion of French American culture in the Southeast, developed a distinctive and sophisticated cuisine that is still celebrated today. Midwestern food on the whole reflects both New England austerity and a pioneer sensibility that depends on pragmatic, hands-on skills to survive. Midwestern food is also pragmatic—in the past, food needed to fill midwesterners quickly and efficiently—so they could get on with the job of settling the land. This attitude is still prevalent in the Mid-west, where the food is characterized as straightforward and hearty, and the larger the portion size, the better.

Also prevalent in the Midwest is scientific farming, in which the farmer attempts to tame the land through science (e.g., machinery, chemicals) and cultivates crops for specific sectors of the food industry. These practices reflect philosophies tracing back to French writer René Descartes who sug-gested that there is a division between the mind and the body, and civilized people need to cultivate the mind. Furthermore, the entire universe works according to logical rules that could be understood and used by humans. This scientific reductionism presented a mechanistic view of the universe, in which everything acts according to logical formulas, including aesthetics and spirituality.

Although American agriculture as a whole has gone in this mechanistic direction, it seems to have been done so for different reason is different pla-ces. California, one of the leaders in scientific farming, tends to be forward looking, valuing innovation and originality and having very little concern for the past. In contrast, the Midwest values tradition and the past and tends to view scientific farming as consistent with classic American values of per-sonal integrity, good business sense, and practicality.

The South never quite seemed to embrace the philosophies prevalent in the Midwest and North, possibly because of its own colonial status (relative to the North), the specific ethnicities and classes settling the region, or the influence of African American culture. Tradition has always been important in Southern culture. The past is seen as the basis for the present, and maintaining memories is valued. Southerners tend to recognize the power of food to carry memory, and family recipes are treasured.

The South is also famous for its hospitality.[2] Throughout the region, cooks tend to make more than enough so that dishes can stretch to serve one more, and a hostess or host would be remiss if any guests were to leave the table hungry. Even strangers are welcome to share meals. Festive meals, particularly, are generous with numerous dishes and many of these are "fancied up" in some way (e.g., sauces, seasonings, nuts).

Resourcefulness in food is also appreciated throughout the South, but particularly in African American communities and in the mountains. A common saying is that when a pig is butchered, everything is used except for the squeal. (Amish and rural Midwesterners also claim this saying.) Gathering foods from the wild (e.g., berries, greens, nuts, and game) is expected, and recycling of foods is assumed. Leftovers are often left on a counter for snacks for later in the day. Other regions claim resourcefulness in their traditional foodways as well. New England views it as part of being frugal, and the Midwest portrays it as part of their practical, pioneer character.

Other features of Americanness are performed through food as well. The rugged individualism of American society is translated into a valuing of personal choice. Contemporary advertising plays upon that idea, often selling mass-produced foods as flexible according to the individual. Burger King proclaims "have it your way" for its marketing campaign slogan. That individualism can be seen in the food habits of the far West, where innovation and originality are also highly prized.

The Puritanism and Protestant work ethic of the eastern United States was carried west by settlers, but the Hispanic and Catholic foundation of southwestern culture set a different stage for attitudes toward food. In the West there tends to be more recognition and acceptance of the physical sensuality and pleasure of food and eating. This is even celebrated in feast days and in literature. The far West, similarly, is further removed from the Puritan ethos, and California has always had a reputation of hedonism and epicureanism—reveling in the glories of good food.

HEALTH ISSUES

Food has always been linked closely to health issues in the United States, and today's diet tends to be questionable. Many blame the fast-food industry, with its inexpensive, quick, and easily available but high-calorie foods; however, numerous other factors have led to a more sedentary lifestyle and less wholesome eating habits and foods. A national taste for fried and deep-fried foods also contributes to health issues. According to 2007 statistics, Colorado has the lowest prevalence of obesity (less than 20 percent), while Alabama, Mississippi and Tennessee have the highest (greater than 30 percent). Overall, the United States has seen a huge increase in obesity over the past 20 years.[3] Other lifestyle factors (e.g., smoking, inactivity, environmental pollution) as well as a genetic predilection toward certain diseases have created a huge surge in the number of conditions related to obesity, particularly hypertension and diabetes.[4]

The regions that are still heavily agricultural, such as much of the Midwest, tend to think of healthy food in terms of food that fills one up and contains lots of protein and carbohydrates. The traditional meat-and-potato diet, with lots of salt and butter but few other spices, tends to be seen as the healthiest. Vegetables tend to be cooked and served with cheese sauce or eaten raw with dips, and salads tend to consist of iceberg lettuce, mayonnaise-based mixtures of meats and vegetables, or Jell-O. Although this hearty diet may have kept pioneer farmers fueled for the day, it now raises numerous medical concerns over cardiovascular diseases and conditions related to obesity, such as diabetes. Fish from the plentiful local rivers and lakes is also a significant part of midwestern foodways, but it is often deep fried and served with rich sauces.

The South suffers from similar health concerns as the Midwest, but the issues there tend to stem from cooking styles as well as content. The heavy reliance on frying, often in bacon grease or lard, is unhealthy and can lead to heart disease. In the Appalachian region, foods are often flavored with bacon grease, so that even the normally healthy greens (e.g., collards, kale, turnip greens) carry health dangers. Historically, poverty and lack of transportation meant that many poor Southerners depended on corn as a staple of meals. Corn, however, lacks niacin, a B vitamin that is vital for human health. Its absence leads to a number of physical ailments as well as depression. Eventually, it can cause death. Interestingly, a form of niacin can be released from corn if the corn is soaked in a lye solution, as was done by Native Americans to make hominy (posole). The Appalachian adoption of hominy actually kept most mountain residents from suffering from pellegra even though many of them were poor and depended heavily upon corn in the diets. Vitamin B is now added to many commercial products, so pellegra is no longer a concern in the South. Unfortunately, soft, white bread made from refined wheat has tended to replace cornbread as an accompaniment to every meal, and this bread poses other health problems. Another unhealthy substitution seen particularly in the mountain area is processed meats replacing country ham and home-raised and home-cured meats. Processing tends to add large amounts of salt, sugar, and nitrates, none of which are considered healthy.

Rural, agricultural areas of the East Coast tend to suffer from the same health issues plaguing the rest of the country. In contrast, many urban areas actually offer more opportunities for walking, access to more variety of cuisines and fresh produce, and more awareness and attention to health than are found in some rural areas. Lower-income urban areas throughout the country, however, usually suffer from a lack of access to reasonably priced, high-quality food and, often, have a culture of snacking and reliance on pre-prepared, highly processed foods.

The Southwest combines Anglo pioneer food traditions with Native American and Hispanic traditions featuring diets of beans, tortillas, and peppers with significant amounts of lard. An interesting discovery is that many southwestern Indians ate a traditional diet (heavy on corn and beans supplemented by cacti and desert game) that was well suited to the local climate and land, and it was their adoption of Anglo food habits that had extremely negative health consequences.[5]

The West Coast tends to have the healthiest food culture in the country. Residents of the mountain states of the Far West as well as the Northwest (including Alaska) share the usual American taste for processed and fried foods and have obesity issues, but they also tend to be more physically active and have a vital outdoors culture of working and recreation. The Pacific Northwest also has a strong culture of eating fish and other seafood, and these are traditionally grilled (preferably on cedar planks) rather than fried. In addition, some cities in the Northwest have also purposefully created healthier environments by promoting walking, public transportation, and farmers' markets.

California, meanwhile, has long promoted a lifestyle full of exercise and healthy eating, not only for personal health but also for maintaining a particular norm for beauty. Slim and trim bodies are part of the California beach culture and Hollywood image. The region also leads the nation in valuing local and organic food production. California cuisine promotes fresh and often unusual vegetables and fruits, including salads as main dishes, a concept now common throughout the United States. California also leads the way in accepting healthier cooking styles and dishes from non–Anglo American cuisines, including grilling, stir-frying, and smoking a wide variety of vegetables and fish. Along with Vermont, the state also promoted vegetarian foods, such as tofu.

Hawaii and Alaska contrast with the West Coast in eating healthily. This may be partly a reflection of native approaches to physical beauty that value large bodies. The traditional diets that produced those types of bodies, however, have been substituted with processed foods that are full of unhealthy fats and sugars.

In general, however, obesity is often perceived as resulting from a lack of self-control and discipline and therefore a reflection of a flawed personality. More stigma seems to be attached to obesity on each coast, but there it is frequently associated with the lower classes. Dieting—that is, following a strict regimen of eating in order to control body weight—seems to be a national American pastime that is usually not specific to regions. One of the most popular diet programs is Weight Watchers, an organization started in 1963 by a housewife in Queens, New York, that offers a supportive group for dieters. Weight Watchers International is now a giant company that owns its own line of food products and oversees the support groups.

The Atkins Diet, developed in the 1970s by Dr. Robert Atkins, who was born and raised in Ohio, but practiced medicine in New York City, was extremely popular throughout the country from 2002 to 2005. Promoting a diet high in fat and protein but low in carbohydrates, it was especially embraced by those regions that tended to rely traditionally on a heavy meat diet. A variation on the Atkins Diet was then developed that had a more regional association, the South Beach Diet. Started in Miami, Florida, in the 1980s by a cardiologist, the plan focused on "bad fats" and "bad carbohydrates" but offered a more varied menu than the Atkins diet. Meanwhile, Californians promoted the Mediterranean diet, based on the traditional foods of the Mediterranean, which had a heavy reliance on olive oil, fresh vegetables, and fish. The famous diet movements of the 1800s that were based in western Michigan and lead to the establishment of the cereal industry seem to have left little legacy.

Gender differences in eating are probably not regional at this point, although more conservative areas tend to have more conservative gender roles. The stereotype is that women eat more daintily, consuming more salads, and lighter food in general, whereas men eat more meat and are expected to have hearty appetites. Historically, women have been more concerned with maintaining specific body weights; however, it is now common to hear the same concerns from men. Eating disorders, such as anorexia and bulimia, are also a national concern. Although in the past these conditions were considered adolescent, female problems, they are becoming more common among males as well, particularly on the coasts, where attention to achieving perfect bodies seems to be most prevalent.

ATTITUDES TOWARD ALCOHOL AND ALCOHOLISM

Americans tend to have ambivalent attitudes toward alcohol that vary widely by region as well as ethnicity, religion, and socioeconomic class.

Historically, the Puritan foundation of American culture tends to show up in negative attitudes toward drinking and overindulging in alcohol, although it is often more of an issue in those regions that attach moral significance to alcohol. The legal drinking age across the country is 21, which often means that obtaining and consuming alcohol becomes a way to rebel, bond with peers, and assert one's independence. Practical concerns about alcohol point to the dangers of drinking and driving as well as to illnesses stemming from chronic abuse. States with the highest incidence of alcohol-related deaths are Alaska, the District of Columbia, New Mexico, Nevada, and North Carolina. States with the lowest incidence of alcohol-related problems include Hawaii, Iowa, Minnesota, and Nebraska.[6]

Although attitudes are changing, the South generally views alcohol negatively and ties the avoidance of alcohol to religious commitment and being a churchgoer. Public drunkenness is seen as a sign of low social class, bad upbringing, and lack of character. In contrast, a joke calling Episcopalians "Whiskypalians" reflects the class distinctions related to different Protestant denominations as well as the differing attitudes toward alcohol held by different denominations. These attitudes even translate into the use of grape juice in place of wine for communion in many Protestant churches.

Even though Kentucky is celebrated for its bourbon, overindulgence in moonshine (corn whiskey) made in home stills and cheap, fruit wines is often looked upon as shameful. On the other hand, New Orleans has always stood out for its looser attitudes toward alcohol, especially during Mardi Gras and on its notorious Bourbon Street, a street that even today is lined with bars, restaurants, and girlie shows. (The entire French Quarter in the city has a reputation based on Bourbon Street, and every morning trucks wash the results of the previous night's overindulgence in alcohol from the streets.) To combat the hangover the next day, a typical New Orleans "cure" is oysters mixed with Tabasco sauce, tomato juice, and vodka. A similar concoction in the prairie states is made with raw egg instead of oysters and is called "prairie oyster."

In contrast, New England, where the Puritans once held sway, has a tradition of British ales and spirits. Irish pubs are common as community meeting spaces, and even the most upstanding housewife and mother might enjoy a nightcap of brandy or wine.

California similarly has a long history of wine production as well as a more liberal attitude toward alcohol, so that wine is a standard part of family meals (as it is in Europe). As one of the prime producers of wine in the United States, wine is a key part of California's identity. Parts of the Midwest (the areas surrounding Lake Erie and Lake Michigan) have a history of wine making as well, but in general, the Midwest is better known for its German-style beer tradition, which in the past was part of family meals and socializing. There, overindulgence of alcohol is celebrated as part of certain ethnic heritages, particularly German, Eastern European, and Irish. The Pacific Northwest is famous for its specialty breweries, and, like California, tends to not attach morality to drinking.

The far West still carries an image left over from its Wild West days where cowboys drank shots of whiskey in the town saloon. A traditional hangover cure is rumored to be a drink of hot water with droppings from jackrabbits.

The Southwest's large Hispanic population enjoys a variety of Mexican alcoholic drinks, particularly, the margarita and tequila. They also commonly use a native soup, menudo, made of tripe, hominy, and chili peppers, as a traditional hangover cure.

Native American populations, particularly those living on reservations in the far West, generally have high rates of alcoholism. The disruption to their traditional cultures created by their forced removals from their lands in the 1830s has never fully healed, and numerous social factors have created an unhealthy environment, both psychologically and medically. Some scholars believe Native Americans are biologically unable to deal with alcohol.[7]

FOOD AND ILLNESS

Chicken soup seems to be a universal home remedy for colds or flu. Hot peppers or chili paste often serve the same purpose in the Southwest and are considered good for the heart and blood pressure. Being able to stand the heat of such hot foods is a sign of masculinity.

The Appalachian region is known for home remedies, such as molasses to "strengthen the blood" if someone is "peaked," or teas and poultices from various herbs, leaves, and roots. Ginseng (called "sang") is still gathered in remote mountain areas (e.g., in North Carolina, Kentucky, and West Virginia) and used to revitalize, although much of it is sold and not kept for home use. Homemade moonshine is also used as a cold medicine—or a cure for "whatever ails you."

In rural areas in the mountains of both the Northeast and South, fresh greens are traditionally eaten in the springtime to "cleanse the blood," and to rid the body of the sluggishness of winter. Wild dandelion greens are also a favorite cure.

NOTES

1. Strong ties with France historically encouraged an interest in the enjoyment of food, and famous epicureans such as Benjamin Franklin (in Philadelphia) and

Thomas Jefferson (in central Virginia) had no qualms about appreciating high-quality food. Jefferson used his Monticello estate to experiment with new crops, growing techniques, and culinary innovations, many of which came from France.

2. It is possible that these customs can be traced to the Irish rules of Brehon, in which welcoming guests to meals was a political and economic obligation, not just a social nicety.

3. Center for Disease Control and Prevention, "U.S. Obesity Trends 1985–2007," www.cdc.gov/nccdphp/dnpa/obesity/trend/maps/index.htm.

4. "Cardiovascular Disease Risk Factors and Preventative Practices Among Adults – United States, 1994: A Behavioral Risk Factor Atlas," *MMWR Surveillance Summaries*, December 11, 1998, 47(SS-5); 35–69. www.cdc.gov/mmwr/preview/mmwrhtml/00055888.htm.

5. Christiana E. Miewald, "The Nutritional Impact of European Contact on the Omaha: A Continuing Legacy," in *Food in the USA: A Reader*, ed. Carole M. Counihan, 109–122 (New York: Routledge, 2002). Gary Paul Nabhan, "Diabetes, Diet, and Native American Foraging Traditions," in Counihan, 231–238 (2002).

6. M. Fe Caces, Frederick S. Stinson, Steven D. Elliott, John A. Noble "Comparative Alcohol-Related Mortality Statistics in the United States by State, 1979–1985," *Alcohol Health and Research World* 15 (Spring 1991): 6. http://findarticles.com/p/articles/mi_m0847/is_n2_v15/ai_12490671/pg_1?tag=artBody;col1.

7. William J. Szlemko, James W. Wood, and Pamela Jumper Thurman, "Native Americans and Alcohol: Past, Present, and Future (Clinical report)," *Journal of General Psychology* 130 (October 1, 2006), no. 4: 435–451. www.encyclopedia.com/doc/1G1-154391007.html.

Glossary

aguduk   Eskimo ice cream. Whipped seal oil mixed with snow berries, roots, and salmon or caribou jerky. Also called *agaduk, akutaq,* or *akudaq.*

aubergine   The French word for eggplant.

barbecoa   Southwestern Hispanic tradition in which the head of an animal is slow cooked, frequently in a pit with charcoal.

Baumkuchen   A layered cake of German origin known as the "king of cakes." The name translates to tree cake, and it gets its name from the many rings that form as the cake is baked; it is typically found in the upper Midwest.

bear claw   Fried dough sprinkled with sugar; found on the West Coast.

beignet   Fried dough, usually sprinkled with sugar, traditional in New Orleans and in Charleston, South Carolina.

benne   African word for sesame seeds.

bizcochito   A cookie unique to Sante Fe, New Mexico.

blini   Buckwheat pancakes topped with butter, jam, sour cream, smoked salmon, or caviar; traditional to Russian Americans in the Pacific Northwest.

burgoo   Kentucky stew usually made for community gatherings. The recipe varies widely, but it always includes a mixture of meats (wild game, poultry, beef, pork, and mutton), vegetables (lima beans, corn, potatoes, okra, celery, tomato, and cabbage), and spices (salt, pepper, cinnamon, nutmeg, and hot sauce).

chitlins/chitterlings   Pig intestines; a soul food tradition.

chowchow   A pepper relish found in the South.

comal   Special griddle used for making tortillas in Mexican American foodways.

fajita   Tex-Mex tradition of marinating and grilling a particular cut of beef and wrapping it in tortillas; the method has been popularized for any grilled ingredient (e.g., chicken, shrimp, vegetables).

Fasnacht   Type of doughnut made by Pennsylvania Germans to celebrate Shrove or Fat Tuesday (Fasnacht Day), the day before Lent begins.

filé   Powder made from sassafras leaves and used as a thickener in Gulf Coast gumbos.

fishy duck   A wild duck that lived off of fish so that its flesh developed a fishy flavor; traditionally consumed by Native Americans in the Pacific Northwest.

fry bread   Native American flat bread originating in the Southwest and now common in Native American foodways.

funnel cake   Fried dough sprinkled with sugar; traditional in Pennsylvania.

geoduck   A type of giant clam found in the Pacific Northwest.

grits   Ground hominy, eaten throughout the South.

gumbo   Traditional stew usually containing seafood, rice, and okra thickened with sassafras leaves powder (filé), traditional in Louisiana and other Gulf Coast areas.

haggis   Scottish meatloaf-like pudding made of oatmeal, chopped liver (lamb or beef), and other ingredients (beef suet, beef heart, lamb shoulder, whiskey) steamed inside a cow's bladder or sheep's stomach; traditional for the Scottish celebration of Burns' Night, commemorating poet Robert Burns.

hominy   Corn kernels soaked in lye so that the husk dissolves and the kernel expands.

Jigg's dinner   A stereotypical Irish American meal of corned beef, boiled cabbage, potatoes, and soda bread.

kolache   Yeast bun filled with poppy seeds or fruit (traditionally, prunes or apricots) among Czech and Slovak Americans. The word has many variants in spelling (e.g., *kolachky*) and covers a range of breads and pastries.

kuchen   German coffee cake.

kulich   Tall, round cake made for Easter by Russian Americans in the Pacific Northwest.

leather britches   Strings of dried green beans typically found in southern Appalachia; they probably came from Cherokee traditions.

lussekatt   Saffron-flavored buns prepared for St. Lucia Day on December 13; this Swedish holiday is commonly celebrated in the upper Midwest.

lutefisk   Dried cod dish traditionally consumed by Norwegian Americans in the upper Midwest.

marzipan   Almond paste used for cakes and confections in German American foodways.

masa/masa harina   Cornmeal in Hispanic foodways, particularly found in the Southwest.

massa sovada A sweet bread used in the Portuguese Holy Ghost Festival in coastal Massachusetts, which takes place one week after Easter.

matzo Unleavened bread, similar to crackers, used in the Jewish holiday of Passover and used with a number of foods.

menudo Traditional Southwestern Hispanic stew featuring tripe and chili peppers.

mochi Japanese rice cake, often filled with bean paste.

muktuk Raw whale skin with blubber, traditionally eaten by Native peoples of Alaska.

muscadine Grape native to the Southeast.

nopalito A dish made of the nopal cactus pad that is eaten in the Southwest in Hispanic and Native American foodways.

oolichan grease Oil made from fermented oolichan fish. Used as a sauce by Native Americans in the Pacific Northwest.

paczki Filled, sweet, fried dough traditionally served by Polish Americans for Shrove or Fat Tuesday.

pan de muertos Sweet bread for Mexican American Day of the Dead.

paschal lamb Lamb-shaped butter or sugar prepared by Eastern European immigrants for Easter.

pascha Ukrainian egg bread served for Easter andtraditionally decorated with a cross.

paska Pyramid of cheese, cream, butter, eggs, sugar, and candied fruits traditional for Easter among Slovak Americans.

piñon Pine nuts.

poi Hawaiian paste made from taro root.

poke Wild green eaten in the Southeast and southern Appalachians. Also known as pokeweed or poke sallet.

poke Hawaiian dish of raw fish, seaweed, salt, and other ingredients.

posole Traditional Southwestern stew of hominy, pork, and chili peppers.

Quinceañera Hispanic tradition of celebrating a girl's 15th birthday.

ramp Wild onion gathered and eaten in southern Appalachia.

scuppernong Grape native to the Southeast.

shoofly pie Pennsylvania German pie made of molasses.

soda bread Irish American quick bread leavened with baking soda.

sofk Florida Seminole Indian drink made from roasted corn.

sopapilla Mexican American fried dough sprinkled with sugar.

speculaa Ginger cookie often shaped into windmills or gingerbread men, traditional in New York State among Dutch and Flemish Americans.

squaw candy   Salmon jerkey or thin strips of sun-dried salmon sweetened with honey, and traditional to the Native Americans of the Pacific Northwest.

stollen   German American tradition of fruit cake usually with an icing.

tamale   Mexican American steamed cornmeal dough wrapped around meats, beans, or cheese.

three sisters   The basic traditional food crops of Native Americans—corn, beans, and squash.

tortilla   Hispanic flat bread made of corn meal or wheat flour.

tripe   Cow stomach.

zamia   Roots from the zamia are dried and ground into bread by American Indians in northern Florida; also known as coontie.

Resource Guide

WEB SITES AND ORGANIZATIONS

Agriculture, Food, and Human Values Society http://www.afhvs.org/

American Breweriana Association http://www.americanbreweriana.org

American Diner Museum http://www.dinermuseum.org/

American Eats: The Food That Built America http://www.history.com/exhibits/americaneats/

American Folklore Society http://www.afsnet.org Provides a listing of traditional arts and humanities programs and organizations by state and region, which often include information on local food traditions.

American Institute of Wine and Food http://www.aiwf.org

Association for the Study of Food and Society http://food-culture.org/

Carolina Cookin' http://www.carolinacountry.com/ccookin.html

Chef John Folse & Company: Louisiana Cooking www.jfolse.com From the "Stirrin' it up" radio show.

Chefs Collaborative www.chefscollaborative.org

The Coal Stove http://www.coalregion.com/recipes.htm Recipes from the eastern Pennsylvania coal region.

Cooking Village http://www.cookingvillage.com/

Cook's Country http://www.cookscountry.com/ From a test kitchen that also publishes *Cook's Illustrated*.

Culinary Historians of Chicago http://www.culinaryhistorians.org Includes links to culinary historian organizations in other states and regions.

Cultural Arts Resources for Teachers (CARTS) http://www.carts.org/ CARTS is a partnership between New York City's CityLore and the National Network for Folk Arts in Education. Includes many resources on food.

Eastern Shore of Virginia Recipes http://www.esva.net/ghotes/ghotes50.htm

Epicurious: America's Best Eats http://www.epicurious.com/restaurants/best_eats/
Jane and Michael Stern's Web site.

Feeding America: The Historic American Cookbook Project http://digital.lib.
msu.edu/projects/cookbooks/

Florida Cuisine http://www.florida-agriculture.com/recipes/

Food History News http://www.foodhistorynews.com

Food Museum Online http://www.foodmuseum.com

Food Site of the Day http://www.foodsiteoftheday.com

Food Timeline www.foodtimeline.org Edited by culinary historian Lynne Olver.

The Gumbo Pages http://www.gumbopages.com/

Iowa Place-Based Foods www.iowaartscouncil.org/programs/folk-and-traditional-arts/
place_based_foods/index.htm

Janice Bluestein Longone Culinary Archive http://www.clements.umich.edu/
culinary/index.html

Key Ingredients: America by Food http://www.keyingredients.org/ The Smithsonian exhibit.

Milwaukee: Beer Capitol of the World www.beerhistory.com

Mississippi Delta Hot Tamale Trail http://www.tamaletrail.com/ Sponsored by the
Southern Foodways Alliance.

Museum on Main Street http://www.museumonmainstreet.org/educate.htm

NOLA.com: Food http://www.nola.com/food/ South Louisiana cuisine.

Pat Willard www.patwillard.com/work3.htm Site of cookbook author, Pat Willard.

Roadfood.com http://www.roadfood.com/

Sauerkraut Recipes http://www.sauerkrautrecipes.com/

Slow Food http://www.slowfood.com The original international Slow Food organization based in Italy.

Slow Food USA http://www.slowfoodusa.org A project that features maps of the
United States by food nation.

Southern Foodways Alliance http://www.southernfoodways.com/

Spice History http://spicehistory.net/

Sugar Maple Program at Cornell http://maple.dnr.cornell.edu/

Tailgaiting America http://www.tailgating.com/

A Taste of Louisiana http://www.lpb.org/programs/tasteofla/

Texas Cooking http://www.texascooking.com/

What's Cooking America http://whatscookingamerica.net/

Yankee Magazine http://www.yankeemagazine.com/food/ New England food

Wines and Times www.winesandtimes.com/wnt/index.php

SCHOLARLY JOURNALS

Food and Foodways
Food, Culture, and Society
Gastronomica: The Journal of Food and Culture

Petits Propos Culinaires

Frequently, folklore journals contain information on regional food. See *Journal of American Folklore*, *Midwestern Folklore*, and *New York Folklore*. See also journals from the American Anthropological Association.

Selected Bibliography

GENERAL WORKS

Gay, Kathlyn, and Martin Gay. *Encyclopedia of North American Eating and Drinking Traditions, Custom and Rituals.* Santa Barbara, CA: ABC-CLIO, 1996.

Katz, Solomon H., ed. *Encyclopedia of Food and Culture.* 3 vols. New York: Charles Scribner's Sons, 2003.

Kiple, Kenneth F., and Kriemhild Conee Ornelas, eds. *The Cambridge World History of Food.* 2 vols. Cambridge, UK: Cambridge University Press, 2000.

Kittler Pamela Goyan, and Kathryn Sucher. *Food and Culture in America: A Nutrition Handbook.* New York: Van Nostrand Reinhold, 1989.

Mariani, John F. *Dictionary of American Food and Drink.* New York: Ticknor and Fields, 1983.

Pillsbury, Richard. *No Foreign Food: The American Diet in Time and Place.* Boulder, CO: Westview Press, 1998.

Smith, Andrew, ed. *The Oxford Encyclopedia of Food and Drink in America.* 2 vols. New York: Oxford University Press, 2004.

Smith, Andrew F. *Encyclopedia of Junk Food and Fast Food.* Westport, CT: Greenwood Press, 2006.

Trager, James. *The Food Chronology: A Food Lover's Compendium of Events and Anecdotes, from Prehistory to the Present.* New York: Henry Holt, 1995.

COOKBOOKS

The American Heritage Cookbook and Illustrated History of American Eating and Drinking. New York: American Heritage Publishing, 1964.

Beck, Ken, and Jim Clark. *Aunt Bee's Mayberry Cookbook*. Nashville, TN: Rutledge Hill Press, 1991.

Brown, Dale. *American Cooking*. Alexandria, VA: Time-Life Books, 1968.

Jamison, Cheryl Alters, and Bill Jamison. *The Rancho de Chimayó Cookbook: The Traditional Cooking of New Mexico*. Boston: Harvard Common Press, 1991.

Kirlin, Katherine S., and Thomas M. Kirlin. *Smithsonian Folklife Cookbook*. Washington, D.C.: Smithsonian Institution Press, 1991.

Longstreet, Stephen, and Ethel Longstreet. *A Salute to American Cooking*. New York: Hawthorne Books, 1968.

Prudhomme, Paul. *Chef Paul Prudhomme's Seasoned America*. New York: William Morrow and Company, 1991.

Saveur Cooks Authentic American. San Francisco: Chronicle Books, 1998.

Smith, Jeff. *The Frugal Gourmet on Our Immigrant Ancestors*. New York: William Morrow and Company, 1990.

Smith, Jeff. *The Frugal Gourmet Cooks American*. New York: William Morrow and Company, 1987.

Stern, Jane, and Michael. *American Gourmet: Classic Recipes, Deluxe Delights, Flamboyant Favorites, and Swank 'Company' Food from the '50s and '60s*. New York: HarperPerennial, 1991.

Stradley, Linda, and Andrea Cook. *What's Cooking America?* Helena, MT: Three-Forks, 1997.

Zanger, Mark H. *American History Cookbook*. Westport, CT: Greenwood Press, 2003.

INTRODUCTION

Allen, Barbara, and Thomas J. Schlereth, eds. *Sense of Place: American Regional Cultures*. Lexington: University Press of Kentucky, 1990.

Anderson, Benedict. *Imagined Communities: Reflections on the Origin and Spread of Nationalism*. Rev. ed. New York: Verso, 1991.

Anderson, E. N. *Everyone Eats: Understanding Food and Culture*. New York: New York University Press, 2005.

Ashley, Bob, Joanne Hollows, Steve Jones, and Ben Taylor. *Food and Cultural Studies*. New York: Routledge, 2004.

Barer-Stein, Thelma. *You Eat What You Are: People, Culture, and Food Traditions*. Toronto: McClelland and Stewart, 2001.

Belasco, Warren, and Philip Scranton, eds. *Food Nations: Selling Taste in Consumer Societies*. New York: Routledge, 2002.

Bell, David. "Fragments for a New Urban Culinary Geography." *Journal for the Study of Food and Society* 6, no. 1 (2002): 10–21.

Bell, David, and Gill Valentine, eds. *Consuming Geographies: We Are Where We Eat*. New York: Routledge. 1997.

Bourdieu, Pierre. *Distinction: A Social Critique of the Judgment of Taste*. Cambridge, MA: Harvard University Press. 1984.

Brown, Linda Keller, and Kay Mussell, eds. *Ethnic and Regional Foodways in the United States: The Performance of Group Identity.* Knoxville: University of Tennessee Press, 1984.

Certeau, Michel de, Lucy Giard, and Pierre Mayol. *The Practice of Everyday Life.* Vol. 2, *Living and Cooking.* Minneapolis: University of Minnesota Press, 1998.

Counihan, Carole M., and Penny Van Esterik, eds. *Food and Culture: A Reader.* New York: Routledge, 1997.

Dorson, Richard M., ed. *Folklore and Folklife: An Introduction.* Chicago: University of Chicago Press, 1972.

Douglas, Mary. *Implicit Meanings: Selected Essays in Anthropology.* 2nd ed. New York: Routledge, 1999.

Kirshenblatt-Gimblett, Barbara. *Destination Culture: Tourism, Museums, and Heritage.* Berkeley: University of California Press, 1998.

Levenstein, Harvey. *Paradox of Plenty.* Berkeley: University of California Press, 2003.

Long, Lucy, ed. *Culinary Tourism..* Lexington: University Press of Kentucky, 2004.

Mintz, Sidney. *Tasting Food: Tasting Freedom: Excursions into Eating, Culture, and the Past.* Boston: Beacon Press, 1996.

Nestle, Marion. *Food Politics: How the Food Industry Influences Nutrition and Health.* Berkeley: University of California Press, 2002.

Pillsbury, Richard. *No Foreign Food: The American Diet in Time and Place.* Boulder, CO: Westview Press, 1998.

Sokolov, Raymond. *Fading Feast: A Compendium of Disappearing American Regional Foods.* New York: E. P. Dutton, 1983.

Shortridge, James R., and Barbara G. Shortridge, eds. *The Taste of American Place: A Reader on Regional and Ethnic Foods.* New York: Rowman and Littlefield, 1998.

Thursby, Jacqueline S. *Foodways and Folklore: A Handbook.* Westport, CT: Greenwood Press, 2008.

Trubeck, Amy. *The Taste of Place: A Cultural Journey Into Terroir.* Berkeley: University of California Press, 2008.

Tuan, Yi-Fu. *Space and Place: The Perspective of Experience.* Minneapolis: University of Minnesota Press, 1977.

Wilk, Richard. *Fast Food/Slow Food: The Cultural Economy of the Global Food System.* Lanham, MD: Rowan and Littlefield, 2006.

Wilk, Richard. *Home Cooking in the Global Village: Caribbean Food from Buccaneers to Ecotourists.* New York: Berg, 2006.

Zelinsky, Wilbur. *The Cultural Geography of the United States.* Englewood Cliffs, NJ: Prentice-Hall, 1973.

CHAPTER 1: HISTORY

Belasco, Warren. *Appetite for Change.* New York: Pantheon Books, 1989.

Belasco, Warren, and Roger Horowitz, eds. *Food Chains: From Farmyard to Shopping Cart.* Philadelphia: University of Pennsylvania Press, 2009.

Berzok, Linda Murray. *American Indian Food*. Westport, CT: Greenwood Press, 2005.

Bower, Anne L., ed. *African American Foodways: Explorations of History and Culture*. Chicago: University of Illinois Press, 2007.

Brenner, Leslie. *American Appetite: The Coming of Age of a Cuisine*. New York: Avon Books, 1999.

Coe, Andy. *Chop Suey: A Cultural History of Chinese Food in the United States*. New York: Oxford University Press, 2009.

Coe, Sophie D. *America's First Cuisines*. Austin: University of Texas Press, 1994.

Crosby, Alfred W., Jr. *The Columbian Exchange: Biological and Cultural Consequences of 1492*. Westport, CT: Greenwood Press, 1972.

Cummings, Richard O. *The American and His Food*. New York: Arno Press and New York Times, 1970.

Denker, Joel. *The World on a Plate: A Tour through the History of America's Ethnic Cuisine*. Boulder, CO: Westview Press, 2003.

Diner, Hasia R. *Hungering for America: Italian, Irish, and Jewish Foodways in the Age of Migration*. Cambridge, MA: Harvard University Press, 2003.

Farmer, Fannie Merritt. *Boston Cooking-School Cook Book*, Boston: Little, Brown, and Company, 1896.

Gabaccia, Donna R. *We Are What We Eat: Ethnic Food and the Making of Americans*. Cambridge, MA.: Harvard University Press, 1998.

Gillespie, Angus K. "A Wilderness in the Meglopolis: Foodways in the Pine Barrens of new Jersey," in *Ethnic and Regional Foodways in the United States: The Performance of Group Identity*, ed. Linday Keller Brown and Kay Mussell, 145–168. Knoxville: The University of Tennessee Press, 1984.

Haber, Barbara. *From Hardtack to Home Fries: An Uncommon History of American Cooks and Meals*. New York: Penguin Books, 2002.

Hess, Karen, ed. *Martha Washington's Booke of Cookery*. New York: Columbia University Press, 1981.

Inness, Sherrie A., ed. *Pilaf, Pozole, and Pad Thai: American Women and Ethnic Food*, Amherst: University of Massachusetts Press, 2001.

Jones, Evan. *American Food: The Gastronomic Story*. New York: Vintage Books, 1981.

Kamp, David. *The United States of Aragula: How We Became a Gourmet Nation*. New York: Broadway Books, 2006.

Levenstein, Harvey. *Paradox of Plenty: A Social History of Eating in Modern America*. New York: Oxford University Press, 1994.

Levenstein, Harvey A. *Revolution at the Table: The Transformation of the American Diet*. New York: Oxford University Press, 1988.

McWilliams, James E. *A Revolution in Eating: How the Quest for Food Shaped America*. New York: Columbia University Press, 2005.

Nathan, Joan. *Jewish Cooking in America*. New York: Alfred A. Knopf, 1994.

Ray, Krishnendu. *The Migrant's Table: Meals and Memories in Bengali-American Households*. Philadelphia: Temple University Press, 2004.

Root, Waverly, and Richard de Rochemont. *Eating in America: A History*. New York: Morrow, 1976.

Takaki, Ronald. *Strangers from a Different Shore*. New York: Penguin Books. 1989.

Williams, Susan. *Food in the United States, 1820s-1890*. Westport, CT: Greenwood Press, 2006.

Witt, Doris. *Black Hunger: Food and the Politics of U.S. Identity*. New York: Oxford University Press, 1999.

CHAPTER 2: MAJOR FOODS AND INGREDIENTS

Albala, Ken. *Beans: A History*. New York: Berg Publishers, 2007.

Albala, Ken. *Pancake: A Global History*. London: Reaktion Books, 2008.

Apps, Jerry. *Breweries of Wisconsin*. Madison: University of Wisconsin Press, 1992.

Baliska, Maria. *The Bagel: The Surprising History of a Modest Bread*. New Haven, CT: Yale University Press, 2008.

Block, Daniel R. "Protecting and Connecting: Separation, Connection, and the U.S. Dairy Economy 1840–2002." *Journal for the Study of Food and Society* 6, no. 1 (2002): 22–30.

DuPuis, E. Melanie. *Nature's Perfect Food: How Milk Became America's Drink*. New York: New York University Press, 2002.

Freinkel, Susan. *American Chestnut: The Life, Death, and Rebirth of a Perfect Tree*. Berkeley: University of California Press, 2007.

Fussell, Betty. *Raising Steaks: The Life and Times of American Beef*. Orlando, FL: Harcourt Books, 2008.

Fussell, Betty. *The Story of Corn*. Albuquerque: University of New Mexico Press, 2004.

Haverluk, Terrence W. "Chile Peppers and Identity Construction in Pueblo, Colorado." *Journal for the Study of Food and Society* 6, no. 1 (2002): 45–59.

Helstosky, Carol. *Pizza: A Global History*. London: Reaktion Books, 2008.

Jenkins, Virginia Scott. *Bananas: An American History*. Washington, D.C.: Smithsonian Institution Press, 2000.

Kraig, Bruce. *Hot Dog: A Global History*. London: Reaktion Books, 2009.

Kurlansky, Mark. *The Big Oyster: History on the Half Shell*. New York: Random House, 2006.

Kurlansky, Mark. *Cod: A Biography of the Fish that Changed the World*. New York: Walker, 1997.

Laszlo, Pierre. *Citrus: A History*. Chicago: University of Chicago Press, 2007.

Mendelson, Anne. *Milk: The Surprising Story of Milk Through the Ages*. New York: Alfred A. Knopf, 2008.

Mintz, Sidney. *Sweetness and Power: The Place of Sugar in Modern History*. New York: Viking, 1985.

Mullins, Paul R. *Glazed America: A History of the Doughnut*. Gainesville: University Press of Florida, 2008.

Pendergrast, Mark. *Uncommon Grounds: The History of Coffee and How It Transformed Our World*. New York: Basic Books, 1999.

Petre, Glen. *The Crawfish Book*. Jackson: University of Mississippi Press, 1993.

Smith, Andrew F. *Hamburger: A Global History*. London: Reaktion Books, 2008.

Smith, Andrew F. *Peanuts: The Illustrious History of the Goober Pea*. Chicago: University of Illinois Press, 2007.

Smith, Andrew F. *Popped Culture: A Social History of Popcorn in America*. Washington, D.C.: Smithsonian Institution Press, 2001.

Smith, Andrew F. *Souper Tomatoes: The Story of America's Favorite Food*. New Brunswick, NJ: Rutgers University Press, 2000.

Smith, Andrew F. *The Turkey: An American Story*. Chicago: University of Illinois Press, 2006.

Weaver, William Woys. *Country Scrapple: An American Tradition*. Mechanicsburg, PA: Stackpole Books, 2003.

Wilson, David Scofield, and Angus Kress Gillespie, eds. *Rooted in America: Foodlore of Popular Fruits and Vegetables*. Knoxville: University of Tennessee Press, 1999.

Wyman, Carolyn. *Spam: A Biography: The Amazing True Story of America's "Miracle Meat"!* New York: Harcourt Brace, 1999.

Zuckerman, Larry. *The Potato: How the Humble Spud Rescued the Western World*. New York: North Point Press, 1998.

CHAPTER 3: COOKING

Avakian, Arlene. *Through the Kitchen Window: Women Explore the Intimate Meanings of Food and Cooking*. Boston: Beacon Press, 1997.

Avakian, Arlene, and Barbara Haber, eds. *From Betty Crocker to Feminist Food Studies: Critical Perspectives on Women and Food*. Boston: University of Massachusetts Press, 2005.

Bourdain, Anthony. *Kitchen Confidential: Adventures in the Culinary Underbelly*. London: Bloomsbury, 2000.

Bower, Anne L., ed. *Reel Food: Essays on Food and Film*. New York: Routledge, 2004.

Bower, Anne L., ed. *Recipes for Reading: Community Cookbooks, Stories, Histories*. Amherst: University of Massachusetts Press, 1997.

Counihan, Carole M. *The Anthropology of Food and Body: Gender, Meaning, and Power*. New York: Routledge, 1999.

DeVault, Marjorie L. *Feeding the Family: The Social Organization of Caring as Gendered Work*. Chicago: University of Chicago Press, 1991.

DuSablon, Mary Anna. *America's Collectible Cookbooks: the History, the Politics, the recipes*. Athens: Ohio University Press, 1994.

Fine, Gary Alan. *Kitchens: the Culture of Restaurant Work*. 2nd ed. Los Angeles: University of California Press, 2009.

Fine, Gary Alan. "Wittgenstein's Kitchen: Sharing Meaning in Restaurant Work." *Theory and Society* 24 (1995): 245–269.

Freeman, June. *The Making of the Modern Kitchen: A Culture History.* New York: Berg, 2004.

Hansen, Signe. "Society of the Appetite: Celebrity Chefs Deliver Consumers." *Food, Culture, Society* 11, no. 1 (2008): 46–97.

Inness, Sherrie A. *Dinner Roles: American Women and Culinary Culture.* Iowa City: University of Iowa Press, 2001.

Ireland, Lynne. "The Compiled Cookbook as Foodways Autobiography." In *The Taste of American Place: A Reader on Regional and Ethnic Foods*, edited by Barbara G. Shortridge and James R. Shortridge, 111–20. New York: Rowman and Littlefield, 1998.

McIntosh, Alex, and Mary Zey. "Women as Gatekeepers of Food Consumption: A Sociological Critique." *Food and Foodways* 3, no. 4 (1989): 317–32.

McWilliams, Mark. "Good Women Bake Good Biscuits: Cookery and Identity in Antebellum American Fiction." *Food, Culture, and Society* 10, no. 3 (2007): 388–406.

Mendelson, Anne. *Stand Facing the Stove: The Story of the Women Who Gave America the Joy of Cooking.* New York: Henry Holt, 1996.

Miles, Elizabeth. "Adventures in the Postmodernist Kitchen: The Cuisine of Wolfgang Puck." *Journal of Popular Culture* 27 (1993): 191–203.

Plante, Ellen M. *The American Kitchen 1700 to the Present: From Hearth to Highrise.* New York: Facts on File, 1995.

Scapp, Ron, and Brian Seitz, eds. *Eating Culture.* Albany: SUNY Press, 1998.

Schenone, Laura. *A Thousand Years over a Hot Stove: A History of American Women Told Through Food, Recipes, and Remembrances.* New York: W.W. Norton & Co., 2003.

Shapiro, Laura. *Perfection Salad: Women and Cooking at the Turn of the Century.* New York: Modern Library, 2001.

Shapiro, Laura. *Something From the Oven: Reinventing Dinner in 1950s America.* New York: Penguin Books, 2004.

Theophano, Janet. *Eat My Words: Reading Women's Lives through the Cookbooks They Wrote.* New York: Palgrave Macmillan, 2002.

Turner, Katherine Leonard. "Buying, Not Cooking: Ready-to-Eat Food in American Urban Working-class Neighborhoods, 1880–1930." *Journal for the Study of Food and Society* 9, no. 1 (2006): 13–39.

CHAPTER 4: TYPICAL MEALS

The Art Institutes. *American Regional Cuisine.* New York: John Wiley & Sons, 2007.

Davidson, Alan, ed. *National and Regional Styles of Cookery.* London: Prospect, 1981.

Fussell, Betty. *I Hear America Cooking: The Cooks and Recipes of American Regional Cuisine*. New York: Penguin Books, 1986.

Grover, Kathryn, ed. *Dining in America, 1850–1900*. Amherst: University of Massachusetts Press, 1987.

Horowitz, Roger. *Putting Meat on the American Table: Taste, Technology, Transformation*. Baltimore: Johns Hopkins University Press, 2006.

Meisselman, Herbert, ed.. *The Meal*. Gaithersburg, MD: Aspen Publishers, 2000.

Stern, Jane, and Michael Stern. *A Taste of America*. New York: Andrews and McNeel, 1988.

Stern, Jane, and Michael Stern. *Two for the Road: Our Love Affair with American Food*. New York: Houghton Mifflin, 2006.

Stradley, Linda. *I'll Have What They're Having: Legendary Local Cuisine*. Guilford, CT: Globe Pequot Press, 2002.

Visser, Margaret: *The Rituals of Dinner: The Origins, Evolution, Eccentricities and Meaning of Table Manners*. Toronto: Harper Perennial, 1991.

Wolf, Bonny. *Talking with My Mouth Full: Crab Cakes, Bundt Cakes, and Other Kitchen Stories*. New York: St. Martin's Press, 2006.

Regions

Northeast

Alperson, Myra, and Mark Clifford. *The Food Lover's Guide to the Real New York: Five Boroughs of Ethnic Restaurants, Markets, and Shops*. New York: Prentice Hall, 1987.

Benes, Peter, ed. *Foodways in the Northeast, The Dublin Seminar for New England Folklife: Annual Proceedings*. Boston: Boston University, 1982.

Booth, Sally Smith. *Hung, Strung, and Potted: A History of Eating in Colonial America*. New York: Clarkson N. Potter, 1971.

Ekfelt, Lynn Case. *Good Food: Served right: Traditional Recipes and food Customs From New York's North Country*. Memphis: Wimmer, 2000.

Farmer, Fannie. The Boston Cooking-School Cook Book. 7th ed. Boston: Little, Brown, 1942.

Hauck-Lawson, Annie, and Jonathan Deutsch, eds. *Gastrolopolis: Food and New York City*. New York: Columbia University Press, 2008.

Hewitt, Jean. *The New York Times New England Heritage Cookbook*. New York: G. P. Putnam's Sons, 1977.

McMahon, Sarah Frances. "'A Comfortable Subsistence': Changing Composition of Diet in Rural New England, 1620–1840." *William and Mary Quarterly* 42, no. 1 (January 1985): 26.

Mosser, Marjorie. *Foods of Old New England*. New York: Doubleday, 1957.

Newstadt, Kathy. *Clambake: A History and Celebration of an American Tradition*. Amherst: University of Massachusetts Press, 1992.

Oliver, Sandra L. *Saltwater Foodways: New Englanders and Their Food, at Sea and Ashore, in the Nineteenth Century*. Mystic, CT: Mystic Seaport Museum, 1995.

Pixley, Aristene. *The Green Mountain Cook Book: Yankee Recipes from Old Vermont Kitchens*. Brattleboro, VT: Stephen Saye Press, 1941.

Rose, Peter G. *The Sensible Cook: Dutch Foodways in the Old and the New World*. Syracuse, NY: Syracuse University Press, 1998.

Stavely, Keith, and Kathleen Fitzgerald. *America's Founding Food: The Story of New England Cooking*. Chapel Hill: University of North Carolina Press, 2004.

Whitehill, Jane. *Food, Drink, and Recipes of Early New England*. Sturbridge, MA: Old Sturbridge Village, 1963.

Mid-Atlantic

Howard, Mrs. B. C. *Fifty Years in a Maryland Kitchen*. 3rd ed. Baltimore: Turnbull Bros., 1877.

Weaver, William Woys. *A Quaker Woman's Cookbook: The Domestic Cookery of Elizabeth Ellicott Lea*. Philadelphia: University of Pennsylvania Press, 1982.

Weaver, William Woys, and Don Yoder. *Sauerkraut Yankees: Pennsylvania Dutch Foods and Foodways*. Mechanicsburg, PA: Stackpole Books, 2002.

Wilson, José. *American Cooking: The Eastern Heartland*. New York: Time-Life Books, 1971.

Yoder, Don. *Discovering American Folklife: Essays on Folk Culture and the Pennsylvania Dutch*. Mechanicsburg, PA: Stackpole Books, 2001.

South

Edge, John T. ed. *The New Encyclopedia of Southern Culture*. Vol. 7. *Foodways*. Chapel Hill: University of North Carolina, 2007.

Edgerton, John. *Southern Food: At Home, On the Road, in History*. New York: Alfred A. Knopf, 1987.

Elie, Lolis Eric, ed. *Cornbread Nation 2: The United States of Barbecue*. Chapel Hill: University of North Carolina Press, 2005.

Ferris, Marcie Cohen. *Matzoh Ball Gumbo: Culinary Tales of the Jewish South*. Chapel Hill: University of North Carolina Press, 2005.

Gutierrez, C. Paige. *Cajun Foodways*. Jackson: University of Mississippi Press, 1992.

Harris, Jessica B. *The Welcome Table: African-American Heritage Cooking*. New York: Simon and Schuster, 1995.

Hess, Karen. *The Carolina Rice Kitchen: The African Connection*. Columbia: University of South Carolina Press, 1992.

Hilliard, Sam. *Hog Meat and Hoecake: Food Supply in the Old South 1840–1860*. Carbondale: Southern Illinois University Press, 1972.

Linck, Ernestine S., and Joyce G. Roach. *Eats: A Folk History of Texas Food*. Fort Worth: Texas Christian University Press, 1989.

Randolph, Mrs. Mary. *The Virginia Housewife: Or, Methodical Cook*. Baltimore: Plaskitt and Cugle, 1838.

Stanonsis, Anthony J. *Dixie Emporium: Tourism, Foodways, and Consumer Culture in the American South*. Athens: University of Georgia Press, 2008.

Taylor, Joe Gray. *Eating, Drinking, and Visiting in the South: An Informal History*. Baton Rouge: Louisiana State University Press, 1982.

Van Willigen, John, and Anne Van Willigen. *Food and Everyday Life on Kentucky Family Farms, 1920–1950*. Lexington: University Press of Kentucky, 2006.

Walter, Eugene. *American Cooking: Southern Style*. New York: Time-Life Books, 1971.

Williams-Forson, Psyche A. *Building Houses Out of Chicken Legs: Black Women, Food, and Power*. Chapel Hill: University of North Carolina Press, 2006.

Upland South/Appalachia

Dabney, Joseph E. *Smokehouse Ham, Spoon Bread, and Scuppernong Wine: The Folklore and Art of Southern Appalachian Cooking*. Nashville, TN: Cumberland House Publishing, 1998.

Long, Lucy. "An Appalachian Meal." In *Musics of the World; Foods of the World*, edited by Sean Williams, 192–196. New York: Routledge, 2006.

Lundy, Ronni, ed. *Cornbread Nation 3: Foods of the Mountain South*. Chapel Hill: University of North Carolina Press, 2008.

Sohn, Mark F. *Appalachian Home Cooking*. Lexington: University Press of Kentucky, 1995.

Wigginton, Eliot, and Linda Garland Page, eds. *The Foxfire Book of Appalachian Cookery*. 2nd ed. Chapel Hill: University of North Carolina Press, 1992.

Midwest

Kaercher, Dan. *Taste of the Midwest*. Guilford, CT: Globe Pequot, 2006.

Kaplan, Anne R., Marjorie A. Hoover, and Willard B. Moore. *The Minnesota Ethnic Food Book*. St. Paul: Minnesota Historical Society Press, 1986.

Kreidberg, Marjorie. *Food on the Frontier: Minnesota Cooking From 1850 to 1900 with Selected Recipes*. St. Paul: Minnesota Historical Society Press, 1975.

Long, Lucy. "Apple Butter in Northwest Ohio: Food Festivals and the Construction of Local Meaning," In *Holidays, Ritual, Festival, Celebration, and Public Display*. Edited by Cristina Sanchez-Carretero and Jack Santino. Spain: Universidad de Alcala, 2003: 45–65.

Long, Lucy. "Greenbean Casserole and Midwestern Identity: A Regional Foodways Aesthetic and Ethos." *Midwestern Folklore: Journal of the Hoosier Folklore Society* 33, no. 1 (2007): 29–44.

Vennum, Thomas, R. *Wild Rice and the Ojibway People*. St. Paul: Minnesota Historical Society Press, 1988.

Walker, Barbara M. *The Little House Cookbook: Frontier Foods from Laura Ingalls Wilder's Classic Stories*. New York: Harper and Row, 1979.

Wilcox, Estell Woods. *Buckeye Cookery, and Practical Housekeeping: Compiled from Original Recipes*. Minneapolis: Buckeye, 1977.

Wilson, José. *American Cooking: The Eastern Heartland*. New York: Time-Life Books, 1971.

West

Brown, Helen Evans. *West Coast Cook Book*. New York: Little, Brown and Company, 1952.

Ronnenberg, Herman. *Beer and Brewing in the Inland Northwest: 1850–1950*. Moscow: University of Idaho Press, 1993.

Williams, Jacqueline B. *Wagon Wheel Kitchens: Food on the Oregon Trail*. Lawrence: University Press of Kansas, 1993.

Williams, Jacqueline B. *The Way We Ate: Pacific Northwest Cooking, 1843–1900*. Pullman: Washington State University Press, 1996.

Hawaii

Laudan, Rachel. *The Food of Paradise*. Honolulu: University of Hawaii Press, 1996.

Southwest

Dent, Huntley. *The Feast of Santa Fe: Cooking in the American Southwest*. New York: Simon and Schuster, 1985.

Linck, Ernestine Sewell, and Joyce Gibson Roach. *A Folk History of Texas Foods*. Fort Worth: Texas Christian University Press, 1989.

Pinedo, Encarnación, *Encarnación's Kitchen: Mexican Recipes from Nineteenth-Century California. Selections from Encarnación Pinedo's El Cocinero Espanol*. Edited and translated by Dan Strehl. Los Angeles: University of California Press, 2003.

CHAPTER 5: EATING OUT

Davis, Netta. "To Serve the 'Other': Chinese-American Immigrants in the Restaurant Business." *Journal for the Study of Food and Society* 6, no. 1 (2002): 70–81.

Grover, Kathryn, ed. *Dining in America, 1850–1900*. Amherst: University of Massachusetts Press, 1987.

Jackle, John A., and Keith A. Sculle. *Fast Food: Roadside Restaurants in the Automobile Age*. Baltimore: Johns Hopkins University Press, 1999.

Kuh, Patric. *The Last Days of Haute Cuisine: The Coming of Age of American Restaurants*. New York: Penguin Books, 2001.

Long, Lucy, ed. *Culinary Tourism*. Lexington: University Press of Kentucky, 2004.

Pillsbury, Richard. *From Boarding House to Bistro: The American Restaurant Then and Now*. London: Unwin Hyman, 1990.

Spang, Rebecca. *The Invention of the Restaurant.* Cambridge, MA: Harvard University Press, 2000.

Sutton, David, and David Berriss, eds. *The Restaurants Book: Ethnographies of Where We Eat.* Oxford: Berg Publishing, 2007.

CHAPTER 6: SPECIAL OCCASIONS

Adema, Pauline. *Garlic Capital of the World: Gilroy, Garlic and the Making of a Festive Foodscape.* Jackson: University Press of Mississippi. 2009.

Frese, Pamela R., ed. *Celebrations of Identity: Multiple Voices in American Ritual Performance.* Westport, CT: Bergin and Garvey, 1993.

Geffen, Alice M., and Carole Berglie. *Food Festival: The Ultimate Guidebook to America's Best Regional Food Celebrations.* New York: Pantheon Books, 1986.

Hauck-Lawson, Annie. "Something's Kosher Here!: Foodways Among Jewish Brooklyn College Nutrition Students." *Journal for the Study of Food and Society* 6, no. 1 (2002): 88–93.

Humphrey, Theodore, and Lin T. Humphrey. *"We Gather Together": Food Festival in American Life.* Ann Arbor: University of Michigan Research Press, 1988.

O'Connor, Kaori. "The Hawaiian Luau: Food as Tradition, Transgression, Transformation and Travel." *Food, Culture, and Society* 11, no. 2 (2008):149–172.

Santino, Jack. *All Around the Year: Holidays and Celebrations in American Life.* Urbana: University of Illinois Press, 1994.

Willard, Pat. *America Eats!: On the Road with the WPA—The Fish Fries, Box Supper Socials, and Chitlin Feasts That Define Real American Food.* New York: Bloomsbury Publishing, 2008.

CHAPTER 7: DIET AND HEALTH

Barndt, Deborah. *Tangled Routes: Women, Work, and Globalization on the Tomato Trail.* New York: Rowman and Littlefield Publishers, 2008.

Biltekoff, Charlotte. "'Strong Men and Women Are Not Products of Improper Food': Domestic Science and the History of Eating and Identity." *Journal for the Study of Food and Society* 6, no. 1 (2002): 60–69.

Douglas, Mary. *Purity and Danger: An Analysis of Concepts of Pollution and Taboo.* New York: Penguin Books, 1966.

Feenstra, Gail. "Local Food Systems and Sustainable Communities." *American Journal of Alternative Agriculture* 12, no. 1 (1997): 28–36.

McWilliams, James E. "'How Unripe We Are:' The Intellectual Construction of American Foodways." *The Journal for the Study of Food and Society* 8, no. 2 (2005): 143–160.

Nestle, Marion. *Food Politics: How the Food Industry Influences Nutrition and Health.* Berkeley: University of California Press, 2002.

Nestle, Marion. *What to Eat.* New York: North Point Press, 2006.

Nutzenadel, Alexander, and Frank Trentmann, eds. *Food and Globalization: Consumption, Markets and Politics in the Modern World.* New York: Oxford University Press, 2008.

Petrini, Carlo. *Slow Food Nation: Why Our Food Should Be Good, Clean, and Fair.* New York: Rizzoli Ex Libris, 2007.

Pollan, Michael. *In Defense of Food: An Eater's Manifesto.* New York: Penguin, 2008.

Pollan, Michael. *The Omnivore's Dilemma: A Natural History of Four Meals.* New York: Penguin, 2006.

Robinson, Jennifer Meta, and J.A. Hartenfeld. *The Farmers' Market Book: Growing Food, Cultivating Community.* Bloomington: Indiana University Press, 2007.

Roth, LuAnne K. "'Beef. It's What's for Dinner': Vegetarians, Meat-Eaters, and the Negotiation of Familial Relationships." *The Journal for the Study of Food and Society* 8, no. 2 (2005): 181–200.

Schlosser, Eric. *Fast Food Nation: The Dark Side of the All-American Meal.* New York: HarperCollins, 2001.

Trubek, Amy B. *The Taste of Place: A Cultural Journey into Terror.* Los Angeles: University of California Press, 2008.

Veit, Helen Aie. "'We Were a Soft People': Asceticism, Self-Discipline and American Food Conservation in the First World War." *Food, Culture, Society* 10, no. 2 (2007): 167–190.

Vos, Timothy. "Visions of the Middle Landscape: Organic Farming and the Politics of Nature." *Agriculture, Food, and Human Values* 17, no. 3 (2000): 245–256.

Winne, Mark. *Closing the Food Gap: Resetting the Table in the Land of Plenty.* Boston: Beacon Press, 2008.

Index

About the Author

Lucy M. Long is Instructor of International Studies and American Culture Studies at Bowling Green State University and has a keen interest in food and folklore. She is the author of *Culinary Tourism: Eating and Otherness* (2004).